# Serving the Empire
## The Karen of Burma

# SERVING THE EMPIRE
## THE KAREN OF BURMA

This edition first published in the United Kingdom in 2023 by DevonPress Knowles Hill, Newton Abbot, South Devon TQ12 2PW United Kingdom.

**PB** ISBN 978-1-7394402-9-9
**HB** ISBN 978-1-7394402-4-4
**Ebook** ISBN 978-1-7394402-5-1

© Richard Duckett, 2023, DevonPress 2023

The rights of this work have been asserted in accordance with the Crown Copyright, Designs and Patents Act 1988.

A CIP catalogue record of this book is available from the British Library.

Publisher: PWN Honeywill
Edited by: R Duckett

All rights reserved. No part of this publication may be reproduced, stored in a retrieval system or transmitted in any form or by any means whether electronic, mechanical, photocopying, recording, or otherwise, without the prior written permission of Richard Duckett. Any person who carries out any unauthorised act in relation to this publication may be liable to criminal prosecution and civil claims for damages.

Cover Image: Morris. Copyright The Trofimov Literary Estate.

Typeset in Adobe Garamond Pro 11/13.2pt. Printed by Print on Demand.

**The translated texts reproduced here appear as unedited text, apart from corrections to typing errors found in the original.**

Unless stated all images are copyright of The Trofimov Literary Estate, Richard Duckett, Bellay Htoo South and Simon Leney.

# Contents

**Acknowledgements** .................................................. 10
**Preface** .................................................................... 12

**Introduction Sally McLean** ................................... 14
**Foreword Dr Rob Lyman** ...................................... 16

**Oral History and this Book** .................................. 18
    Statement of Oral History Collector, Naw Bellay Htoo
        South ................................................................ 26
    Statement of Oral History Collector, Thra Charles ....... 28

## Part One

Pre-War, **Introduction** ........................................... 36
**Pre-War** .................................................................. 47
    Saw Johnny Htoo .................................................. 47
    Saw Aye Kyaw ....................................................... 49
    Saw Fair Play ......................................................... 50
    Saw K'Hsaw ........................................................... 50
    Saw Kay Ray .......................................................... 50
    Saw San Aye .......................................................... 51
    Mr Peter Andrews ................................................. 52
    Mel Du .................................................................. 52
    Saw Daniel Tun Baw ............................................. 53
    Saw Htoo Mar ....................................................... 53
    Saw Baw Nay ......................................................... 53

The First Burma Campaign, December 1941–
    June 1942, **Introduction** ................................. 54
**The First Burma Campaign, December 1941–
June 1942** ............................................................... 56
    Saw Champion ...................................................... 56
    Saw Johnny Htoo .................................................. 58
    Saw Michael Shwe ................................................. 58
    Saw Aye Kyaw ....................................................... 60
    Saw Smile Paul ...................................................... 61

Saw Fair Play ........................................................... 63
Saw Htaw Tha Heh ................................................. 64
Saw K'Hsaw ............................................................ 65
Saw Kay Ray ........................................................... 66
Saw Bunny .............................................................. 67
Saw San Aye ............................................................ 67
Mr Peter Andrews ................................................... 68
Saw Maw Ler ........................................................... 69
Mel Du .................................................................... 72
Saw Baw Nay ........................................................... 72

**Sworn Statement**
Ukyme Hti Nigon .................................................... 73

War Service, June 1942–October 1945,
**Introduction** ........................................................ 74
**War Service, June 1942–October 1945** .............. 77
Saw Champion ........................................................ 77
Saw Johnny Htoo ..................................................... 78
Saw Michael Shwe ................................................... 79
Saw Aye Kyaw .......................................................... 80
Saw Smile Paul ........................................................ 82
**Sworn Statement** of Saw Rupert ......................... 82
Saw Smile Paul continued ....................................... 82
Saw Fair Play ........................................................... 88
Saw Htaw Tha Heh ................................................. 89
Saw K'Hsaw ............................................................ 91
Saw Kay Ray ........................................................... 91
Saw Bunny .............................................................. 92
Saw San Aye ............................................................ 93
Mr Peter Andrews ................................................... 93
Saw Maw Ler ........................................................... 94
Mel Du .................................................................... 98
Saw Daniel Tun Baw ............................................... 99
Saw Baw Nay ........................................................... 99

Address by Karen Leaders to Forces 136 Officers and Men,
    Kya-in Village, September 1945 .......................... 101
Address by Karen Leaders to Forces 136 Officers and Men,
    Mewaing, October 1945 ...................................... 106
Address of Welcome by Saw Po Htin ...................... 109

**Sworn Statements**
Kyaw Po, Jemadar Toe Kin and U Tun Baw ................. 112

Post War to Independence, October 1945–4
January 1948, **Introduction** .......................... 116
**Post War to Independence, October 1945–4
January 1948** ................................................. 118
Saw Johnny Htoo ................................................. 118
Saw Michael Shwe ............................................... 118
Saw Aye Kyaw ...................................................... 119
Saw Smile Paul .................................................... 121
Saw Fair Play ....................................................... 121
Saw Kay Ray ........................................................ 125
Saw Bunny ........................................................... 125
Saw San Aye ........................................................ 126
Saw Htoo Mar ..................................................... 126
Saw Baw Nay ....................................................... 126

'The Humble Memorial of the Karens of Burma' ........... 127
Karen letter to His Excellency The Governor of Burma,
  March 1947 ..................................................... 130
Karen letter to His Excellency the Governor of Burma,
  June 1947 ........................................................ 133

After Independence, **Introduction** ...................... 135
Saw Samson, letter to The Telegraph, March 1949 ........ 137
Letters from Saw Ohn Pe to Major Dennis Ford, 1949-51 145

**After Independence** ........................................... 145
Saw Johnny Htoo ................................................. 145
Saw Aye Kyaw ...................................................... 145
Saw Smile Paul .................................................... 146
Saw Fair Play ....................................................... 147
Saw San Aye ........................................................ 158
Saw Maw Ler ....................................................... 159
Mel Du ................................................................. 159
Saw Daniel Tun Baw ............................................. 159
Saw Htoo Mar ..................................................... 161
Saw Baw Nay ....................................................... 162

## Part Two

**Interviews by Raymond Brown** .................. 166
    Saw Thu Po Mu ............................................. 166
    Saw Mahler ..................................................... 169

**Interviews at Mae La Camp, 18 January 2009** .. 173
    Sein Aye ........................................................ 173
    Maung Sein .................................................... 176
    Saw Hla Tin ................................................... 178
    Saw Percy ...................................................... 181
    Saw Dway Maung ......................................... 182

**Ban Surin Camp, November 2012** .................. 185
    Saw Harcher .................................................. 185
    Saw Thart'gay ................................................ 186
    Saw Ba Kyaw ................................................. 188

**VJ Day Interviews, 2015 by Mark Fenn** ............ 192
    Tha Din ......................................................... 192
    Saw Ba Aye .................................................... 193
    Tancy McDonald ........................................... 194

**Epilogue** ............................................................ 202
    Naw Bellay Htoo South: Brief Report from NLB 2022 .... 202
    TTT Report ................................................... 203

**Sources and Bibliography** ................................ 219

**Richard Duckett** ............................................... 225
**Naw Bellay Htoo South** ................................... 225
**Robert Lyman** .................................................. 226

**Index** ................................................................ 227

# Acknowledgements

From the time the first interviews and recordings were made until the publication of this book is a period of almost 25 years. It has, therefore, been a long time in the making and there are a number of people who have played their part along the way.

Firstly, to Lt.Col. Sam Pope RM (retired) and all with whom he worked at the Burma Forces Welfare Association for finding the veterans and their families, and then having the presence of mind to begin recording their experiences of serving the British Empire. Their goal of providing welfare to these old soldiers and/or their families so many decades after Burma gained its independence was no small undertaking, especially given the history of the country since 1948. The mantle was then taken up by the charity Help for Forgotten Allies (H4FA), and the work continues despite the march of time and the February 2021 coup. In the December 2020 UK honours list, Sally McLean, founder and chair of H4FA for over twenty years was recognised with the award of MBE for all her hard work in bringing aid to people in desperate need of medical supplies, food, and education - often in remote refugee camps hidden in the jungle or over the border in Thailand. The work of H4FA continues into 2023 with 36 veterans and 145 widows receiving grants, providing some dignity and quality of life in their final years.

Special thanks to the two oral history 'collectors', Naw Bellay Htoo South and Thra Charles, and Bellay's on-going work as seen in the reports included in the epilogue here. The translation of the testimonies from Karen into English was made possible by a grant from the Gerry Holdsworth Special Forces Charitable Trust, thereby enabling these important yet marginalised voices to reach a wider anglophile audience.

As ever, wherever SOE makes an appearance, so does the name Steven Kippax. Thanks again to him for unfailing support in providing digitised files normally within (two?) hours of an email request. During Covid lockdowns and subsequent archive inaccessibility this was especially valuable. It was also Steven who put me in touch with Sam Pope, thereby getting this project into my hands.

Immense gratitude is also due to Steve Rothwell, who really needs to write up all his amazing work on the Burmese colonial units. That there is still a huge gap in the historiography here is incredible in itself, and I know no other person with such an intimate knowledge of this part of Britain's colonial history. Steve is always so generous with his time and expertise, and he has been a great help in clarifying and providing much needed information for this book.

Thanks to Paul at Devonshire Press for taking on the publication of this project, and all those final bits of hard work that finally brought this history into the public arena.

'And lastly, much love and gratitude to my two girls, Kara and Emily; I'm a lucky man to have such a wonderful wife and daughter.'

# Preface

The longest land campaign of the Second World War was fought in Burma against the Japanese between December 1941 and August 1945. The soldiers who fought in this campaign came from all over the Empire; India, Kenya, Uganda, Nyasaland, Nigeria, The Gambia, Ghana and of course Burma itself. The second largest ethnic group in Burma, now more widely known as Myanmar, are the Karen people. Most Karen remained loyal to the British Empire throughout the colonial period, and many of their menfolk served in military units such as the Burma Rifles (Burifs). They usually made up fifty percent of each battalion of the Burifs at the outbreak of the Second World War, and many of these servicemen went on to fight with irregular or clandestine units such as the infamous Chindits, or the Special Operations Executive (SOE), known as Force 136 in the Far East. At least 12,000 Karen were recruited and served as guerrilla fighters behind the lines with SOE, in addition to the thousands who served with regular forces. Seeing action in such a range of the Empire's military and paramilitary forces, the Karen inevitably contributed great value to the campaigns in Burma, both in the defeat of 1942 and in the victory of 1945. There can be no doubt that huge sacrifices were made in their resistance to the Japanese, and then that many Karen felt let down by the terms of Burma's independence in 1948.

In this book, for the first time, the experiences of Karen servicemen have been told using their voices to reveal a unique insight into the role of the Karen in serving the British Empire before, during, and after the Second World War. Exclusive veteran interviews and access to private collections, as well as sworn statements given to war crimes investigators during 1945 and 1946, collated here, paint a fascinating picture of a people who have remained beyond the periphery of mainstream historical consciousness despite their proud yet tragic contribution to the annals of the British Empire. Theirs is a tale of loyalty and fortitude, of resistance against oppression and torture, and a determination for their core values and culture to be restored, protected, and preserved – over several decades.

Saw Johnny Htoo (note the 'Spider Group' armband).

# Introduction
# Sally McLean

I first met Bellay Htoo South in 1998 at the Euro Burma Office, Brussels where I was working. She had come to testify in a European Parliament Human Rights hearing on Burma. As a young teacher she and her family had been driven out of Karen State by the brutality of the Burma Army or Tatamadaw. We remained in touch; she and her husband Ashley South were a patient and invaluable source of information. During her years of living in the UK and then in Thailand we continued to work together to provide funds to Karen organisations working to educate, inform, feed and shelter their people in the face of the brutal oppression of the military junta. The tatmadaw's stated aim, according to some sources, was to annihilate the Karen. As a notably large ethnic nationality, with well developed political systems and a successful army the Karen constitute and always have, as this book demonstrates, a particular threat to the forces of evil.

Bellay and I have been friends for 25 years now. Both devoted to the cause of the Karen and the Golden Book; last year I had the privilege of travelling with her to visit Mae La refugee camp. Bellay kindly agreed two years ago to become a trustee of Help for Forgotten Allies, the charity I founded in 1997, and as I am getting older she is now picking up the slack.

Her patient work of recording the aural testimonies of 2nd WW veterans has been invaluable. This work was done on a shoestring and involved long hours of difficult and dangerous travel to achieve. Without her dedicated work their stories would have been lost. There are now only around 30 veterans receiving annual welfare grants through our organisation, and some of these in the Ayerwaddy Delta, have not had their stories recorded yet, but it may well be the case that they are now too old to be able to recount them. When Bellay did her painstaking work the men were still clear minded enough to remember their experiences and recount them to her.

We continue at H4FA to enjoy the benefit of Bellay's reports on her distribution of grant money, and on other projects notably providing young IDP Karen mothers forced to give birth while on the run in the jungle from the Burma Army, with essentials. The Maternity Bags project. Her love of her people and family, her sense of humour, her endurance and humility during long difficult journeys in the rainy season on muddy roads, on the back of motorbikes, and on swollen rivers shines through the reports and her courage is an inspiration.

# Foreword
# Dr Rob Lyman

This is an impressive and much needed book. Authentic voices from the men and women of the hill tribes in India and Burma telling of their experiences of the Second World War are few, at least those that are told from their own cultural and societal perspective. Oral cultures don't make it easy to capture the past, which is why the known histories of so much of this region is only generations old. This is why the author and the collectors of the oral testimonies in this book are to be congratulated. These recollections of the men and women in this book are powerful reminders of the seismic events of the war on the people of the Karen Hills, and for the first time give them a voice, in print, to an audience outside of Burma/Myanmar that would otherwise be ignorant of their existence. The book will ensure that their otherwise forgotten voices will last far beyond the couple of generations that was the fate of their parents and grand-parents.

Of especial interest to historians is the testimony of these men and women to the great anti-Japanese uprising across the Karenni, fermented by SOE, in the early months of 1945, which stopped the Japanese Army from capturing Toungoo and enabled the southward rush of General Slim's 14th Army towards Rangoon. The courage of this uprising was remarkable given that large numbers of Karens – over 12,000 – fought to liberate Burma from the Japanese. The success of the uprising was equally significant, given that without it, Slim would not have managed to reach Toungoo, and thus Rangoon, before the rains fell, and the war would have dragged into yet another monsoon period without a denouement. The role that large numbers of Karen men and women played to help in the success of Slim's reconquest of Burma, and in the liberation of their country, has for too long been forgotten. In the pages of this remarkable book, they burst back into life.

Dr Robert Lyman FRHistS
October 2023

# Oral History and this Book

This book is, primarily, a compilation of oral testimonies. 'Oral history is the recollections of a single individual who participated in or was an observer of the events to which s/he testifies.'[1] All of the testimonies are drawn from the experience of ex-servicemen from the Karen people of Burma. After the majority Bamar, the Karen are the most populous ethnic group in Burma (now increasingly referred to as Myanmar). During colonial times, the Karen were considered a martial race by the British, and therefore were prominent in the various military and paramilitary units that were used to keep order and defend the colony. The bulk of the testimonies were collected by two members of the Karen community, Naw Bellay Htoo South and Thra Charles, between approximately 1999 and 2002. As Bellay acknowledges in her statement which follows this brief exploration of oral history and how it relates to this book, the Karen people have long enjoyed a tradition of 'oral history'. This oral tradition is important to the cohesion and identity of ethnic groups, often because they have not had access to the facilities required to record their community's histories in the written form.[2]

The collection and production of oral testimonies from minority ethnic communities, and other marginalised groups such as the working class, has been termed 'Recovery History'.[3] 'Recovery History' in Britain was pioneered by Paul Thompson in the 1970s. He argued that 'once the life experience of people of all kinds can be used as its raw material, a new dimension is given to history.'[4] The creation of documents that constitute archives, and the creation of historiography based on those documents, Thompson argued, was the domain of the elites, meaning that most of the participants in history didn't have a voice. Practitioners of oral

---

[1] Gary Y. Okihiro, 'Oral History and the Writing of Ethnic History: A Reconnaissance into Method and Theory.' *The Oral History Review*, vol. 9, 1981, p.34.

[2] Laurie R. Serikaku, 'Oral History in Ethnic Communities: Widening the Focus.' *The Oral History Review*, vol. 17, no. 1, 1989, p.71.

[3] Penny Summerfield, 'Oral History as an Autobiographical Practice', *Miranda* [Online], 12 | 2016, http://journals.openedition.org/ miranda/8714 ; DOI : 10.4000/miranda.8714.

[4] Paul Thompson, *The Voice of the Past: Oral History* (OUP: Oxford, 1978), p.4.

history, therefore, are often described as giving 'a voice to the voiceless'.[5] It is this act of giving a voice to the voiceless that, according to Thompson, made history 'more democratic.'[6]

To be truly democratic, perhaps this book should have included the voice of Burma's other unheard communities. The majority Bamar population, although possibly not 'heard' so much in the West, became the ruling population from independence in 1948. As such, nationalist leaders were able to write their histories, some of which are available in English. The work of leaders such as Ba Maw, U Nu, and U Maung Maung, are probably the best known.[7] With the onset of civil war from (approximately) 1949, Burma's minority communities, such as the Karen, Kachin, Chin, and Shan, have not had the same opportunity to record their histories. These Karen testimonies now having been collected, this book aims to address at least one 'democratic' gap in our knowledge.

Part of Thompson's work to ensure the democratisation of history was to develop a methodological approach to the gathering of oral testimonies. The concern was to ensure a fair and balanced representation of the people for his study of the Edwardians.[8] The reader will find no such sampling methodology in these pages. Although thus far the testimonies in this book have been referred to as originating from the Karen people, this does not differentiate between, for example Sgaw or Pwo Karen. The only methodology used to select for an interview was finding a veteran, or the spouse of a veteran, from the Second World War, and to establish whether there was an entitlement to welfare in (belated) recognition of their service. What this means is that the testimonies recorded here are almost entirely random. As a result, the interviews concern men who served in the regular colonial units, including the Burma Rifles, the Burma Frontier Force, the Burma Auxiliary Force, the Burma Military Police, the Burma Intelligence Corps, Burma Signals and Burma Ambulance; as well as irregular units such as the Chindits and the Special Operations Executive. Within these units, the role of the men varied, from 'postman' to medic, from rifleman to guerrilla fighter; and

---

[5] Summerfield, 'Oral History as an Autobiographical Practice'.

[6] Thompson, *The Voice of the Past: Oral History*, p.7.

[7] Maw, Ba, *Break – Through in Burma: Memoirs of a Revolution, 1939-1946* (Yale University Press, 1968); Nu, Thakin, *Burma Under the Japanese* (Macmillan: London, 1954); Maung Maung, U, *Burmese Nationalist Movements 1940. –. 1948* (Kiscadale: Edinburgh, 1989).

[8] Thompson, *The Voice of the Past,* pp.123-27.

their level of responsibility ranges from camp helper to officer. In terms of age, Saw Ba Kyaw was thirteen in 1945, while Saw Johnny Htoo was in his thirties. There is a clear variation in level of educational achievement, as well as geographical spread in terms of place of birth. Seen in these terms, the testimonies collected here perhaps constitute a more representative sample of the Karen experience than might have been expected. This is important, because the aim of this book is to provide a voice for the Karen, allowing the reader to gain a sense of what it was like to serve the British Empire before, during, and after the Second World War, as well as their experience beyond independence.

Gary Okihiro has written that '[t]he oral historian is not merely a publicist of individual perceptions; the ultimate goal is the reconstruction of historical reality.'[9] With regards to this book, the first part is certainly accurate; this is intended to publicise the Karen role. At a time when the world has seen huge 'Black Lives Matter' rallies, and the associated tearing down of statues and memorials; when teachers are working hard to 'decolonise' their history curriculums, the pressure to hear the 'voice of the voiceless' has probably never been so great.[10] What this book does not seek to do is the 'reconstruction of historical reality', but it is hoped that the testimonies included might contribute to that endeavour elsewhere, providing the source material for that to be possible. With this in mind, what the reader will find within this volume is an attempt to give this set of memories some context, some clarification, and to make any necessary corrections. In a format much like the popular 'Forgotten Voices' series commissioned by Britain's Imperial War Museum, the book has been divided into chronological sections to cover the war in Burma, and beyond, with each section prefaced with a short contextual introduction.[11]

---

[9] Okihiro, 'Oral History and the Writing of Ethnic History', p.36.

[10] In 2020, in the midst of a global pandemic, BLM campaigners targeted statues like that of the slaver Edward Coulson, which was pulled down and dumped in Bristol city harbour. Even the grave of Guy Gibson's dog, the mascot of the famous 'Dambuster' RAF squadron, was replaced with a headstone which didn't bear the canine's offensive name.

[11] Regarding Burma, *see* Julian Thompson, *Forgotten Voices of the Burma Campaign* (Ebury Press: London, 2009). It should be noted that this volume does not include the testimony of Burma's indigenous population. One Anglo-Karen, Neville Hogan, is included. Rod Bailey's *Forgotten Voices of the Secret War: An Inside History of Special Operations During the Second World War* (Ebury Press: London, 2008) has a section on

In *The Voice of the Past,* Thompson wrote 'there can be no substitute for a full transcript' of an oral source.[12] The transcription process should be carefully done to preserve, as far as possible, the full sense of the testimony, the subtleties, the emotions; 'grammar and word order must be left as spoken' and words shouldn't be inserted so it makes sense because the character of the speech will get lost. Bearing this in mind, there has been minimal tampering with the transcripts as delivered, save to correct spelling mistakes such as names, and dividing the transcripts up to fit the chronological structure of the book. To tamper with the recording in its transcription is to distort the source. Distortions are a major concern of oral historians, with a broad range of ways in which it can happen. At least two means of distortion are worth discussing in relation to this work.

Firstly, oral historians agree, perhaps unsurprisingly, that translations allow for much more distortion of an oral testimony. Joanna Bornat wrote:

> Oral history's commitment to voice and self-expression has accepted the compromise which transcription introduces, but to add translation is to create another layer of distance from the original interview exchange. Cultural complexity, and attempts to balance generalisation against cultural relativism, add further deterrents.[13]

It is hoped that this may have been ameliorated to some extent by the fact that, in the first place, the interviews were conducted by Karen interviewers. The transcripts were then published in the Karen language in a book for the Karen community. This means that the community from which the narrator comes has been both a producer and a consumer of the testimonies, which Serikaku advises as the most beneficial way to conduct oral history with ethnic communities.[14] The transcripts were then translated for this publication by a Karen who speaks English,

---

the Far East with testimonies from those who served with SOE in Burma, but there is no Karen contribution.

[12] Thompson, *The Voice of the Past*, pp.198-99.

[13] Joanna Bornat, 'Oral History and Remembering.' *Research Methods for Memory Studies*, edited by Emily Keightley and Michael Pickering (Edinburgh University Press: Edinburgh, 2013), p.40.

[14] Laurie R. Serikaku, 'Oral History in Ethnic Communities: Widening the Focus.' *The Oral History Review*, vol. 17, no. 1, 1989, p.71.

rather than an English speaker of the Karen language.

Secondly, and linked to the above, another major source of distortion is the relationship between the interviewer and narrator. Such variables as the interviewer's dress, where the interview takes place, the type of questions, the motives of the interviewer, and how well trained an interviewer is as an oral history practitioner, have all been cited as possible causes of distortion.[15] These are all things that the interviewer can control, however, and use to determine the content of an oral source.[16] The content can also be impacted by the *who* rather than the *how*. In America, a 1942 survey found a significant difference in answers when Afro-Americans were interviewed by another Afro-American compared to a white person.[17] While this highlights race relations in America, it is also instructive in the consideration of how a narrator will respond to an interview by someone from within their community compared to an outsider. As already noted, the majority of these interviews were carried out by members of the Karen community, but the latter interviews were not. Readers may judge for themselves the interesting contrast in the presentation of the transcripts, and possibly the nature of the content. The point, made quite clearly by Thompson, is that in both scenarios the potential for distortion is something to be aware of.

What these points about distortion should reveal is that oral history does not present some 'Holy Grail' of historical veracity. Like any source available to an historian, the oral testimony needs to be treated with due care and diligence. 'Positivism' in the early days of oral history was based on the idea that here was access to the past which had not been exploited, the benefits of which could be seen in challenges to prevailing views such as the perception that the Suffragettes were a distinctly middle class affair.[18] Detractors of oral history have argued about the subjectivity of the testimony, but oral history practitioners argue that subjectivity applies to any source. The difference is that with documents the subjectivity of the source is fixed. As Alessandro Portelli has written, 'oral history will never be the same twice', just as in normal speech we don't

---

[15] Okihiro, 'Oral History and the Writing of Ethnic History', p.37.

[16] Alessandro Portelli, 'The Peculiarities of Oral History', *History Workshop*, no. 12, 1981, p.103.

[17] Thompson, *The Voice of the Past*, p.115.

[18] Bornat, 'Oral History and Remembering', p.32-33.

explain something verbatim for a second time.[19] A relationship can be built between an interviewer and a narrator, and as it is built, for example, so might trust be gained leading to increasing levels of disclosure. An on-going dialogue is able to be constructed with a living person, as opposed to a document, so gaps can be filled, questions asked, points clarified, and more memories provoked. One of the old soldiers in this collection, Saw Mawler, was interviewed twice. Both transcripts are included here, providing clear differences in what was recalled and/or shared.

One of the more obvious criticisms that has been consistently directed at oral sources is the problem of memory.[20] Although issues of reliability still have not disappeared, Summerfield points out how there has been a shift from interest in the reliability of the memory to how memory is constructed and narratives composed: how do 'interviewees construct themselves through narratives that arise in dialogue with an interviewer, and how [do] personal experience and public histories interact in the production of memory stories'?[21] Some of this construction can perhaps be seen in the response of Saw Ba Kyaw, who gave a 'proud military salute' upon meeting his interviewer. If arguments about memory may be distilled into Portelli's observation that "[t]here are no 'false' oral sources' because 'untrue statements are still psychologically true', it is then down to the historian to decide which sources s/he will use to construct their account of the past.

So why is this book important? Thompson wrote, back in 1978, that:

> by bringing recognition to substantial groups of people who have been ignored, a cumulative process of transformation is set in motion. The scope of historical writing itself is enlarged and enriched; and at the same time its social message changes.[22]

If history is the re-creation and the re-telling of the past, it is indeed a cumulative process. If significant participants have not had their voice heard, for whatever reason - gender, race, class, ethnicity, sexuality - then that cumulative process will always be incomplete. If our history is incomplete, then so is our understanding of it. By creating sources like

---

[19] Alessandro Portelli, 'The Peculiarities of Oral History', p.103.

[20] *See* Thompson, *The Voice of the Past*, pp.100-114.

[21] Summerfield, 'Oral History as an Autobiographical Practice'.

[22] Thompson, *The Voice of the Past*, p.7.

these oral testimonies, which bring voices to the voiceless, our understanding is progressed. To properly achieve this progression, 'the historian must shed the intellectual arrogance which presumes that s/he knows better than the historical actors themselves or that non literate peoples have no conception of history.'[23] Forty years have passed since Thompson wrote of enriching history and Okihiro wrote of how that needs to be done by shedding intellectual arrogance, yet the year 2020 has shown that the 'voiceless' do not always perceive that their contribution to, and their place in, history has been acknowledged. If we agree with Okihiro that '[t]he writing of ethnic history is both necessary and possible' then why is it still missing from books such as the 'Forgotten Voices' series?[24] This is not to say that oral history has all the answers; Okihiro once again:

> While oral history does not maintain that each individual's view of history is legitimate or that every voice must be heard, it does agree that by going directly to the people for historical documents, a more valid variety of history can be written.[25]

It hoped that, in at least some small but cumulative way, the Karen testimonies contained in this volume can contribute to the construction of a 'more valid variety of history'.

To add further depth and texture to the oral testimonies, it was decided that other Karen sources would be added to the book. Researching the Special Operations Executive in Burma led to meeting Burma veteran's children or grandchildren, and access to a, perhaps surprising, amount of papers that never made it into the archives. These included notes and reports brought home from operations, but more impressively, correspondence between Karen and British veterans spanning the decades after the Second World War. That such a close bond had been created between these soldiers is unsurprising really, considering that in many cases these men had served behind the lines with each other for up to nine months; what is surprising is that the friendship and concern for the plight of the Karens so obviously persisted for the rest of their lives. Simple time, let alone physical distance and a civil war, seem to have been thwarted as obstacles by

---

[23] Okihiro, 'Oral History and the Writing of Ethnic History', p.27.

[24] Okiniro, *ibid*, p.42.

[25] *Ibid*, pp.45-6.

friendship forged through combat experience, and a sense of shame and injustice provoked by the decolonisation of Burma. A modern equivalent might be the sense of betrayal caused by the British withdrawal from Afghanistan in August 2021, which left friends of the British Army at the mercy of the Taliban.

It was felt that these letters, like the oral testimonies, provided an authentic voice, and filled gaps in our understanding of how the Karen perceived their world after the British left Burma. When placed alongside the transcripts of Karen speeches given at victory parades, and documents retrieved from the archives petitioning the Governor and the Secretary of State for Burma for consideration of their concerns for the future, it is hoped that the reader will agree that a very evocative and powerful story emerges. In addition, the fluke find of a misnamed file in the UK's National Archives revealed the sworn testimonies of Karens who had been tortured by the Japanese during the war. Their signed affidavits were to be used in war crimes trials which never took place, but the Karen experience of Japanese brutality described therein provides a sharp insight into what the Karens suffered in the defence not only of their own communities, but of the British Empire - something they evidently loved and respected. Where the oral histories are often a recital of remembered facts about their lives, the sworn testimonies, the speeches used to open victory ceremonies, and the letters from across the decades provide the emotion; they enable entry into a tragic story that will hopefully connect you, the reader, to a remarkable people whose voices have never been heard, at least outside of their own community.

# Statement of Oral History Collector, Naw Bellay Htoo South

Oral history has been a custom of Karen people since the beginning. Therefore, there was not much literature on the history of the Karen published. Most of the time, our ancestors orally handed down about Karen stories, legends, poems (or Htah) from generation to generation. The history and knowledge of our ancestors is gradually fading out because the younger generations do not know the value and understand those poems anymore. Therefore, both secular and religious leaders as well as teachers have researched and collected and explained the poems, stories and experiences of our forefathers. Therefore, I enthusiastically collected the information about the experiences of Karen soldiers in World War Two during the war between the British and Japanese in Myanmar. As they are not living with us forever we arranged interviews with them and recorded their answers and wrote it as they said. Some veterans are not in good health but they tried their best to answer all our questions during the interviews. A few stories were collected from Tham Hin camp and some from Myanmar. The data might not be accurate and complete because they have told us what they could remember.

The vision of this oral history book is for the present and future generations to read and understand the experience of these Karen soldiers. This book will be there forever for us to learn about the history of our forefathers when they are not here to tell us about themselves.

I had my own story that motivates me to collect this information. When I was four or five years old, I used to see my grandfather's younger brother from my mother's side who we called Phu Hla Kyi Par (Saw Meh Du) who was blind. I asked my mother why he was blind and why do we have to help him to walk with a walking stick? My mother said the Japanese had tortured him until he was blind during World War Two.

This story is always stuck in my mind. Now, my mother has written about it. In 2001, I had a good opportunity to work with the Burma Forces Welfare Association (BFWA). My duty was to meet veterans and widowers from World War Two at Tham Hin Camp. I took this opportunity to collect data about their experiences. Moreover, I got some information from BFWA records. We did not get any support while we were collecting the information from the veterans but, if you try enthusiastically, you will be successful in any case.

Lastly, I would like to thank the Open Society Institute (now the Open Society Foundation (OSF)) who supported me to attend workshops to observe the compilation of Oral History in South Africa and moreover, I would like to thank Dr. Mandy Sadan and Dr. Michael Gravers for their advice concerning Oral History which enriched my understanding about data collection.

Furthermore, thanks to the British Forces Welfare Association's Lieutenant Colonel Sam Pope OBE who allowed me to have information about some of our forefathers and thanks to Mrs. Sally Steen who supported with recording facilities. And thanks to Thra Aung Moo Day and Thra Charles who helped collect and write about the lives of soldiers during World War Two and then thanks to Thramu Lar Say Wah Heh who helped me in typing and translating this document.

Thanks to Dr Ashley South who encouraged, supported and advised me not to be disheartened during the process of data collection about the Karen soldiers who fought in World War Two and thanks to Saw Soe Moo's grandmother who let me know about my grandfather's brother. Finally, I would like to thank all the readers and I hope this book will be beneficial and valuable for future generations.

Naw Bellay Htoo South

# Statement of Oral History Collector, Thra Charles

For Burma, World War Two lasted from December 1941 to August 1945, altogether three years and nine months. In Myanmar, people say it was an English-Japanese (Ko Lah Wah – Short Leg) War.

The Japanese bombed Pearl Harbor on 7 December 1941 and America finally became an ally of the British. Eight days later, on 15 December 1941, the Japanese army seized Victoria Point in southern Burma, (now called Kawthaung). The colonial defence forces for Burma had been reorganised before the Japanese launched their attack. The following armed groups were under the administration of Burma Rifles (Burifs):

1. Burma Military Police (BMP)
2. Burma Auxiliary Force (BAF)
3. Burma Army Signals (BAS)
5. Burma Territorial Force (BTF)
6. Burma Frontier Force (BFF)

The Burma Rifles battalions were normally comprised of four companies, two Karen and one each of Kachin and Chin. This meant it was roughly made up of 50% Karen, 25% Chin, and 25% Kachin. There were other ethnicities in the various units, such as Bamar, Gurkha and Indians. Among the Karen soldiers, the most famous who became leaders were educated people such as Smith Dun, Hanson Kya Doe, and Sar Pho. Among the three, Smith Dun and Kya Doe had been sent to Sandhurst, England for officer training. Altogether there were about 20,000 soldiers, 4,000 of which were based in Yangon.

The Japanese army was dominant, so the British army withdrew to India in 1942. While the whole British army including Karen soldiers withdrew to India, there remained an English officer, Captain Seagrim with his Karen Levy soldiers who were holding positions at Papun on the Than Lwin River bank at a place called Kho Lo District. The Japanese tried to capture the English officer.

After the British army evacuated, the Japanese army governed the whole of Burma and the Burma Rifles personnel who did not leave for India went back to their villages. The Bamar dominated Burma

Independence Army (BIA), who had invaded Burma with the Japanese to liberate their country from British colonial rule under the Japanese. Later, the BIA changed its name to Burma Defence Army (BDA), remaining under the command of General Aung San. Dr. Ba Maw became Prime Minister of the country as a puppet of the Japanese. During that time, the Japanese army searched for Captain Seagrim in the Karen Hills and BIA soldiers burnt villages, captured and tortured Karen people and raped Karen women. On top of that, they made Karen women serve as sex-slaves for their soldiers.

In 1944, the Japanese captured Captain Seagrim who gave himself up because a lot of Karen villagers were being captured, tortured and interrogated about his whereabouts. Now a Major, Seagrim was executed in Rangoon along with seven Karens. They were Lieutenant Ba Kyaw, Saw He Be, Saw Htun Lin, Saw Sar Ni, Saw Pay, Saw Peter and Saw Ah Din. Before Major Seagrim surrendered himself, two other British officers who had been parachuted into the Karen Hills in 1943 to work with Major Seagrim, were shot dead at their hiding places in the jungle. Their names were Captain Jimmy Nimmo and Captain Eric McCrindle.

After the war finished in 1945, the British governed again until they gave Burma independence on 4 January 1948. During World War Two, many lost their lives including people from Europe, Asia, Karens and other races in Burma. After World War Two, the British built a war cemetery to pay tribute to the fallen soldiers, especially in Yangon and Thailand. Major Seagrim and his Karen comrades were buried in Yangon War Cemetery.

The British Commonwealth Ex-services League (BCEL) was formed and collected information about the veterans and in 1999 they started supporting ex-soldiers and the wives of those who were killed during World War Two. Due to the limitations of the budget and the number of people to support, they cooperated with Burma Force Association (BFA). According to the list, there were 2000 veterans and wives of those who had passed away. Not only Karen but also Chin, Kachin, Karenni and others. This is not a complete story of World War Two but a chance to read the stories of Karen soldiers who are still alive, or who gave their lives, and to remember and be proud of their sacrifice.

Thra Charles

IDP veteran Mau Pleh Hser.

Peter Mitchel and Veterans, 17th February 2013.

Karen Veteran couple.

Veteran Saw Pha Cha Law.

Veteran Saw Ler Hay.
Portrait by Wendy Aldiss.

Veteran Saw Polar.

# Part One

Photo credit | mohigan

# Pre-War, Introduction

Having written a history of the Special Operations Executive (SOE) in Burma during the Second World War, I was honoured to be asked if I could help to get the stories of the Karen soldiers presented here published in the United Kingdom.[26] While researching the role of SOE's Force 136 in Burma, I was struck by the number of people from Burma who participated in that conflict but who don't seem to have had their voices heard – in the west at least. It is estimated that around 20,000 Burmese, from all ethnicities, fought with Force 136 to free their country from Japanese Imperialism.[27] An estimated 12,000 of that number were Karen.

Thousands more Burmese fought with other clandestine organisations such as the American Office of Strategic Services (OSS) and the British Secret Intelligence Service (SIS); irregular units such as the Chindits, the Chin Levies and Kachin Levies, as well as V Force and Z Force; and in regular formations such as the Burma Rifles, Burma Frontier Force, Burma Military Police and the Burma Regiment. Their motivation to fight varied. Some people fought against the Japanese from the beginning, in the hope that the British would be reinstalled as the colonial power, while others changed their mind over the course of the Japanese occupation. The latter, mostly from the majority Burman, or Bamar, population, realised that defeating the Japanese was one of many steps required to gain the independence that the Japanese had failed to provide with the 'independence' they granted Burma in August 1943. So while most of the indigenous population of Burma were quite obviously anti-Japanese by 1945, it did not necessarily follow that all were pro-British. This, however, did not preclude the British from recruiting them in both regular and irregular roles in order to prosecute the war.

Although almost all of the ethnicities that call Burma their home

---

[26] Richard Duckett, *The Special Operations Executive in Burma: Jungle Warfare and Intelligence Gathering in World War Two* (IB Tauris: London, 2017).

[27] In an effort to commemorate all those who fought with SOE in Burma, I have been compiling a Roll of Honour. Some fifteen files of training records of Burmese and other non-Caucasian personnel have been consulted to contribute to this record. *See* 'The Men of SOE Burma' [online,] https://soeinburma.wordpress.com/the-men-of-soe-burma/

fought in the war, and all certainly lived through it in one way or another, this work is based on the transcripts of interviews carried out from the Karen community only. It should be made clear that this is not for any political reason. Seeking greater understanding and clarification of the past is the pursuit of all historians, and it is hoped that this book will add to our collective comprehension of this aspect of the Second World War. It is only by revealing these 'hidden' histories – particularly the under or unheard colonial voices - that we will better understand the Second World War in Burma. It should also help us to understand what has happened in the turbulent decades since the war's conclusion.

The effort to give more prominence to the voices of marginalised veterans is not new. In 1997, the BBC *Timewatch* programme broadcast a series entitled *Forgotten Allies* which featured an episode on Burma.[28] In 2019, Grammar Productions premiered their film about 'forgotten' Burmese allies, based on two years of research in Burma, locating and interviewing former soldiers in a race against the march of time. The Grammar Productions team was greatly assisted by the charity Help for Forgotten Allies (H4FA).[29] A 'chance meeting' in 1998 had led to the founding of H4FA, whose aim is to provide welfare for surviving veterans or their immediate family. At the same time as H4FA was being established, the Burma Forces Welfare Association was formed, also with the aim of providing welfare to the surviving ex-servicemen and their widows. Both organisations gained charitable status and worked in Burma and along the Thai border to find veterans and provide much needed assistance. It was during this time that the interviews in this volume were recorded, as the two charities identified those who were entitled to welfare based on their wartime service.

The interviews were originally made into a transcript in the Sgaw Karen language, which was then published in 2009 as *Days Not To Be Forgotten*.[30] Later, the transcripts were translated with funding from the Gerry Holdsworth Special Forces Trust, with the intention of being published in English.[31]

---

[28] BBC *Timewatch*, 'Forgotten Allies', available [online], https://www.youtube.com/watch?v=xTJ3q5yg38Q

[29] Help for Forgotten Allies [online], http://www.h4fa.org.uk/about-us

[30] *Days Not to be Forgotten* published by Drum Publications, *see* http://www.lulu.com/shop/drum-publication-group/days-not-to-be-forgotten/paperback/product-5524024.html

[31] The Gerry Holdsworth Special Forces Trust [online], http://holdsworthtrust.org/

In an effort to give context to these accounts and find out more about the men interviewed, the records kept in the British Library and the National Archives in London, were the primary sources of information. Since a significant number of the interviewees joined Force 136, a suitable starting point seemed to be the fifteen files of 'Training Cards and Reports' which altogether contain the details of approximately 600 non-Caucasian personnel who served with the Special Operations Executive (SOE).[32] This ended up being much more difficult than anticipated because of the British record keeper's misspelling of Burmese names. Whether through Anglicisation, a lack of familiarity with non-Anglophone names, or typing errors, on many records there were several different spellings of a name, sometimes on a single page. This inconsistency of spelling names made it difficult to ascertain whether the 'Saw Johnny' presented here was the same man as 'Saw Johnnie' in the records. In the end, it was clear that he could not be the same person.

Another interviewee who provided a challenge was Lieutenant Saw Smile Paul. Those men who achieved a commission on a level with British officers were few. There should have been a record of Lieutenant Saw Smile Paul receiving his commission, or the award of the British Empire Medal he speaks about in his interview, but searching the London Gazette for his Anglicised name as well as his Karen name yielded no results. His prominent role with the Force 136 guerrillas in Operation Character also led me to expect an 'easy find' in the SOE files. Eventually, reference to Saw Smile Paul was found at the end of one of the British officer's reports where special mention was made of a handful of Karen who had been invaluable in the success of operations in their specific area.

In a number of the interviews, the old soldiers recalled the names of their commanding officers. The difficulties posed by the Anglicisation of Karen names was now reversed; very often, the spelling of British officer's names was inaccurate, based on memory and/or phonetics, and some therefore proved quite tricky to decipher from the translation. To try and trace the correct name and career of the officers of the Burma Rifles mentioned, the British Library's India Office Records provided many of the details, however, also extremely useful in this regard, was Steve Rothwell, whose work and collegiality on the units of the Burma Army has been incredibly helpful.

---

[32] The National Archives (hereafter TNA), HS 1/29. –. HS 1/43, 'Training Cards and Reports'. The records vary, but most have a standard form, and some have a photo of the recruit.

The complementary research to accompany these interviews has been put into footnotes to keep the transcript free from interruptions. The transcripts themselves have been sectioned into a chronological structure, so that the reader could get a sense of the different phases of the war in Burma and each soldier's place in it. Each chronological section of the book has a brief overview of the next period to be covered by the interviewees, and each interviewee has a brief header to remind the reader of their story up until that point. Some of the transcripts go beyond 1945 and offer insight into what happened after the war.

Many Karen servicemen, and the British officers and men who served with them, felt let down by the British government in the post-war years. Burma gained independence swiftly, a little over two years after the cessation of hostilities, on 4 January 1948. The form independence took was not perceived by the Karen as safeguarding their interests. There was a fear of what would happen to the Karen living under a majority Burman administration. These fears were amplified both by the creation of a unitary state, and when the Burmese government decided not to be part of the Commonwealth. It was not long before civil war began, officially, in 1949. Some former British officers and colonial officials formed a group called the 'Friends of the Burma Hill People', but they were unable to do much to help as their intentions ran contrary to British Foreign Office policy. As the conflict in Burma between the various factions and ethnicities deepened, except for some private correspondence between Karen and British individuals, contact all but ceased and the service of Burma's Second World War veterans was subsumed by more immediate survival needs.

In what follows, the transcripts have remained, as far as conducive to coherence and accuracy allowed, unaltered from the translated versions. It was felt that as little editing or correction of details as possible would retain as much authenticity of the oral source as possible, and so let the reader 'hear' the voice of these Karen servicemen after nearly eight long decades of silence.

### Pre-war

In March 1824, the British East India Company went to war against the Burmese empire. Burmese troops were on the offensive in the Arakan and Assam, probing into north eastern India, towards Calcutta. To regain the initiative, British forces landed in Rangoon to engage the Burmese army on terrain it was more comfortable fighting in. After a determined resistance, British forces eventually forced a surrender. In the

Colonel Sam Pope (centre standing) of the Burma Forces Welfare Association with Karen veterans at Mae La, circa 2000. Photo courtesy of Col. Sam Pope (centre).

Saw Aye Kyaw (standing) with un-named Karen veterans. Photo courtesy of Col. Sam Pope, Burma Forces Welfare Association.

Umpiem Mai Refugee Camp. Photo courtesy of Col. Sam Pope, Burma Forces Welfare Association (and below).

Widow of Daniel Tun Baw. Photo courtesy of Col. Sam Pope, Burma Forces Welfare Association.

resulting treaty, the Burmese kingdom lost the long 'tail' of southern Burma, Tenasserim; in the north west of the country, they lost the Arakan (now referred to as Rakhine). These areas became part of the British Empire, run by the British East India Company.

Between 1826 and 1852, resistance to East India Company rule continued with frequent skirmishes where the Burmese Kingdom met company territory.[33] Tensions resulted in a second war in 1852-53, which concluded with the East India Company's annexation of lower Burma. This left the Burmese Kingdom in control of a vast swathe of territory cut off from the sea in central Burma. Four years later in 1857, the Indian Mutiny led to the East India Company's possessions being formally taken over by the British Crown. This meant that the Third Anglo-Burmese War in 1885-6 was fought on behalf of Her Majesty's Government, and the Burmese lost the last part of their Kingdom. This

---

[33] *See*, for example, Parimal Ghosh, *Brave Men of the Hills: Resistance and Rebellion in Burma, 1825 - 1932* (Hurst: London, 2000), chapter 1; James Lunt, *A Hell of A Licking: The Retreat from Burma 1942-2* (Collins: London, 1986), pp.24-9.

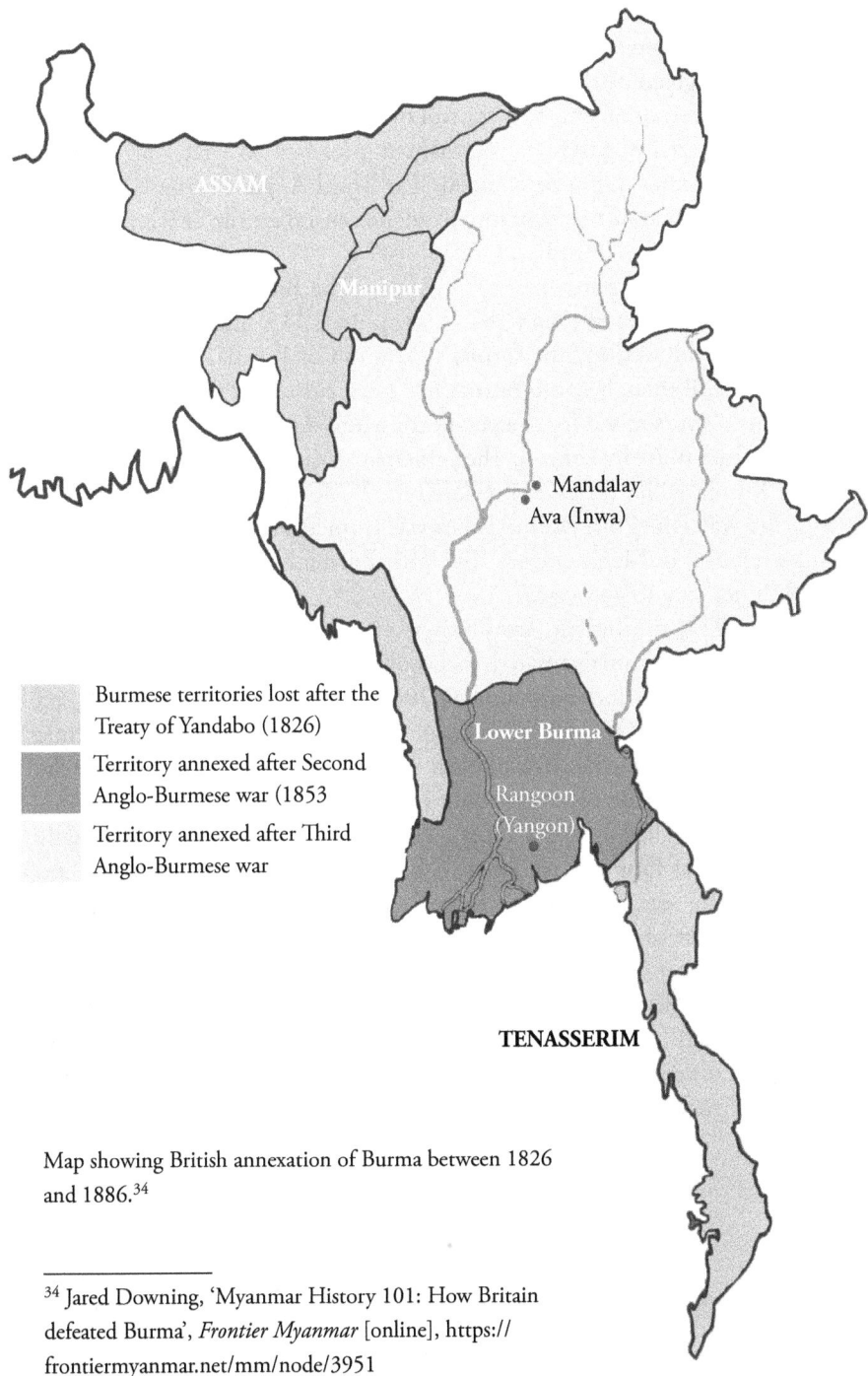

Map showing British annexation of Burma between 1826 and 1886.[34]

---

[34] Jared Downing, 'Myanmar History 101: How Britain defeated Burma', *Frontier Myanmar* [online], https://frontiermyanmar.net/mm/node/3951

war occurred during the period known as 'New Imperialism', when competition between European powers for overseas possessions was at its peak. As agreed at the Berlin Conference of 1884-5, European powers were required to take formal control over any overseas territory that they wished to claim, leaving a permanent presence so that war between European states might be avoided. The Third Anglo-Burmese War thus marked the end of Burmese independence and the exile of King Thibaw, Burma's last king, to India.

For the next approximately fifty years, the British ruled Burma as a province of India through the Viceroy. In 1935, the Government of India Act allowed for the formal separation of Burma from the Raj in 1937. Until then, because Burma had been ruled as a province of India, the main units raised for the pacification and defence of the colony were under Indian Army control. The principal army formation in Burma was the Burma Rifles (often abbreviated to 'Burifs'), established during the Great War. The 70th Burma Rifles was formed in 1917, in time to join the fighting in Mesopotamia. The 85th Burma Rifles was established in 1918, too late to go overseas.

In 1922, the Indian Army was reorganised. The two Burma Rifles regiments were amalgamated to become the 20th Burma Rifles. This meant that the 2nd Battalion of 70th Regiment (2/70) became 2nd Battalion, 20th Burma Rifles, or 2/20 Burif. While the ethnic composition of the Burifs had been inclusive from 1917, from 1927 the decision was made to recruit only from the Karen, Kachin and Chin - Burma's so-called 'martial races'. Thus, a Burif battalion was usually composed of four companies, two Karen and one each of Kachin and Chin. The decision to exclude Burmans was reversed after the Government of India Act came into force in 1937, but recruitment of ethnic Burmans, or Bamar, remained low. It was a similar story with the other paramilitary units formed for colonial rule: the Burma Military Police (BMP), and the Burma Frontier Force (BFF) battalions were largely composed of either the Burmese 'martial' races or the Indian 'martial' races.

| Ethnicity | 1938 | 1939 |
|---|---|---|
| Gurkha | 2390 | 2328 |
| Sikh | 1523 | 1543 |
| Punjabi Mussalman | 1386 | 1424 |
| Dogra Rajput | 140 | 32 |
| Garhwali Rajput | 433 | 438 |
| Kumanonis | 356 | 450 |
| Karen | 134 | 183 |
| Kachin | 598 | 725 |
| Chin | 618 | 620 |
| Shan | 131 | 159 |
| **Total** | **7716** | **8086** |

The ethnic composition of the Burma Frontier Force in 1938-39.[35]

Between October 1939 and July 1941, expansion and redesignation meant that the Burma Army consisted of the following:

**1st Battalion**
Formed 1st April 1937 from the 1st Battalion, 20th Burma Rifles. Included Burmans.
**2nd Battalion**
Formed 1st April 1937 from the 2nd Battalion, 20th Burma Rifles.
**3rd Battalion**
Formed 1st April 1937 from the 3rd Battalion, 20th Burma Rifles.
**4th Battalion**
Formed 1st April 1937 from the 10th Battalion, 20th Burma Rifles.
**5th Battalion**
Raised 1st April 1940. One company was Burman.
**6th Battalion**
Raised 15th February 1941. One company was Burman.
**7th (Burma Police) Battalion**
Raised 1st November 1940, at Mandalay from a nucleus of men of the Burma Police and Burma Military Police; composition was Gurkha, Sikh, Punjabi Mussalman and Burman.

---

[35] *See* British Library (hereafter B.L.), IOR V/24/1684 Annual Reports BFF, Rangoon Government Printing & Stationery.

**8th (Frontier Force) Battalion**
Raised 1st October 1940, composed of Sikhs and Punjabi Mussalmans serving with the Burma Frontier Force.

**9th (Reserve) Battalion**
Formed on 24th July 1941, a holding unit responsible for training recruits who passed out of the 10th Battalion.

**10th (Training) Battalion**
Raised on 1st July 1941, a training unit at Maymyo.

**11th (Territorial) Battalion**
Formed on 1st April 1937 from 11th (Territorial) Battalion, 20th Burma Rifles, Indian Territorial Force.

Saw Johnny Htoo, photo adapted from unpublished memoir of Henry Stonor.

**12th (Lower Burma) Battalion**
Raised on 1st October 1939, composed of Burmans and Karens. Headquarters and two companies were raised partly by transfer of men from the 11th Battalion. Two further companies were raised in 1940.

**13th (Shan States) Battalion**
Raised on 1st December 1939, to guard RAF aerodromes; officered by Shans, Karen and Burmans, the majority being Shans.

**14th (Shan States) Battalion**
Raised 15th May 1941, to guard RAF aerodromes; officered by Shans, Karen and Burmans, the majority being Shans.[36]

In the interviews which follow, many of the men served in the battalions set out above, serving as infantrymen, signallers, or non-commissioned officers. Others served with the navy, the ambulance section of the Burma Army Medical Corps while others were still at school when the war started.

---

[36] *See* B.L., L/MIL/17/7/11-13, Burma Army List, 1941; Steve Rothwell, 'The Burma Rifles' [online], https://homepages.force9.net/rothwell/burmaweb/burif.htm

# Pre-War

## Saw Johnny Htoo[37]

On 19 October 1932, I joined 10/20 Burma Rifles battalion, in Maymyo (Pyin Oo Lwin).[38] My regimental number was 4074. After I attended recruit training, I was assigned to 3rd battalion Burma Rifles. At that time, our battalion Major was Major F.O.N. Ford and the battalion commander was Lieutenant Colonel Buddet; I don't remember the correct spelling of his name.[39] At that time, I was just an NCO instructor. I attended a small arms training course in India, at Panchamari. After I passed Q1 (quality first class), the highest level, I came back to 3rd Burma Rifles battalion in Mandalay and was assigned as a military instructor. I

---

[37] Saw Johnny Htoo photographed by Henry Stonor (known as Tony) served in Burma after the Second World War, when he established a strong affection for the Karen. He became a lifelong supporter and campaigner for the Karen in their struggle against the Burma government. Photo from *'Henry Stonor (Henri Mon Ami: 11 May 1926 - 26 February 2006',* unpublished memoir compilation. Possibly from an article entitled 'Man of Parts: the Nebulous Nineties' in *The Magazine,* date unknown. Tony mentions that he met Saw Johnny Htoo again in 1991 when touring Thai-Burma border.

[38] Maymyo was the British Hill Station to the east of Mandalay which provided a more agreeable climate for British colonial administrators during the dry season. It was also the home of the Burma Rifles (Burifs), the first battalion of Burifs having formed there in 1917.

[39] Major Frank O'Neill Ford OBE, was born 26 September 1894. He was a career soldier, serving with the Burma Rifles in the Mesopotamian Campaign during the Great War. By 1921 he was company commander of 5/70 Burifs, a Kachin and Chin battalion. He served almost exclusively in Burma from 1920 through to his retirement in 1947. During the Second World War, he won the Order of the British Empire (OBE) for commanding the Kachin Levies between 1943 and 1945. See B.L., IOR/L/MIL/14//12001, Ford's personal record. Lieutenant Colonel Ernest Wyndham Burdett DSO, MC, was born 5 September 1887. He was commissioned in August 1907 and served in India before the Great War. During the Great War, when he won the Military Cross, he fought in the Mesopotamian Campaign from October 1914 until he was captured in April 1916. During the interwar period he served in India and Burma, winning the DSO during the Burmese Rebellion of 1930-32. He retired as officer commanding 3/20 Burifs in April 1936. See B.L., IOR/L/MIL/14/11926, Burdett's personal record.

passed Roman Urdu second class in Military Education and English first class in the 1934-35 academic year.

During the Wa States Expedition I was included and lost one of my men by the name of Saw Tha Htay, after we had battled for three hours, with the Wa people.[40] They lost thirty killed and forty went missing. At that time, our Company Commander was F.O.N. Ford and our column Commander was Colonel R.C. Fletcher.[41] The battalion rewarded me with a double barreled shotgun and a certificate of honour.

---

[40] Between 1934 and 1936 there were several Wa States expeditions. The Wa States are in northeastern Burma, bordering Yunnan Province, China. At this time, the northern Wa territory was not under British administrative control, and the border between China and Burma was contested. On 13 January 1934, the Burma Corporation, with Government of Burma protection in the form of a column of Burma Military Police, sent a team of engineers to investigate the prospect of mining in the area. Although in terms of future mineral exploitation the expedition was a disappointment, the need to agree a border and administer the area led to later expeditions.

[41] In 1936, when he led a column into the Wa States, Roger Cormell Fletcher was a Major. He was in charge of a 'southern punitive column' into the Wa States from January to June 1936, see B.L., L/PS/20/D230, 'Report on route of southern punitive column by Major R.C. Fletcher, I.A.', 21 July 1936. He was promoted to Lieutenant Colonel and took command of 3/20 Burifs, succeeding Burdett in October 1936.

Saw Aye Kyaw in 2004 with Bellay Htoo's son.

## Saw Aye Kyaw

I was born in the Delta region, Pyapon Township, Kyite Latt, Ka Dite Village, in 1920 and studied in Yone Dauk Middle School.[42] I left school in 1938 and served at B.A.M.C H.Q, British Army, Sale Barracks (Gaw Yar Gone) and the OC's [Officer Commanding] name was Major Shanker.[43] Soon after Dr. Mg Mg Gyi was appointed, I served in the Ambulance Section and those who were in the Nursing Section had to attend training at Mingaladon, Maymyo and Mandalay. The Ambulance Section had to attend training at Sale Barracks and right before the war with Japan there was recruitment for new soldiers and I became a Sergeant, called Havildar in the Indian Army.

---

[42] The 'Delta region' is where the Irrawaddy River meets the Andaman Sea. Pyapon is approximately 75 miles southwest of Rangoon. 'Kyite Latt is most likely 'Kyaiklat' which is its own Township in modern Myanmar, with Pyapon being a District of the Ayeyarwady Region.

[43] Sale Barracks were in Rangoon, on the site of Alanpya Pagoda (also known as Signal, Sale or McCreagh's Pagoda). The pagoda and barracks were named after Major-General Sir Henry Sale, 1782-1845. As a Major, Sale helped capture Rangoon in the first Anglo-Burmese War 1824-1826. 'BAMC' probably stands for Burma Army Medical Corps. Major Bhavani Shanker, commissioned 1926, see B.L., IOR/L/MIL/14/69428. Dr Maung Maung Gyi was also a Major in the Indian Medical Service.

## Saw Fair Play

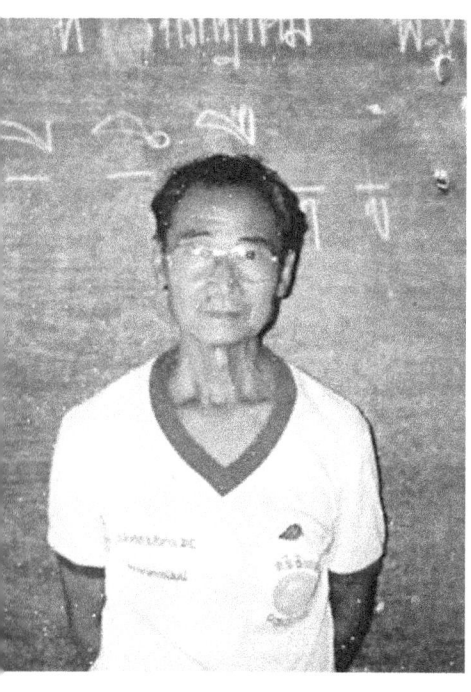

I, Saw Fair Play John, was born on 22 October 1924 in Kyawt Mae Taw, Dawei [Tavoy] region. I'm a Karen and a Christian. I studied in one of the Burmese schools but I did not understand anything, so my parents sent me to a village school called Pa Saw Law in Dawei Khee village. They put me into Grade 4 but I had to restart again from the Kindergarten as I did not understand any-thing and I was punched in the stomach by my cousin teacher. I got sick and was sent back to Dawei. I studied again in Mawro Karen High School Tavoy and passed up to Grade 8.

Saw Fair Play. Photo courtesy of Col. Sam Pope, Burma Forces Welfare Association.

## Saw K'Hsaw

I was staying at Phaw Mu Doh Village, which was a small township in Papun, Kro Lo District (now Mu Traw District). In 1941, I went into Mone jungle (now Mone Township) in Upper Myanmar. I worked under the supervision of managers from Timber Union at Bombay Burma Trading Corporation Ltd.[44]

## Saw Kay Ray

I was born on 16 December, 1916 and I went to school until I finished Grade 8. I joined the British army on 11 June, 1937 as part of the Burma Military Police (B.M.P). My regimental number was 2797 when I first joined Burma Military Police and the Commander was Major Chappell.[45] The Instruction Officer was Major Bennett, when I was at

---

[44] The Bombay Burmah Trading Corporation was founded in 1863, originally to trade in tea between Burma and India. See A.C. Pointon, *Bombay Burmah Trading Corporation, 1863-1963* (Millbrook Press: Southampton, 1964) and Anthony Webster, *Gentleman Capitalists: British Imperialism in Southeast Asia 1770-1880* (IB Tauris: London, 1998).

[45] Major Hereward Chappell, born 21 April 1898, was commissioned in April 1916. In

Burma Frontier Force (B.F.F), and my regimental number was W-640.[46] I was only 20 when I joined B.M.P. After serving one and a half year, I was transferred to Pyaw Bwe front line.[47]

## Saw San Aye

My name is Saw San Aye I am now 76 years old. I am from Tharyarwady [also spelt Tharrawaddy] region. I joined 1st Burma Rifles, Training Company, British Army in 1938. My regimental number was 7279. Lieutenant Colonel J.C. Martin MC was our Battalion Commander.[48] The other officers were Second Battalion Commander Major Rosely, Adjutant Captain Stringer, Company Commander Major Blaber and Platoon Commander Captain Moore.[49] I served in Mingaladon for one

---

the Great War he served in Mesopotamia and Salonika. In the inter-war period he was posted to Waziristan and later Burma where he served with the Burma Military Police (BMP) from 1931. In 1938 was appointed commandant of 2nd Rangoon battalion, BMP. After the retreat from Burma, he commanded the 4th, and later the 2nd Battalion, the Burma Regiment. *See* Steve Rothwell, '1st and 2nd Rangoon Battalions, Burma Military Police' [online], https://homepages.force9.net/rothwell/burmaweb/RangoonBattalionsBMP.htm

[46] Hon. Lieutenant Colonel Maurice Bennett, born 1896, served in the Great War and later badged Royal Signals, was in charge of the BFF's wireless equipment. *See* Steve Rothwell, 'Reserve Battalion, Burma Frontier Force' [online], https://homepages.force9.net/rothwell/burmaweb/ReserveBattalionBFF.htm

[47] The Reserve Battalion of the Burma Military Police was based at Pyawbwe, but in 1937 it became the Reserve battalion for the Burma Frontier Force. *See* Rothwell [online], ibid. 'Pyaw Bwe' or 'Pyawbwe' is approximately 42km south of Meiktila in central Burma. The frontline reached here in mid-April 1942, though it is unclear when Saw Kay Ray moved there.

[48] Lieutenant Colonel James Elliot Leslie Martin, born 5 June 1898, was commissioned in July 1918. He served with the 26th (later 15th) Punjab Regiment until 1940 when he was transferred to the Specially Employed List. Through much of the 1930s he was attached to the BMP and served as Assistant Commandant of the Chin Hills Battalion. He commanded 1st Rangoon BMP from 1941. – 1942. *See* Steve Rothwell, '1st and 2nd Rangoon Battalions, Burma Military Police' [online], https://homepages.force9.net/rothwell/burmaweb/RangoonBattalionsBMP.htm

[49] Major Geoffrey Lionel D'oyly-Lowsley (most likely Major 'Rosely' above), born 10 January 1900, was commissioned in 1918. He served on the North West Frontier Province of India before being seconded to the Burma Rifles in 1937, with whom he served until 1942. Died 12 September 1944. *See* Steve Rothwell, '4th Battalion, The

year and then served under the command of Subedar Major Kan Choke (Karen) and Subedar Htwe Kyaw (Karen) in Maymyo in 1939.[50]

I attended Training in Hopone, Shan State from January to March 1941 and in June I was sent to Taunggyi, and then from Kyai Ton Mountain and to the army into the Loi Mwe army base.[51]

## Mr Peter Andrews
On 14 June 1940, I joined the Burma Army Signals in Maymyo and my regimental number was W/759.

## Mel Du, also known as Pu Hla Kyi Pa
Village Headman Mel Du was the eldest son of Saw Pho Mya. There were four siblings and they were Saw Mel Du, Naw Ko, Naw Par and Saw Maw Lay. His hometown was Lerwetkhi village in Lerdoh region. He was educated in Lerdoh Primary School and became a monk for three years in Tarkholaw Monastery. Later on, he came back to his village and married Tar Po Lo, his cousin. The villagers made him Village Headman as he could read and write Burmese and he could speak English a little.

---

Burma Regiment' [online], http://www.rothwell.force9.co.uk/burmaweb/4th_burma_regt.htm and Commonwealth War Graves Commission [online], https://www.cwgc.org/find-war-dead/casualty/2177166/d'oyly-lowsley,-geoffrey-lionel/ Captain A.J. Stringer was seconded from 10 Gurkha Rifles to serve with 1st Battalion Burma Rifles from 1937. –. 1942. Captain F.J.W.H. Moore joined the 1st Battalion Burma Rifles in March 1938. Major Hugh Kenneth Blaber was born 22 August 1899 and commissioned into the Indian Army in 1918. He served with the Burma Rifles from 1919 until retirement in 1949 as Honorary Colonel. See Steve Rothwell, '9th (Reserve) Battalion, The Burma Rifles [online], https://homepages.force9.net/rothwell/burmaweb/9th_burma_rifles.htm See also 'Blaber Family Genealogy' [online] http://www.blaberfamily.org.uk/trees/blaber04/b343.htm

[50] Mingaladon is now the international airport for Myanmar, located approximately 15km north of Yangon. Subedar Major Kan Choke went on to become an Honorary Lieutenant, winning the Military Cross and the Burma Gallantry Medal for his work with the Special Operations Executive's Force 136. See 'The Men of SOE Burma' [online], https://soeinburma.wordpress.com/the-men-of-soe-burma/ and TNA, HS 1/31 for Kan Choke's record.

[51] Loi Mwe is in the Southern Shan States, about 20km south east of Keng Tung, in the east of Myanmar. During the colonial period, the British built a hill station there. It is approximately 40km from the border with Vietnam (then French Indochina) and Thailand (Siam).

That's why he became Village Headman and took responsibility of Lerwetkhi village. He had two children, the elder daughter Naw Hla Kyi and son Saw Hto Thaw Aye.

## Saw Daniel Tun Baw

Saw Daniel Tun Baw, the son of Porry Tun Baw and Naw El Si was born on 14 May 1923 in Taungoo, Central Burma. He was the sixth son among eight siblings. He was educated in Taungoo Karen High School. He passed each grade and passed high school in 1940. He studied at Agricultural College for two years and joined the British Navy in 1942 after World War Two started.

## Saw Htoo Mar

Saw Htoo Mar was born on 28 March 1925 in Kyo Doe (Kyaukchaung) village, Beik town, Tanintharyi Division, Southern Myanmar.[52] His father was Saw Lu Bay and his mother was Naw Htee Yee. His parents were working peacefully and honestly as farmers. There were five siblings (four boys and a girl) and he was the second son. He grew up in the village and studied at the village. He was interested in fighting a war from a young age. He passed every grade and when he got to Grade 6, his parents could not afford it anymore and he had to stop his education. So, he helped his parents.

## Saw Baw Nay

Saw Baw Nay, the son of Saw Shwe Htoo San and Naw Dar Dai was born on 23 February 1922 at Paycha village, Palaw town, Mergui region, Tanintharyi Division. His father was a clerk in an English mining company and his mother was a housewife and had an orchard to support the family. He was the eldest son among four siblings.

He studied at Paycha village and after passing Grade 4, his father sent him to Klawmawsoe School in Dawei (Tavoy) to continue studying. After he passed Grade 7, he had to stop studying in order to help his mother and took over some of the family responsibilities when his father was ill. His father died that year so he helped his mother to look after the younger siblings.

---

[52] Tanintharyi Division was known as Tenasserim during the colonial period. The town Beik is also called Myeik today, but was known as Mergui.

# The First Burma Campaign, December 1941–June 1942, Introduction

The Japanese had been fighting the Chinese since 1937, so war in the Far East was already three years old by the time the French surrendered to the Third Reich in June 1940 . The consequences of French capitulation in Europe were significant to how the war unfolded after Japan finally attacked the American, British and Dutch empires in the Far East, and the American Pacific Fleet at Pearl Harbor in December 1941. Part of the reason for the third Anglo-Burmese War, and Siamese independence from colonial rule, had been British fears of French expansion into Burma from French Indochina. After France was occupied by the Nazis in 1940, 6000 Japanese troops were able to occupy French Indochina. This not only meant that Japanese troops were now stationed in territory neighbouring Burma, but one of the supply routes of American aid to Chinese Nationalist forces fighting the Japanese was closed.

During 1940, both the Japanese and Siamese exploited the war situation for their own gains. The Siamese Army fought against French troops in Indochina, with help from the Japanese Army, enabling Siam to increase its territory by around 21,000 square miles. In return for their help in extending the Siamese border, when the Japanese government asked to move troops through Siam on 8 December 1941, the Siamese agreed. Japanese soldiers were thus able to attack Tenasserim in southern Burma, taking Victoria Point (now Kowthoung) and the RAF airfield there by 11 December. Along with their invasion of Malaya and Siamese belligerence, by taking Victoria Point, the Japanese had in effect severed the air link between Singapore and India.

From Victoria Point, the Japanese started pushing north towards Bokpyn, Mergui and Tavoy, the latter of which was taken by 19 January. Wavell's forward strategy of trying to defend Tenasserim was in tatters as seasoned Japanese troops came up against Burma Rifles units which had been skimmed for officers to fight Germany and then hurriedly expanded between 1939 - 1941. On 22 February, a week after Allied forces surrendered Singapore, what General Slim and others have described as the turning point in the first Burma campaign occurred when the bridge over the Sittang was prematurely blown up.⁵³ With Rangoon now exposed, the Japanese concentrated their efforts in securing the port city so that divisions freed up from Singapore and Malaya could be shipped in.

Plans to try and bring the Japanese to battle once Allied forces had concentrated in central Burma came to nothing as the Japanese continued to hold the initiative. Causes of the Japanese success was at the time blamed on an extensive Burmese Fifth Column, by war correspondents as well as the military.⁵⁴ The Special Operations Executive's Oriental Mission had hurriedly put men into the field to form left behind units, which some of the Karen interviewees, such as Saw Smile Paul became involved with.⁵⁵ There have been plenty of dissections of British reverses in the Far East, including Burma specifically, but probably the most serious failings occurred due to a combination of colonial politics, a lack of military resources due to the needs of the European and North African theatres, and command and control issues in Burma. Nevertheless, as the interviewees show, in the main, the Karen and their Burma units often fought on determinedly. Of approximately 20,000 personnel in Burma Army units such as the Burma Frontier Force or Burma Rifles, about 6120 made it out to India by June 1942.⁵⁶ Those left alive who didn't make the trek out to India followed orders to return to their villages, hide their weapons, and await the British return.

---

⁵³ William Slim, *Defeat into Victory* (Pan: London, 1999), p.14; Louis Allen, *Burma: The Longest War* (Phoenix Giant: London, 1998), p.43.

⁵⁴ *See* Philip Woods, *Reporting the Retreat: War Correspondents in Burma* (Hurst: London, 2016), pp.109-11 for a more recent analysis of this debate.

⁵⁵ For more on left behind guerrilla groups in the first Burma campaign, *see* Richard Duckett, *The Special Operations Executive in Burma* (IB Tauris: London, 2017), pp.52-69.

⁵⁶ TNA, WO 106/2677, 13 June 1942.

# The First Burma Campaign, December 1941–June 1942

Saw Champion. Photo courtesy of Col. Sam Pope, Burma Forces Welfare Association.

**Saw Champion**

My name is Saw Champion. I was born in a year 1918. In 1941 when I was 23 years old, I enlisted in the British Burma at No.1.A.T. (Animal Transport) company commanded by O.C Subaltern La Zun Dan.

My regimental No. is 15692. After two months training, the company was ordered to transfer to Rawkamun lake near Maulmein. On the month of October 1941, the company was attached to No.6 Burma Rifle battalion in order to transport heavy guns and ammunitions for we learnt that the invading Japanese troops were approaching the Thai-Burma border. The disposition of the battalion was at Zaha village just close to Tavoy aerodrome.

On 15 December, at about noon, about 70 Japanese air fleet comprising fighters and bombers surprisingly arrived at the site where we were stationing at, raided by bombing and machine gunning at us and the aerodrome and its surroundings. We had got some casualties and the runway of the aerodrome was destroyed. 150 drums of gasoline were directly hit. The huge flame and smoke burst out of the exploding drums that could be seen from Tavoy town.

On 2 January 1942, the No.6 Burma Rifle battalion and our attached company about 800 in strength took the defence position Thung-Thone-Lone (Kyaik Mai Hill) where we engaged with the invading Japanese troops of one of the columns advanced from Bangkok. Fierce fighting broke out between us that the fighting lasted for 4 days. We bravely fought with all our might and energy. However, using human wave operation of the forces of the Japanese compelled us to retreat from our position. We had 42 casualties at the battle. 1200 Japanese soldiers were also died in action. During the event Subaltern Ba Sein (Karen), Subaltern San Ba (Karen) and Subaltern Major Hta Kho Khine (Chin) commanded the defence forces.

The battalion retreated to Myit-ta village near Mergui junction at where the fierce fighting occurred again for two days. After the battle the battalion was ordered to withdraw to Tavoy.

At the time when we were preparing our defence line at Tavoy, the Japanese troops attacked us again. The fighting lasted for two days. After the battle, our troops withdrew to Maulmein, leaving the corpses of our comrades at the battle field. 2 soldiers killed in action and about 150 discouraging soldiers deserted from the battalion. After restored our failing health and moralities, for 20 days at Maulmein, we were ordered to change our position. We crossed the Salween river by the ferries and sampans to Martaban, situated on the opposite bank of the river, at where the Punjab battalion (12 Army) came to join with our battalion.

Soon after we had taken our defence position the Japanese troops arrived and attack our position. Close quarter battle occurred between the two opponents which resulted in heavy casualties on both sides. The fighting lasted for two days. The Japanese used assorted arms and also Japanese air planes supported them in time. Therefore, our troops retreated to Thaton where we stayed for a week.

During these days, our troops were hard to control for they were demoralised that the Japanese were so swift in advancing their troops equipped with high morality and military equipment and also overwhelmed the air space with their bombers and Zero fighters.

During 1942 in early days, the Japanese divisions invaded Burma along the Thai-Burma border from the South to the Northern part of Shan State. The British Burma forces was in full retreat to the Northern part of Burma step by step. Our battalion was also ordered to retreat from the area.

1. We stayed in Thaton for a week and retreated and were staying in Kyaik-Htoe for 4 days.
2. Kyaik-Htoe to Sittaung.
3. From Sittaung to Pegu before the Punjab battalion demolished the Sittaung bridge.
4. Stayed two days at Pegu and withdrew to Taungoo and stayed for five days. During our stay at Taungoo, the Chinese Nationalist troops arrived to Taungoo for defending the area.
5. From Taungoo our troop was ordered to withdraw to Mandalay, the second city of Burma.
6. From mandalay to Maymyo in Northern Shan State where we stationed for month.

7. Battalion commander La Zun Dan gave out the order to withdraw to India.
8. Then, we started our long march from Maymyo to Mandalay, from Mandalay to Mon-Ywa, from Mon-Ywa to Ka-Lay-Wa to Ta-Mu.
9. At Ta-Mu, our troop engaged with the Japanese advancing column and fighting occurred for two hours. Forty two soldiers including me were captured by the Japanese. Some of our troops who were taking a position at Rue-Chaung escaped. We, the prisoner of war were sent to Mandalay prison via Mon-Ywa.

## Saw Johnny Htoo
*Saw Johnny Htoo had joined the Burma Rifles in 1932, and taken part in military expeditions in to the Wa States in 1936-7:*

When I came back to Maymyo, I was transferred to Mingaladon, Rangoon and in 1939, I was appointed as Jemedar.[57] During World War II, we withdrew to India from Katha. Our Column Commander was Lieutenant Colonel Abernethy.[58] When I was in India, I joined the Chin Levies.[59]

## Saw Michael Shwe
*Saw Michael Shwe, the son of Saw San Shwe, was born on 24 May 1924. On 14 September 1941, he joined the Signals detachment of the Burma Frontier Force, at Pyawbwe:*

The Japanese air force bombed Rangoon on Christmas day, 1941 so the brigade was moved to Anni Sa Khan in Maymyo (Pyin Oo Lwin) and I

---

[57] Saw Johnny Htoo was promoted to Jemadar 2 September 1939. He was serving with 3rd Battalion Burma Rifles.

[58] Lieutenant Colonel Peter Paul Abernethy was officer commanding 4th Battalion Burma Rifles. See B.L., IOR L/MIL/14/242; Steve Rothwell, 4th Battalion, 'The Burma Rifles' [online], https://homepages.force9.net/rothwell/burmaweb/4th_burma_rifles.htm

[59] The Chin Hills separate India from Burma. The Chin Levies were an irregular force hastily organised in the Chin Hills for the defence of India in 1942. For more on the Chin Levies, *see* Lieutenant Colonel Balfour-Oatts, *The Jungle in Arms* (NEL Books: London, 1976); Harold Braund, *Distinctly I Remember: a Personal story of Burma* (Wren Publishing: Victoria, 1972).

finished Wireless Operator training at Anni Sa Khan.⁶⁰

The brigade withdrew to Myitkyina, Kachin State by train when the Japanese came into Burma. After a few days, the whole brigade walked to India. After many days, when we got to the Ledo-Hukawng valley, we had been walking for about 105 miles through the route which led to India. It was raining and there were thunderstorms, therefore, we had difficulty in walking as the roads were very slippery. By the Grace of God, the OC, Major Hayfield, gave the soldiers three months' salary.⁶¹ At the same time, they gave wireless sets to connect with military headquarters in India. The group consisted of

1. Subedar Saw Phoe Aung
2. Havildar Saw Tun Nyein
3. Naik Saw Ba Win
4. Lance Naik Sum Lut La
5. Signalman Saw Chit Phay
6. Signalman Saw Noe Ghii
7. Signalman Speuccer
8. Signalman Saw Nelson
9. Signalman Saw Maung Sint
10. Signalman Saw Aung Shaing
11. Signalman Saw Marshal Shwe
12. Private Saw Noe Ray (Subedhar Saw Phoe Aung's body guard).

At that time, the brigade was withdrawing to India. Our group got lost and was separated from our brigade; unexpectedly we met Division Commander Haswell with a dog in a jeep.⁶² He told our group leader that the Japanese were now in Myitkyina and said to follow him to

---

⁶⁰ Probably 'Anisakhan', which now gives its name to the airport in Pyin Oo Lwin.

⁶¹ Major H.V. Hayfield, on loan from the Royal Signals to the Burma Frontier Force from March 1940, joined the Reserve Battalion based at Pyawbwe.

⁶² Lieutenant Colonel Francis William ('Jack') Haswell, born 9 February 1898, received his commission in 1917 and saw service in France and Belgium during the Great War. He served in Burma from 1932 as officer commanding the Chin Hills Battalion of the Burma Military Police. From 1937 he was in charge of the Chin Hills Battalion of the Burma Frontier Force, and then commandant of 2ⁿᵈ Battalion the Burma Rifles before becoming commandant of 9ᵗʰ (Reserve Battalion) the Burma Rifles until March 1942. He was then ordered to raise the Chin Levies for the defence of India. See B.L., IOR L/MIL/14/18958; TNA, WO 373/79/310; Steve Rothwell, '9ᵗʰ (Reserve) Battalion, The Burma Rifles' [online], http://www.rothwell.force9.co.uk/burmaweb/9th_burma_rifles.htm;

Sumprabum, Kachin State. After a few days rest in Sumprabum, we continued to Putao – Fort Hertz, Northern Kachin State. At that time I got a high fever and malaria so Lance Naik Sum Lut La and Signalman Maung Sint looked after me. We arrived safely at Fort Hertz, Putao area after a difficult journey.

By God's will, while I was cooking in the evening, Division Commander Haswell ordered us to go and report at the Fort Hertz airport in full uniform. When we got to the airport, we saw a small military cargo plane (Dakota) which was there. We were ordered to put down all our weapons, bullets and all heavy things and to get into the aircraft. Once the aircraft took off, it was a surprise because it was our first time travelling by plane. The weather was fine. After many hours, we arrived safe and sound in Tinsukia town, India. When we got off from the plane, the lady volunteer group welcomed us with tea and delicious food. But Division Commander Haswell stayed behind at Fort Hertz, Putao forward area to establish Northern Kachin Levies - NKL - with Signalman Saw Chit Phay to help him. We heard that Division Commander Haswell died at the end of 1942.[63]

## Saw Aye Kyaw

*Saw Aye Kyaw had achieved the rank of Havildar, serving with the Burma ambulance:*

The company I led was sent to Mawlamyine camp situated in a rubber plantation near Mudon. There were other companies stationed close to us. We secured our position in our camp until the Japanese came into Thailand then we were ordered to move to the border at Mya Hti (Myawaddy) and Moei River. The Japanese crossed the border and passed by the British Army with the help of the village guides, therefore we had to move back.[64] After the battle at Mawlamyine, we withdrew to Rangoon.[65] The Japanese air forces were flying every day. The Allied air

---

[63] Lieutenant Colonel Haswell did not die during the war. He retired from the Army in 1949.

[64] Accounts of a Burmese Fifth Column assisting the Japanese, sometimes acting as guides such as in this example, was not unusual.

[65] The Battle for Moulmein developed at the end of January 1942. Four Burif battalions (2, 3, 7 & 8) plus 4/12 Frontier Force Regiment (Reserve) defended the town. See General S. Woodburn Kirby, *The War Against Japan, Vol.2: India's Most Dangerous Hour* (Military & Naval Press: Uckfield, 2004), pp.30-33.

force was the AVG.[66] We got the order to withdraw from Rangoon because of the lack of air force and air superiority. We passed many places and had to sleep where we could sleep including monasteries and schools for two to three nights. While we moved forward, wounded soldiers were sent to us. We cleaned their wounds, put medicine and treated the front line soldiers who were wounded and sent them on as more injured soldiers were sent to us.

All the army from Taukkyan retreated and only one British unit was left and there were many wounded soldiers. That was the day we had to do first aid the most. After sending them on, we had to retreat through Pyay, Aunglan, Thayet, Minbu, Magwe and we got to rest for a few days and after that we continued to Meiktila and Amarapura by car. When we got to Sagaing, we stopped for a few days and opened a First Aid Centre. There, we treated the patients and sent them to Manipur, by road to India, and gradually we moved to Kalewa and Tamu by ship or car and sometimes on foot. We passed many places but I do not remember their names. There were many Indian people along the road and some of them were ill and no one was there to look after them. They were along the entire road. We arrived to Shillong, Assam by car. We could rest for a couple of months at that place. We got days off, so sometimes, we could go and watch movies and eat food at restaurants in the town.

## Saw Ni K'mwe Paul AKA Lieutenant Saw Smile Paul

*Saw Ni K'mwe Paul was 81 when he was interviewed in 2001. Sixty years before, he had joined Captain Seagrim to fight as a guerrilla with the Special Operations Executive, known in the Far East as Force 136 from March 1944:*

I was among the Karen soldiers who joined together when the British Army retreated to

Saw Smile Paul (left) and Mya Yin. Photo courtesy of Col. Sam Pope, BFWA.

---

[66] The AVG was the American Volunteer Group, better known as 'The Flying Tigers'.

Northern Myanmar and I met with Captain Seagrim, Pu Htun Khaung at the Karen hills.[67] When Captain Seagrim formed the Karen Volunteer Force, my brother-in-law Saw Ba Tin was a Medical Officer and my brother-in-law, Htin Kyaw, was an intelligence agent tasked with getting information about the enemy. The Karen from the hills around Papun wholeheartedly joined Captain Seagrim's force. A lot of my relatives were in the force.[68]

*The Japanese soon began to arrest any Karen they thought had cooperated with the British. In a sworn statement given after the war, Saw Po No Gyi of Thandaung township stated that he had been arrested on 8 May and taken to Toungoo where he was locked in the bathroom of the railway officer's house:*

I was questioned by Sgt AKISTA (said to be killed by villagers at YADO). He accused me of co-operating with the British and helping Major SMITH, Conservator forestry.[69] I refused to give any information and was then strung up by my hands to a beam, and left to hang in this position for three hours. After this, I was sent back to the bathroom, where I remained for 21 days.

Before I returned to the bathroom, I saw Sgt Mjr SEIJO beat and torture SAW E MG in the next room. He made him kneel down with his hands tied behind his back and in this position, beat him. After this he rolled bamboos up and down his leg. Later he was returned to the bathroom in a very weak position.

During the time I was confined in the bathroom, I saw Sgt AKIYAMA take SAW WI DI Headman of KYETTAIK out into the yard outside, hang him up on a tree and beat him brutally. After he was beaten, SAW WI DI was dragged into the bathroom by some Burmese constables, (whose names I don't know) and after ten minutes he died.[70]

---

[67] 'Pu Htun Khaung' (Pwo Karen) means 'Grandfather Longlegs', which is the name the Karen gave Major Hugh Seagrim. Hpu Taw Kaw is the same name but in Sgaw Karen.

[68] Major Hugh Paul Seagrim, DSO, GC was recruited by the Special Operations Executive's Oriental Mission in January 1942. He was tasked with raising Karens as a guerrilla force which would attack Japanese lines of communication. *See* Richard Duckett, *The Special Operations Executive in Burma,* especially chapters one and two; Ian Morrison, *Grandfather Longlegs* (Faber: London, 1947); Philip Davies, *Lost Warriors* (Atlantic Publishing: Croxley Green, 2017).

[69] Smith was recruited by SOE's Oriental Mission in 1942, about the same time as (then) Captain Seagrim. There is a short report by Smith in TNA, HS 1/27.

[70] TNA, WO 325/63, 'STATEMENT', Saw Po No Gyi, witnessed by Major P.R. Barrass,

## Saw Fair Play

*Saw Fair Play hadn't been doing very well at school, and had been punched in the stomach by his teacher:*

On the last of our exams, thirty planes from the Japanese air force bombed and fired at our school compound and airport. The Burma Rifles fired back but we did not know there was a battle. The teacher said the British air force was training and asked us to wave scarves and clothes. The whole town was not afraid and no one was harmed. Only 1000 gallons of aircraft fuel from the airport was destroyed. This happened suddenly and a British Buffalo plane dared not to take off.[71]

The teachers knew that it was World War Two and the Japanese air force was bombing day and night so the British had to move their aircraft to Rangoon. Therefore, the Primary School and High School was closed. We did not have to sit for the exam and hide in the bomb shelter. Once, one Japanese plane fired and on its return a Buffalo plane attacked it and it was damaged and crashed at Maytarkalelki. The Japanese plane burst into flames and was destroyed and the four Japanese who parachuted to Sarukhi town were dead. The Buffalo plane arrived safely at Dawei and demonstrated a victory roll above our school compound and flew to Rangoon. Some of my friends and me registered in the BAF, the Burma Auxiliary Force.[72] The Burmese were not allowed to join. Only Karens and Anglo-English were allowed to join.

The Japanese entered Burma first from Thailand via Baw Ti to Ka Saw Wah region. We got to Myit Rar via Ka Saw Wah and fought with the Burma Rifles for three hours and after that the Burma Rifles withdrew to Dawei. The Japanese and Burma Rifles came face to face for over three weeks from Ka Saw Wah to Dawei. The Dawei battle was from six in the morning to noon and Burma Rifles withdrew to Ye. The Burmese officers who went to Japan were also included in the Japanese army.[73] During the

---

GSO 2 (I) 19 Indian Division.

[71] This raid possibly took place on 17 January 1942; Tavoy was occupied by the Japanese on 19 January. *See* General S. Woodburn Kirby, *The War Against Japan, Vol.2: India's Most Dangerous Hour*, p.28.

[72] For more on the Burma Auxiliary Force, *see* Steve Rothwell, 'The Burma Auxiliary Force' [online], https://homepages.force9.net/rothwell/burmaweb/BAF.htm

[73] This is a reference to the 'Thirty Comrades', Burmese Nationalist leaders including Aung San who invaded Burma with the Japanese. *See* Angelene Naw, *Aung San and the Struggle for Burmese Independence* (NIAS: Copenhagen, 2001).

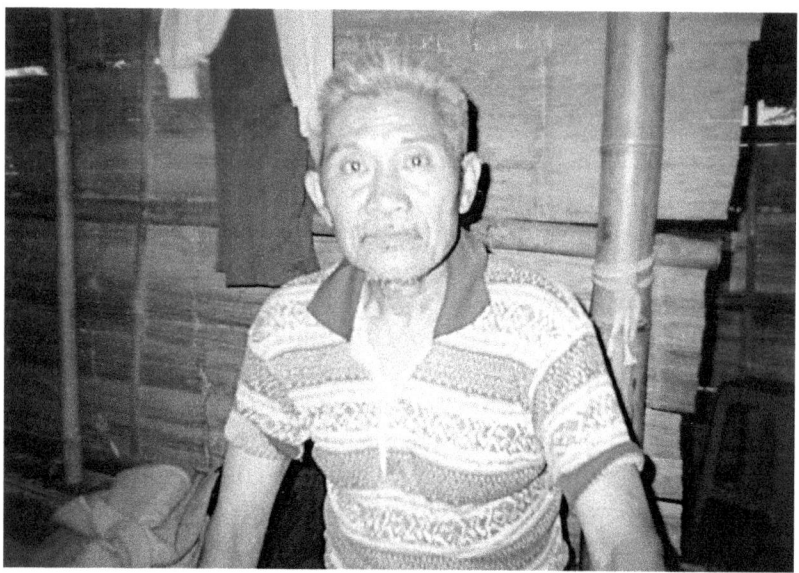

Saw Htaw Tha Heh. Photo courtesy of Col. Sam Pope, Burma Forces Welfare Association.

Dawei battle, one Japanese plane and one Buffalo plane had a Dog Fight for two hours above the school compound and turned back.[74] We withdrew from Beik and arrived at Tha Nyaw Si village at twelve at night and then arrived at Eh Eh village in the morning.[75] The Chin Burma Rifles platoon and a few BAF were in our group. A few days later on, the local people sent us to Ma Li Island via sea route.[76] While we stayed there for a month's time, there was no ship passed by. The Burmese and Japanese armies were furiously searching for the British Army, therefore I came back to Dawei.

### Saw Htaw Tha Heh (AKA Saw Kway Kwi)
*I was born in 1928 in Kler Lwe Htu (Naung Lin Bin) region and I was educated at Kler Lwe Htu American Baptist School:*

When World War Two started we heard that the Japanese army was coming into Myanmar (Burma). I recall that the school windows were

---

[74] A two hour dog fight seems unlikely.

[75] Beik was a local name for Mergui, now called Myeik. Tavoy, Mergui and Victoria Point all had important airfields.

[76] Ma Li Island, Mali Kyun today. Also known as Tavoy Island.

sealed with paper tape to prevent it from shattering because of the bombing.

As we were just children, we had no worries or any sort of fears. But shortly we learned that our teachers (American lady teachers are called Ma Ma, added in front of their name) Ma Ma Feather and Ma Ma May would be leaving. After a few weeks we felt some sort of earthquake very frequently and the elders told us that the Japanese army were bombing all over the country from small towns to big cities even Yangon (Rangoon). After a few days, the English troops that were stationed at our village (Thay Kar Kyaw) had fallen back to Kyauk Ta Gar and Tha May Oo Ku villages near Sittaung River.[77] Then we heard the sound of small arms, big arms and even machine guns, bombing from planes, shooting. After the battle that lasted three days and three nights we learned that English troops from the north had been forced to fall back to Taungoo.[78] Shortly after, there were Japanese troops coming into Wel Pyar Khu, Ka Ma Dee Kway, See Pay Ku and Thay Kar Khaw villages and then they moved to Taungoo where the English army was stationed.[79]

## Saw K'Hsaw
*Saw K'Hsaw had been working for the Bombay Burmah Trading Company in Mone Township:*

By late 1941 and early 1942, the Japanese were coming into lower Burma. During that time, one of the managers named N.R. Johnson asked me to go to B.B.T.C.L [Bombay Burmah Trading Company Ltd] at Shwebo and the second manager asked me to come along with him to the Chindwin River to clear the campsite for the British Army. In March and April, we had to arrange for the armies in Kalewa and Mawlaik to retreat.

In May 1942, the second manager left Mawlaik and went back to India. I was staying in Mawlaik until the Japanese occupied the whole of Burma. In August 1942, I went back to my village and the villagers told me that a British soldier was ill and was living in the forest nearby. Once I heard the news, I went straight to the forest and saw that the soldier had

---

[77] Also spelt Sittang River. There is a Sit Taung on the Sittang, and a Sittaung on the Chindwin River.

[78] Also spelt 'Toungoo'.

[79] The battle for Toungoo was largely a Chinese affair, defended by the 200th Division of V Army.

a high fever and was seriously ill. Saw San Say (Pre-war-SIP [Superintendent Police]), our leader, told me to bring him back to the village. But this soldier could only walk for ten steps and could not walk anymore as he was so tired. It was so difficult to carry him all the way home from the forest. I made boiled rice for him but he would say "I'm fed up of eating gruel rice" and would not eat. I took care of him for one week and he died. We took his corpse and buried it nearby Paw Mu Doh village. As he was a soldier, at the burial ceremony we fired a gun three times out of respect. When he was alive he told me that he was a British soldier from the Supply Corps and had come from Dawai. When the Japanese army came into Dawai, he had to move to Mawlamyine. When he arrived in Mawlamyine, he heard that the Yangon-Mandalay highway was cut off. He came north and then to Papun. He heard that Major Seagrim was at Papun so he tried to join with them. But when he got to Phaw Mu Doh he could not walk anymore and he was so weak he collapsed. He stayed at Phaw Mu Doh till he died.

This soldier was Lesley Cryer from Ireland. I felt sad when he told me about himself and was in tears. I kept his badge but lost it later when fleeing during the war.[80]

## Saw Kay Ray

*Saw Kay Ray had joined the Burma Military Police in 1937, which was soon redesignated a reserve Burma Frontier Force battalion, based at Pyawbwe:*

I served as Signalman until the Japanese captured Singapore. I was transferred to Myeik, Tenasserim region as Signalman for five months and then the Captain called me back to Pyawbwe.

On the way back, I had to follow the British troops withdrawing to India from South to North. This withdrawal was via Monywa, Kalaywa, Tamu to Lanpriopi (Palel), Assam border. After a couple of weeks, we were sent to Dimapur via Imphal by truck.

---

[80] The soldier was Private Leslie Cryer of 2 Battalion, the King's Own Yorkshire Light Infantry. He had become separated from his unit and made his way north where he was put in contact with Captain Seagrim. See Philip Davies, *Lost Warriors,* pp.78-80. Although he remains buried in the Karen Hills, he is remembered in Taukkyan War Cemetery, Rangoon: https://www.cwgc.org/find-war-dead/casualty/2507760/cryer,-leslie/

## Saw Bunny

I am the son of Reverend Lun Shwe. I have one son and three daughters and they are school teachers, an office clerk and one is helping at home. I was born on 4 March and after I passed Grade 7 from Papun Karen Mission Middle School, I joined the British Army as a volunteer soldier with Major Seagrim's company. I joined the army where Major Seagrim was in command in January 1942 and appointed as an infantry soldier reporting information between Papun and Lerdoh.[81]

## Saw San Aye

*Saw San Aye had been near the Siamese border in the Southern Shan States, serving with 1 Burifs:*

I served on the Burma-Thailand border in the Burma Frontier Force till 1942.[82] The Japanese did not come into Burma via that route so we were transferred to Mawlamyine to help the army at Karutu and Kawkareik where the battle was being fought. After that we withdrew to Bago and held back the Japanese for two days at Nyaunglebin (Kler Lwe Htu). The Japanese air force attacked us but we were able to shoot down some planes.

While one of our Company was on patrol, we came across the Burma Independence Army (BIA) with the Japanese and in the ensuing battle five Karen soldiers, one driver, one Company Commander and three Chin soldiers were killed. We had to draw back to Ngarhtetkyi and two battalions which were under the command of the Brigade Major came to reinforce us. We took positions at Kyauktaga. The battle was fierce and took three days and three nights. A Chinese company and Rajputs from Pyuntasa also reinforced us at that battle. Thirty Rajput soldiers were killed as the battle was very fierce.

Subedar Moezit and seventeen soldiers were killed when the Japanese fought against the 5th Burma Rifles at Kyauktaga. Later, we received the order to withdraw to Taungoo.[83] After the battle, our company and the

---

[81] At this time, Seagrim's rank was Captain. Saw Bunny must have been one of Seagrim's first recruits as he only arrived in Papun in January 1942.

[82] Saw San Aye was more than likely with Frontier Force column 1. *See* Steve Rothwell, 'F.F.1, Burma Frontier Force [online] http://www.rothwell.force9.co.uk/burmaweb/FF1.htm

[83] Apart from Ngarhtetkyi, the other place names can be found on the map tracing the line of the railway and road north from Rangoon. A line of retreat Bago-Pyuntasa-

Chinese company were ordered to defend the Mawchi road and the Officer-in-Charge was Captain Thompson of the Bengal Rifles.[84] Jemedar Pan Mya and sixteen soldiers were captured fighting the Japanese at Paletwa.[85] There was one company with us when we withdrew in the night. It took two days and two nights when we withdrew to Mawchi and from there to Loikaw, Karenni state. We rested there and it took three or four days to withdraw to Mong Pawn, Shan State and from there to Loilem, and then to Naung Peng (Sakanthar) and then to Momeik, Northern Shan State.

Captain Thompson knew the Battalion Commander of 15th Shan Battalion who was also the Momeik Sawba (ruler).[86] That Sawba helped to send our troops to Nyaung U, some by car and some by raft. Captain Thompson said that he would stay in Nyaung U and we had to inform him if the British Army came back.

## Mr Peter Andrews

*Peter Andrews had joined the Burm Army Signals in Maymyo in June 1940:*

In 1941-42, when the Japanese came into Burma, I got to India while withdrawing with the 2nd Burma Rifles from Meik (Mergui).

---

Nyaung Lay Pin-Kyauktaga-Taungoo can be followed. There is no record of a Subedar Moezit on the Commonwealth War Graves soldier search.

[84] Captain A.L.B. Thompson was in the 1st Battalion the Burma Rifles, and part of SOE's Oriental Mission.

[85] There are two places called Paletwa in Burma, a town in the west of the country in Chin State, and the other a bridge just east of Taungoo where the road to Mawchi starts. The Jemadar is more than likely Pan Nya who was 1st Battalion Burma Rifles, *see* Commonwealth War Graves [online] *https://www.cwgc.org/find-war-dead/casualty/2630698/pan-nya,-/* . *See* TNA, HS 1/27 for Capt. Thompson's account which includes action at the Paletwa Bridge and details of a Jemadar who was beheaded, p.3.

[86] *See* Steve Rothwell, 'Southern Shan States Battalion, Burma Frontier Force' [online] http://www.rothwell.force9.co.uk/burmaweb/SouthernShanStatesBattalionBFF.htm for more on the Shan States Battalion mentioned here. Momeik is also known as 'Mong Mit'

## Saw Maw Ler[87]
*Saw Maw Ler, born 11 November 1921 was 80 when he was interviewed in 2001:*

I joined the Burma Army in 1941 and have [taken a] wireless operators course. My unit commanding officer was Major O.W. Bowing; later he was promoted to Brigadier and became C.S.O. Eastern Army during the Burma campaign.[88]

After a year in Burma Army Signals I passed out wireless operator course and then sent to Moulmein to work as wireless operator in Brigade HQ. After about six months I was then sent to Mergui south of Tavoy as [a] wireless operator attached to 2nd Burma Rifles.[89] There is a unit called B.F.F. (Burma Frontier Force) south of Mergui at a place called Bokpyin which they now called Kawthaung.[90] It was the southern tip of Burma. Saw Maw Ler, born 11 November 1921 was 80 when he was interviewed in 2001:

> The B.F.F. was the first Burma Army unit to go into action with Japanese forces. The Japanese army are in that area on Thai side. Our duty at Mergui is to make contact with B.F.F. at Bokpyin, 4th Burma Rifles at Tavoy and G.H.Q at Rangoon. After a month of fighting, B.F.F. commander Major Love was killed in action so 2nd Burma Rifles have to send a company to Bokpyin to reinforce B.F.F.[91] After a month of heavy fighting in Bokpyin Japanese make a

---

[87] There are many variations in spelling of Burmese names, which makes researching Burmese soldiers quite a challenge at times. Saw 'Maw Ler' as presented here is Saw 'Mauler' elsewhere.

[88] Brigadier, later Major General, William Oswald Bowen. Born 10 November 1898, died 14 January 1961. A pioneer of VHF radio communication during the Second World War, he was Chief Signals Officer for Burma Army in 1942 and then for XIV Army. *See* http://www.unithistories.com/officers/Army_officers_B04.html

[89] 2 Burif were sent to Mergui in October 1941

[90] From 1824 to 1948, Kawthaung was known by the British name of Victoria Point. Bokpyin is about halfway between Mergui (now called Myeik) and Kawthaung / Victoria Point.

[91] Major S.W.A. Love was killed attacking the Japanese at Bokpyin in January 1942. *See* James Lunt, *A Hell of a Licking: The Retreat From Burma, 1941-2'* (Collins: London, 1986), pp.92-3. D Company of 2 Burif was sent to Bokpyin on 26 December 1941 and was withdrawn on 5 January 1942.

surprise attack on Tavoy and capture Tavoy so army south of Tavoy are cut off.[92] Colonel [O'Callaghan] C.O of 2nd Burma Rifles sent a message to G.H.Q in Rangoon that Tavoy has fallen to Japanese so troops south of Tavoy will try to recapture Tavoy and then retreat to Moulmein. A reply from G.H.Q said that don't try to recapture Tavoy. If you try that none of you will reach Moulmein. All of you will be dead and none of you will reach Moulmein but evacuate Mergui and go to an island west of Mergui called Elephant Island and in a couple of days a ship will come and take you back to Rangoon.[93]

A troopship called S.S. Anderson came back from Penang and took us back to Rangoon. We are posted in university compound in a building called Pegu House. [After] about a month Moulmein was capture[d] by Japanese and advance towards Pegu.[94] [The] Japanese airforce [was] also bombing Rangoon day and night. All civilians in Rangoon are ordered to evacuate Rangoon and move to rural area. [The] Japanese advance was halted north of Pegu at a place called Myitkyo. All are quiet in all fronts.

About a week on an early morning we got information that five or six Japanese soldiers are sighted on [the] Rangoon Prome road near a place called Wanetkone [Ywathitkon?]. We are then order[ed] to pack up immediately and [be] ready to move. At about 1 A.M we move out from Rangoon and heading toward[s] Taukkyan. When we arrived [in] Taukkyan we heard sounds of bombs, shells and guns - then we are told that the road was block[ed] by Japanese. All troops in Rangoon are rushed [to] that area to clear the Japanese but they cannot. [The] next day, tank brigade and troops from Pegu front are re-call[ed] and order[ed] to clear the road. [The] Japanese air force are also active the whole day bombing and strafing. [The] commander of the Burma Army general Hutton seemed to be in great worry. The day ended with the road unclear.[95] On the 3rd day at about 10AM we are told that the road was

---

[92] Tavoy fell on 19 January.

[93] The battalion was withdrawn on 21 January, reaching Rangoon on 25 January, see Steve Rothwell, '2nd Battalion, Burma Rifles' [online] http://www.rothwell.force9.co.uk/burmaweb/2ndburma.htm

[94] Moulmein fell on 31 January.

[95] Saw Maw Ler is referring here to the 7 March block the Japanese put on the road to enable the rest of their army to flank Rangoon and capture the city on 8 March 1942. Hutton was right to be worried, for if the Japanese had not been so focused on

clear so we the GHQ staff are getting first priority to move out. When we arrived at the battle area we saw that hundred[s] of Japanese and some of our military corps[es] are near the road side as well as tanks and Bren carriers are overturn[ed] and some are still burning. From this we are retreating step by step to Tharawaddy, Prome, Magway, Yenangyaung, Meiktila then finally in about a week we arrived to Maymyo. At Meiktila we saw that some Chinese troops are retreating from Toungoo.

[After] about two months in Maymyo we are then ordered to leave Maymyo and go to Shwebo. We stay at Shwebo for about two months. [During] this time we are subjected to heavy bombing almost every day. I think Japanese knew that British G.H.Q is at Shwebo. Road[s] in Shwebo are black with fallen branches, uprooted trees and shattered houses. [A] [w]ave of 29 bombers bombed Shwebo almost every morning at about 8am. After all our troops south of Sagaing Bridge completely withdrew to north of Irrawaddy River Sagaing bridge was blown up and destroyed and we are order[ed] to move to Kalewa a town on Chindwin river. We the G.H.Q staffs are able to go by trucks up to Shwegyin, a little town on Chindwin river. From there we travel on boat to Kalewa. All rifle units are retreating on foot. Thousand[s] of Indian civilians are also travelling on foot to India. Hundred[s] of them died on the way because of disease and hard journey. From Kalewa we travel to Tamu and then Imphal. [The] Japanese air force are also active up to Imphal. At Imphal we lost another two men hit by the bombs. They were signalman Maung Nyo and cook[?] Bahadur.

From Imphal we proceeded to Kohima and [indecipherable] and now we are safe in India. We then proceeded to Ranchi a town in Bihar state. Being summer, all school[s] are close[d] so we are sent to a school called Bishop West High School to stay there. We are then given a month['s] rest and sent to Muree a town north of Rawalpindi a hill station and spent our leave there. After leave we come back to Ranchi and this time we are ready for any duty for reoccupation of Burma.

*In this interview, Saw Maw Ler was somewhat less detailed about his experiences in the first Burma campaign:*

I, Saw Maw Ler was born on 11 November 1921. I am the son of Saw David and Naw Say Myai. I joined the British army in 1941. I was a Wireless Operator 1st Grade during the war. Our Company Commander

---

capturing Rangoon, they could have captured him, the Rangoon garrison and 17 Division. *See* Louis Allen, *Burma: The Longest War* (Phoenix: London, 1998), p.54.

was Major. O.W Bowing and he became CEO of Eastern Brigade. I joined 2nd Burma Rifles in Meik (Mergui) in 1941; my Battalion Commander was Colonel Calogan.[96] When the Japanese army captured Dawei (Tavoy), we withdrew on SS Andrew to Rangoon.[97] We withdrew via Rangoon to Pyay, Yenanchaung, Meiktila, Mandalay, Shwebo, Kalewa, Tamu via Imphal, Kohima, India border up to Ranchi. We sheltered at the Bishop West High School.[98]

## Mel Du AKA Pu Hla Kyi Pa
*Mel Du was the village headman of Lerwetkhi:*

Soon after the Japanese came into Burma and fought against the British Army. At that time, the British Army was withdrawing. The Headman and friends helped a British officer who requested it by hiding him from one village to another. The officer he helped was Major Seagrim.

## Saw Baw Nay
*Saw Baw Nay had had to withdraw from school to help his mother after his father got ill and subsequently died:*

In 1942-43, the Japanese came into Burma to fight the British as the Burmese requested. At that time, most of the Karens were working at the departments of British subsidiaries. That's why the Burmese accused the Karens as being pro-British and ill-treated them.[99]

---

[96] Lieutenant Colonel C.H.D. O'Callaghan, 2nd Punjab Regiment was officer commanding 2 Burif from 28 December 1941.

[97] Elsewhere, Saw Maw Ler names the ship the 'SS Anderson'. The most likely ship is the SS Sir Harvey Adamson, which helped evacuate troops from Mergui in 1942. The ship survived the war but disappeared, losing all on board, in 1947, sailing from Rangoon to Tavoy. *See* P&O Heritage 'Ship Fact Sheet: Sir Harvey Adamson' [online] http://www.poheritage.com/Upload/Mimsy/Media/factsheet/94487SIR-HARVEY-ADAMSON-1914pdf.pdf

[98] The Bishop Westcott High School for boys was founded in 1928. In April 1942, the school was commandeered by the military and the pupils were evacuated to Allahabad. *See* the school's website, 'Bishop Westcott Boys School' [online] https://bishopwestcottboysschool.com/abut/hist_bg/1939_1948.htm

[99] By 'subsidiaries', presumably what is meant here is the British firms working in Burma. It is well known that Burmese from the Scheduled Areas were favoured for military service over Burmans who were excluded from 1927. *See* BL, IOR V/24/1684,

# Sworn Statement of Ukyme Hti Nigon

*One such person was Ukyme Hti Nigon, a village Elder. He was a building contractor in Toungoo, who was arrested on 21 June 1942. Initially arrested for refusing to collaborate with the Japanese, he was later accused of being a British spy, and tortured:*

I was taken to the KEMPEI TEI Headquarters, and put in a cell, seven feet by twelve feet, where thirteen other men were already imprisoned. I was imprisoned for one month. During this period, I was subjected to many tortures. One of these was suspension from a beam by my thumbs. A second was water torture. This consisted of my being securely tied, placed across a stool, and my head lowered into a tub of water. Whilst in this position, red-hot needles were jabbed into my neck. I was on several occasions beaten about the head and body. Another torture was Jap jujitsu. In all, I was tortured about twenty times, and they were all executed by Sgt-Major SEIJO and Sgt AKISTA. My food at this time consisted of one bowl of rice and a portion of salt daily. SAIJO approached me on frequent occasions with the charge that I was a British Agent, which accusations I denied. On the final occasion that SAIJO asked me to collaborate, and I refused, I was, on his orders, taken to the village cemetery. After being blindfolded and handcuffed, I was placed in front of a weapon pit, expecting to be shot. AKISTA then asked me again to work for them. By this time, I was faint and weak, and in order to escape death, I agreed. I was then taken to jail, where I remained a further month. During this period, five or six men were shot at random every day, to instil in the populace the fear of the KEMPEI TAI. Two of these men were CHIT PE and AUNG KO, who were shot for non-collaboration, but the names of the others are unknown to me.

I was released in September 1942 and I joined the Police Force.

I SWEAR that SAIJO and AKISTA were responsible for the deaths, which occurred during my imprisonment.[100]

---

Annual Reports BFF, Rangoon Government Printing & Stationery; BL, L/MIL/ 17/7/11-13, p.48.

[100] TNA, WO 325/63, 'STATEMENT' of Ukyme Hti Nigon, witnessed by Corporal Tin Win, 603 Indian Field Security Section and Sergeant Wiltshire, also 603 Indian FSS. Undated.

# War Service, June 1942–October 1945, Introduction

After the retreat from Burma, the British and Allied armies maintained a front facing the Japanese from the Arakanese coast running roughly northeast following the mountainous ranges that separate India from Burma. The area of Burma north of the town of Sumprabum, including Fort Hertz (Putao) remained in Allied hands. Behind this front, which was screened by the Kachin and Chin Levies, the Burma Army licked its wounds and reorganised.

The Japanese did not push on into India, or try to advance on the airstrip being built at Fort Hertz. Concentrating on consolidating their victories up to June 1942, the Japanese reorganised the Burma Independence Army and began enacting policies to pacify the Burmese population. The main manifestation of this was the granting of independence to Burma in August 1943, and the appointment of Ba Maw as premier. It was not long before Burmese nationalists began to get restive, recognising the sham independence for what it was.

Meanwhile, there was a limited offensive in the Arakan launched during December 1942. The aim was to capture Akyab Island and its airstrip. By January, the offensive was stalling and by May both sides were back where they had started in December. During this campaign, the Chindits had been launched into Burma on their first operation, codenamed *Longcloth*. While *Longcloth* did not achieve any immediate significant strategic gain, in terms of confidence and morale, sorely needed after the latest reversal in the Arakan, it was used to show that British troops could match the Japanese in jungle warfare.[101] Perhaps more importantly, it convinced the Japanese that they could launch an offensive against India.[102]

Adding to the confidence won by the Chindits, there was a complete reorganisation of leadership in the theatre. In August 1943, Admiral Mountbatten was appointed Supreme Commander Southeast Asia, and

---

[101] *See* Philip Woods, *Managing the Media in the India-Burma War: Challenging a 'Forgotten War'* (Bloomsbury: London, 2023), especially Chapter 5 'Media Coverage of Operation Longcloth, pp.53-63.

[102] *See* Christopher Sykes, *Orde Wingate* (Collins: London, 1959), p.542.

General Slim was put in charge of XIV Army. The armed forces finally began to gain some self-belief as these new leaders put their programmes into effect, rallying the morale of the men through concerted training, malarial protection, entertainment and news. At the same time, the Special Operations Executive was inserting secret agents as well as officers and NCOs behind the lines, making contact with the Kachin in the north, the Karen in the east, and Burmese nationalists in Arakan and southern Burma. The foundations for victory in 1945 were constructed during this important period of 1943 into early 1944.

In February 1944, the Japanese launched their bid to invade India. This began with an offensive in the Arakan to try and draw Allied troops south from the main offensive, Operation U-Go, which was pointed at Imphal and the railhead at Dimapur. In Arakan, the Allied armies successfully defeated the Japanese offensive using the new tactics of staying put when surrounded. In the now infamous 'Battle of the Admin Box', troops relied on being supplied by air to keep on fighting rather than retreat. With this battle won, the main attack fell on Imphal and, further north, developed around a small town called Kohima. These two battles are regarded as the turning point for the Allies in the war in Burma. In these twin battles, the Japanese suffered more casualties than any other battle in which they fought in the Second World War.

With the Japanese defeat at Imphal and Kohima and a lack of resources to effect amphibious landings in southern Burma, the decision was taken in late 1944 to chase the Japanese over the Indian border and into Burma. Working in cooperation with the Special Operations Executive, General Slim launched Operation Capital, an ambitious plan to bring the Japanese army to battle and destroy it on the flat country north of Mandalay. When Mandalay was liberated, Slim decided to try and reclaim Rangoon before the monsoon arrived in May 1945. This offensive was codenamed *Extended Capital.* From February 1945, Special Groups of SOE, now known as Force 136, were parachuted into Burma to raise the Karen on the left flank of XIV Army's advance, in support of *Extended Capital.* Codenamed Operation Character, approximately 12,000 Karen volunteered to fight as guerrillas and made a valuable contribution to ensuring the success of Slim in re-taking Rangoon by 3 May.

While the Army was reorganised in preparation for the anticipated invasion of Malaya, the Karen serving with Force 136 continued to fight. Approximately 70,000 Japanese were cut off in Burma by the drive to Rangoon. During July, these Japanese troops attempted to break out to the southeast of the country, crossing the Sittang River on bamboo rafts and any boats they were able to scavenge. The Karen guerrillas in SOE were waiting, and, assisted by the Burma National Army and the British Indian Army, there was a terrific slaughter in the immediate weeks prior to the atomic bombs being dropped on Japan.

After the Japanese surrendered on 15 August 1945, many Karen continued to serve in the jungle with SOE until October and November 1945, fighting Japanese soldiers who didn't believe their emperor had capitulated, and ensuring law and order prevailed in the power vacuum left between war and peace.

# War Service, June 1942–October 1945

## Saw Champion

*Saw Champion had joined No.1 Animal Transport Company in 1941. After seeing fierce fighting attached to 6 Battalion Burma Rifles in Tenasserim, Saw Champion had retreated north with Allied forces, trying to reach India. Saw Champion was captured by the Japanese and sent to prison in Mandalay as a POW.*

At the time, the Japanese prison authorities asked the convicts to do force labour outside the prison wall. After 20 days in the prison, I disguised as one of the convicts to give force labour outside the prison wall and then escaped.

Japanese military intelligence (Cam-pa-tai) looked for me in Mandalay town where I hid for 3 days and then left to Maymyo by the merchant's truck. From there I journeyed to the country side village named Taung-gaung – Taung-gani where I hid for six months.

One winter night I came to Maymyo to find the truck going to Taungoo. Fortunately, I found it and travelled to Taungoo. While I staying in the out skirts of Taungoo town, I was recruited by British Army officer who told me to revolt the Japanese. Arms and ammunition and military equipment would be supported by the allied forces. According to the officer, guerrilla Force 136 commanded by Major Poe had been formed and was operating in Mawchi mine area.

Therefore, I enrolled in Force 136 and we launched our mobile operation using guerrilla warfare tactics. We annihilated the Japanese troops retreating from the front lines by using surprise attacks, ambushed and setting booby traps and mines. Japanese casualties were immense. I revolted the Japanese Fascist forces for 4 months till the Japanese Army unconditional surrender on September 1945.

As the allied forces arrived and orderly controlled the Taungoo town, I came to Taungoo to look for my old veterans who were surviving in the bloody World War II. I found some of my friends from No.1 A.T. (Animal Transport) company and we went to report at No.5 Holding and Enquiry supervised by Major Smith. I enlisted at No.1 Karen rifle organised by British Army. I got more modern training given by English, Australian and Canadian instructors.

## Saw Johnny Htoo

*Saw Johnny Htoo had managed to escape to India and join the Chin Levies, operating on the Indo-Burmese border:*

After two years, I attended parachute training in India in order to come back to Burma.[103] The instructor was Colonel Toke. I remembered one soldier asked the instructor "Officer, what should we do if we cannot open our parachute?" The Officer answered "If the parachute does not open, for sure you have to know that this may be your last jump." In 1939-40, our group was sent back to Burma and I was appointed as group leader.[104] My secret name was Bud Four.[105] Unfortunately, we missed the location where we had to jump and we blindly jumped into another area. After two days and two nights, we were captured by the Japanese in Pathein Delta. The Japanese sent us from Pathein to Yangon within a night. We were tortured the whole way. When we arrived at Paungde town which is close to Yangon, as I could not tolerate anymore, I held the hand of the soldier who was torturing us and he asked "Why did you hold my hand?" I said, "When I held your hand, I compared our skins and I knew that we are both Asian." "Are you a Christian?" "Yes" and he said he was a Christian too. Then he told me "If you are a Christian, you shouldn't lie" then I knew that he was a Christian officer and I told him "I am not lying I am telling the truth but you didn't believe me and tortured us tremendously which we had never been tortured like this before."

Why I came back to Burma was to contact Saw Bonny Bwal who had lost contact with us for six months. I was put into Rangoon jail and was kept in one of the cells and while I looked up at the wall, I saw the names Major H.P. Seagrim and Lieutenant Saw Ba Gyaw who was my old friend

---

[103] All parachute training for members of clandestine organisations was carried out at Chaklala near Rawalpindi in modern day Pakistan, or Jessore in India. Jessore was a Special Operations Executive (SOE) training base, whereas Chaklala catered for all, e.g. SOE, SIS, Z Force. The SIS files will probably never be released, but a total of 2,170 SOE personnel were trained in these two schools from May 1944 to the end of the war. *See* TNA, HS 7/115, 'History of Training', Part II.

[104] Note the dates here are clearly incorrect. Judging by later comments, he was most likely parachuted into Burma in 1944.

[105] The codename 'Bud Four' implies an SIS operation, as SOE operatives were assigned B/B codenames, for example B/B226.

in 3rd Burma Rifles were written on the wall.[106] Major H.P Seagrim G.C., D.S.O., M.B.E was the person Karen people called Phu Htaw Khaw (Grandfather Long Legs). I was detained for three months and afterwards I met with Saw Bonny Bwal.

After our group was released, we had to follow the Japanese as cooks. The duty of the Japanese was to look for the camp of British Force 136. My friend Saw Thet Wah and I tried to escape and we met with Karen Levy soldiers and followed them to a mountain called Mount Si Phoe where Lieutenant Colonel Peacock (Chief Officer of the region) and Major Saw Butler who were in command of British Force 136 were. I worked with them until 15 August 1945, the year the war ended.[107]

## Saw Michael Shwe

*Saw Michael Shwe had withdrawn to Fort Hertz in northern Burma, where, suffering from malaria, he had been flown to India:*

At the end of the year, we moved from Tinsukia to Dibrugarh recreation camp. We reorganised with our main navy brigade in Dibrugarh. Then, I took one month leave in Lahore region, Amritsar Punjab town to travel.

Again the battalion was reorganized at Hoshiarpur. Burma Frontier Force Signals and Burma Army Signals were combined under the command of Major Carlyn. In 1943, we had to attend strong military training again to be ready for front line action. After the training, we were given one month's leave and I spent it in Darjeeling Hill Station, Nepal.[108] And then, BFF Signals soldiers were reorganised in Hoshiarpur. They were:

1. Havildar Saw Ba Lay
2. Naik Saw Kar Ri
3. Signalman Saw Tun Oo
4. Signalman Saw Aung Tun Khin
5. Signalman Johnny Win
6. Signalman Saw Benny.

---

[106] Seagrim and Ba Kyaw (more often spelt 'Gyaw') were incarcerated in Rangoon jail sometime in August 1944, and executed in September.

[107] Lieutenant Colonel Peacock was an SOE / Force 136 officer. He was in charge of the Otter area of Operation Character. His headquarters was located on Mount Sosiso (2,237m) which is between Toungoo and Mawchi.

[108] Darjeeling is in West Bengal, India.

After a month's leave, we had to serve under the command of Naik Saw Kar Ri at 14th Army Corps D Signals Light W/T Detachment Station in Imphal, Manipur. The other people were Naik Saw Johnny Win, Signalman Saw Benny, Signalman Saw Aung Shaing, Signalman Saw Michael Shwe, O.C (Officer Commanding), Captain R.E. Kitson (Royal Signals) 2.I.C.(2nd in command) Lieutenant Vault (India Signals). At the end of 1943, we were transferred to Northern Kachin Levy (N.K.L) under the command of Major De Silva and second-in-command Major Rosnar and we had to move station from one place to another until the Chinese battalion K.M.T [Kuomintang, Chinese Nationalist forces under Chiang Kai-Shek] captured Myitkyina which was led by General Stilwell in August 1944.[109] We were recalled to Headquarters in Shillong, Assam in October 1944. We received an order that those who were in the list had to report to Lieutenant Colonel Mayne, Inter Services Liaison Department (I.S.L.D) at Calcutta, India.[110] While serving at I.S.L.D, we had to attend parachute training at Jorhat, India. We parachuted into Papun, Karen mountain range behind the enemy's camp under the mission named *Blast*.[111] Our mission was to get enemy information and head to Dawei (Tavoy). By the blessing of God, before the mission ended, the Japanese surrendered on 14 August 1945. We had to report at I.S.L.D Yangon Headquarters and got leave to meet our family which had been parted during the Second World War for four years. I joined my old battalion in Maymyo in 1945, Christmas time.

## Saw Aye Kyaw

*Saw Aye Kyaw had retreated up the western side of the Pegu Yomas from Rangoon, tending to the wounded, until he eventually reached India:*

The people who lived on Assam Mountains, called Kasie people were like the Karen people and they chewed betel and smoked pipes.[112] There were no motor roads so they would bring pigs, ducks and poultry and vegetables from their home, carried them on their back and would go to the town market once a week in groups to sell or exchange for rice, salt

---

[109] For more on the North Kachin Levies, *see* Ian Fellowes-Gordon, *Amiable Assassins* (Panther: London, 1958).

[110] ISLD was the cover name for MI6, the Secret Intelligence Service (SIS).

[111] Most ISLD missions into Burma had codenames beginning with the letter 'B'.

[112] The Karbi people are a group living in the Assam Hills, for which the name 'Kasie' might have been given here.

or other food, they put it into the big basket on their back and went home. They built their houses on the side and on top of mountains and their houses were not too high, but low. During winter, they lit fires inside the house and slept near the fire. Some of those who lived in town attended Missionary Schools and became Christians.

The villagers would carry things on their back, chew betel and smoke pipes and communicate in Hindi as their language was different. Although there were Christians, we did not get to Church. We were sent to outside Poona where the army was stationed. We met with Punjabi, Gurkha and Chin and Rakhine privates who underwent military training at Burma Rifles, Burma Army and Signal M.T. After that, we had to stay and attend military training at Hoshiarpur, Punjab.

While I was in that region, a group of people were selected to go to the front line near Imphal, where the Japanese army came to attack the British but they had to retreat because it was a mountain region and supplies could not be sent and the local Naga people had no rice. After a few months there I was allowed to come back to Headquarters in Poona. I asked leave to meet my friends in Calcutta and to enquire about serving in US Force 101.[113] After some months of military training at a tea leaf plantation, eight of us were selected.[114] We flew by plane in the night and parachuted near Kanyutkwin town, on Yoma Mountain.[115] While we went and found out information about the enemy from those villagers near the route where the Japanese had military operations we engaged three Japanese. They were travelling towards Thailand by cart.

During that time, the Japanese were heading east and were being attacked by guerrillas so many were injured. The three Japanese could have been officers. They carried swords and a Japanese flag. My men waited at the top of the hill by the end of the cart track. When the cart arrived at the end of the track we opened fire and all three of them were killed. The cart driver ran away with fear and came back scared as we called him back. He was exhausted. We got documents, swords and the flag. We never experienced this situation again.

---

[113] 'US Force 101' is most likely a reference to OSS Detachment 101. The Office of Strategic Services (OSS) later became the CIA.

[114] Detachment 101's training base was on a tea plantation in Nazira, northeast India.

[115] Ka Nyut Kwin is a town just east of the Pegu Yomas, approximately 200km north of Yangon.

## Saw Ni K'mwe Paul AKA Lieutenant Saw Smile Paul

*Saw Ni K'mwe had joined Captain Seagrim's levies to fight as a guerrilla behind the lines:*

The Japanese arrested, jailed, and tortured Karen villagers, in order to capture their enemy Hpu Taw Kaw (Grandfather Long Legs).[116] The Japanese would arrest whoever they suspected, so the Papun villagers were so frightened.

Later on, the Japanese would ask for the whereabouts of Major Nimmo and Major McCrindle and arrested most of the Karen villagers and imprisoned them in Monastery in Kyaukkyi (Lerdoh). They would torture the arrested people to get answers. My older brother was arrested, tortured and hung upside down, his knees were hit with metal bars and he could not stand the pain anymore so he gave information about a gun that he had hidden.

*After the war, several Karen made sworn statements to place on record the ill treatment that they had received from the Japanese. The Headman of Bawgaligyi, Saw Rupert, was one such man. His statement infers that it was the torture that caused Major Nimmo's camp to be attacked:*

In February 1944 I heard from my brother MAYSHA that a CAPT NIMMO of Force 136 was in hiding nearby. The same month SGT AKIYAMA of TOUNGOO KEMPEI TAI came to my house and arrested me. He then told me to lead him to where CAPT NIMMO was hiding. On the way SGT AKIYAMA kicked me in the face, and beat me in order to make me divulge this officer's position. On approaching CAPT NIMMO's hide-out firing broke out, and he was killed. Immediately afterwards I was taken to TOUNGOO jail where I was detained for five months.[117]

*Saw Rupert was detained in Toungoo for five months before being taken to Rangoon where he was sentenced to eight years imprisonment for helping Nimmo. Back to Lt. Saw Smile Paul:*

So, I decided to give myself up to the Japanese to save the villagers and relatives. I gave my brother-in-law one Tommy gun, 303 hand grenades,

---

[116] 'Grandfather Longlegs' was the name the Karen gave to Major Hugh Seagrim.

[117] TNA, WO 325/63, 'Statement by SAW RUPERT, Headman of BAWGALIGYI on 9 Mar 46' witnessed by Major P.R. Barrass, GSO 2 (I) 19 Indian Division.

one rifle and a double barrel shotgun which was given to me by Phoo Htun Khaung. Later on, I escaped. The situation in Kyaukkyi was unstable, so I returned to Chinatown, Yangon. The Japanese asked my mother-in-law and said that they would find Hpu Taw Kaw (Seagrim). The Japanese soldier Kawabata entered our house to harm my mother-in-law. Finally, the Japanese put a number of Karen people on trial for interrogation.

Karen people didn't want him to, but Captain Seagrim could not stand seeing Karen being tortured any more so he gave himself up to the Japanese. The Japanese Colonel promised that he would not harm him. He did not keep his promise, he killed Captain Seagrim and his fellow soldiers at Kyantaw, Yangon.[118] My two friends, who were bodyguards of Seagrim, Saw Maung Kyaw Gyi from Burma Rifles and Airman Saw Ei Doe Myaing were killed and buried together in the same pine coffin.[119] When I heard that I went to the hills and asked the headman to send me to the place where Hti Yoo Bo Hta had parachuted in. With the help of village headman Saw Gay Mu, I met with Colonel H.W Howell, Captain R.J. Barron, Captain Wilson, Sergeants Roe and Henney.[120] Colonel Howell asked Captain Barron and Sergeant Henney to lead a [Force] 136 Guerrilla unit.[121]

---

[118] 'Kyantaw' is most likely 'Kyun Taw', as the cemetery in which Seagrim is buried is between Kyun Taw Road in the west, and the main Pyay Road to the east.

[119] It's not clear who Maung Kyaw Gyi and Saw Ei Doe Myaing were, but Saw Maung Kyaw is mentioned often but briefly in a documents in Major Seagrim's personnel file; TNA, HS 9/1334/7, *see* for example report of Major Jones, 'Major Seagrim's buried documents', 12 December 1945.The names of the Karen who were executed with Seagrim are: Lieutenant Ba Gyaw, Saw He Be, Saw Tun Lin, Saw Sunny, Saw Pe, Saw Peter and Saw Ah Din. Those who were sentenced to eight years in prison were; Saw Po Hla, Saw Ta Roe, Saw Digay, Thra May Sha, Thra Kyaw Lay, Saw Rupert, Saw Henry, Saw Po Myin, Saw Tha Say and Saw Yay. See Philip Davies, *Lost Warriors,* pp.214-5.

[120] Lieutenant Colonel Hugh Warton Howell was in charge of SOE's Operation Character, team Hyena, from 24 March 1945. Captain Robert Barron was in charge of Hyena sub-area White. Captain J.W. Wilson was in charge of sub-area Orange. Sergeant Henney was W/T operator with Capt. Barron, while Sergeant Roe was one of three W/T operators at Hyena HQ.

[121] 'On the 8th May 45 I received orders from Lt Col HOWELL to proceed down to the plains and organise levies in the area', TNA HS 1/10, 'REPORT ON OPERATION HYENA WHITE by CAPTAIN R.J. BARRON, p.2.Captain Barron's month is wrong, it was April.

We spent the evening at Kyaukkhine region and waited for the parachutists from India to land at Phaw Mhu Hta village. At 8 pm, Major Torry, Major Ba Chit and some soldiers parachuted in.[122] We took them to Mawchi Mountain where Colonel Howell was.[123] Captain Barron and Sergeant Henney went by bullock cart. The Japanese army waited to ambush the British soldiers but could not see us as it was dark. We told Captain Barron and Sergeant Henney to lie flat on the bullock cart and covered him with hay. When the Japanese passed us we went to Myat Yine village and warned the local people at 4am in the morning. On the way to Yeleh, we saw one Burmese and avoided him for our security. At Yeleh village, we had to ask the Pastor to find alcohol as Captain Barron would like to drink. The Pastor asked "Does the English [man] drink?" I answered "The English [man] is not a missionary." I went to Kywe Ta Lin village where my father and relatives lived. Two or three days later, I received a message from Colonel Howell that military equipment had been delivered at Major Torry's base and we needed to collect it from Major Torry.

We headed to the east of Kywe Ta Lin village to wait for more parachutists. At 5pm, only a Liberator Bomber arrived. At that time, Lieutenant Marlam gave us one hundred .303 Rifles together with bullets.[124] Then we received a message to return to Kywe Ta Lin. The Japanese troops controlled the area and Kempeitai, Japanese Intelligence, had received news about our activities. At Pastor Phar Khu Say's house in Kyaukkyi our volunteer army, led by my brother-in-law Saw Tin Kyaw and Major Turrell, fought against the Japanese army who were holed up in there.[125] They fought the whole night. In the end, we threw hand

---

[122] Major Saw Torry and Major Ba Chit arrived on 9 May 1945 according to Capt. Barron's report, but it was night of 9-10 April, *see* TNA, HS 7/106, 'REPORT ON OPERATION "HYENA" By Lieutenant Colonel H.W. HOWELL', p.23. Major Torry later led sub-area White, and Ba Chit was in charge of sub-area Green.

[123] Lieutenant Colonel Howell had his HQ on Chawido Hill, *see* TNA, HS 7/106, Lieutenant Colonel H.W. Howell, 'Report on Operation "Hyena"', p.5.

[124] Captain Joseph Marlam. *See* Richard Duckett, 'The Men of SOE Burma' [online] https://soeinburma.wordpress.com/the-men-of-soe-burma/

[125] In Turrall's report, the Pastor is named Saw Nya Say, and his house was the Kempetai's HQ in Kyaukkyi. *See* TNA, HS 7/106, Major Rupert Turrall, 'Report: Character Operation – Hyena Red', 23 October 1945, p.7. Saw Nya Say was awarded the British Empire Medal: https://www.thegazette.co.uk/London/issue/37959/supplement/2249/data.pdf Saw Tin Kyaw is mentioned in the following terms in Major

grenades into the house to burn the chillies under the house which gave a bad smell and killed all of them. Two days later, we got news from Colonel Howell that the Japanese marched to Kyaukkyi. They arrived at Kyaukkyi at midnight and simultaneously attacked us. The Japanese were defeated as we counter attacked. The Japanese retreated to north of Kyaukkyi to Shwe Kyin as dawn broke. We captured Kyaukkyi and returned to Kywa Ta Lin Village. We got news from Colonel Howell that they would drop bullets at Mar Pi Village, east bank of Kyaukkyi stream. We prepared to specify Mar Pi village as the Drop Zone. It was 9pm when we got there. Soon, three Liberator Bombers dropped bullets, food, cheese, tea, money and alcohol for Karen, British and Indian troops. We transported the supplies the whole night. We had to carry the heavy weapons such as 81 mm mortar and Bren guns secretly.[126]

Early morning, the Captain announced that the Military Headquarters had promoted me to Warrant Officer and gave me a pistol and a star. That morning, we captured a Japanese soldier who asked for rice at the village. The villagers gave him rice and asked him to surrender but he refused. He had a grenade in his right hand and rice in his left hand so the villagers shot him. We got information that the Japanese were coming to Yay Twin Gone and the main base at Kywe Ta Lin. We had to march there before the Japanese arrived. We received information that the Japanese were a mile away from the village. Captain Barron and I looked for the Japanese with a telescope outside the village and they saw us through their binoculars so they went back to the forest. The villagers searched where the Japanese were heading for. They reported that the Japanese were heading to Yin Tite Kone village, south east of our village. When we followed the Japanese, the villagers reported that they were sleeping in the hay on the bank of the dried fish pond. Captain Barron told Sergeant Henney and me to wait at the village and he would inform us if he needed help. After a few hours, we heard the blast of the grenades and shooting by the river. Soon, we saw Captain Barron and his soldiers. The Captain was wounded in the left ear and thigh and Private Maung

---

Turrall's report: 'SAW TIN GYAW who "wanted to go and kill Japs" had proved, in practive [sic], most reluctant to be at the taking of his town', p.8. More on Saw Tin Gyaw on p.9 indicates that he was a member of the Burma Defence Army. *See* 'Report: Character Operation – Hyena Red'.

[126] According to Major Turrell's report, they received a Liberator drop of weapons, ammunition and money on 18 April at Hlelangu. *See* HS 7/106, 'Report: Character Operation – Hyena Red', Appendix VIII, 'Supply Drops'.

Lay was hurt a bit around the lips, but not seriously.[127] The Japanese retreated to the forest with their wounded. We sent Captain Barron to Yay Twin Kone by bullock cart. The wounds were serious and we worried that would get infected, but the Japanese were everywhere. It was not safe in Yay Twin Kone village. Therefore, we moved to Kywe Ta Lin. At Kywe Ta Lin, the Officer Thet Tun and U Boe Chin asked for weapons so we gave them one hundred 303 Rifles together with bullets.[128] The villagers said the British battalion in Mandalay had advanced to Yangon.[129]

We arranged to send Captain Barron to Penwegon where the British Army was situated. That was the Japanese retreating route. Thus, we had to go to Mar Pi there was no Japanese army. From there, we went to Kyone Kyi, the eastern bank of the Sittang River. We marched to Tha Min Inn Kone village while looking for the Japanese. The villagers said the Japanese had moved to the eastern bank of the Sittang River.

We moved from Tha Min Inn Kone to about a few miles from Yangon-Mandalay highway. We had to wait a long time for the trucks from Yangon to Mandalay. There was no space on the truck only for Captain Barron and I could get on, Sergeant Henney would like to go by truck but the Captain ordered him to track along with the soldiers. We arrived to Nan Thar Kwin at 4 pm and we sent Captain Barron to Yangon by Lysander plane. He ordered Sergeant Henney and me to wait for the order from Headquarters. The Headquarters staff and privates arrived at 9 at night and ordered us to go to Anti Fascist People's Freedom League (AFPFL). Sergeant Henney arrived to Penwegon at 9 pm. Sergeant Henney got angry when the Indian soldiers did not permit him to pass. We slept at AFPFL Headquarters with the privates for the night. Sergeant Henny returned to Nan Thar Kwin.[130] I returned to Yay Twin

---

[127] 'Capt. BARRON was wounded at YINDAIKKON on the 29 April 1945, and whilst at KYAUGYI the wound became worse' therefore he was evacuated. *See* TNA, HS 7/106, 'OPERATIONAL REPORT WHITE, HYENA AREA', 29 November 1945, p.4.

[128] Thet Tun and Bo Chin are recorded as being 'leading citizens' who were elected to the military department of Kyaukkyi township's governing body on 17 April 1945. This was an SOE initiative after the attack on the town just described. *See* TNA, HS 7/106, Major Turrall, 'REPORT CHARACTER OPERATION - HYENA RED, 17 October 1945, p.9.

[129] Rangoon, now Yangon, was occupied by the Allies on 3 May 1945.

[130] Sergeant Henney did not return to operations, and since he had taken the W/T crystals, Major Torry was without communications with HQ until 20 July when

Kone with the Headquarters staff. I lost contact with Howell for some time while I was staying there.

Major Torry came to Penwegon Headquarters.[131] He wrote a letter to the Army Headquarters requesting supplies and asked me to do the rest. I said to the private who questioned me at the entrance of the Police Commissioner Office "I came from Force 136" and the Captain heard me while he was having a bath and permitted me to come in. I told him about the letter of Major Torry.

After reading the letter, he told the Brigade Major to give me what we needed and the Brigade Major told the Supply Point Captain to give what we need. I got a truck load of stuff. We got tinned food, beer, sugar, coffee, Indian food and English food. Major Torry was quite pleased with what I had done. Within a couple of days, Colonel Howell sent Sergeant Moore. The Japanese passed Sittang River during the monsoon when the water level was rising.[132] They came from the Pegu Yomas and marched to Yangon-Mandalay highway road. The Japanese would ask for chicken, rice and whatever food from villages they passed as they were out of rations. One night, we caught one Japanese private and sent him to Penwegon.[133] When I got to Headquarters, the Captain gave me 500 rupees because I caught the Japanese private alive. Major Torry said he had never heard anyone being given a bonus. I asked Colonel Howell whether it is true or not. I said English never lie. When I telegrammed to Colonel Howell, I knew it was true.

I got 500 Rupees for capturing the Japanese soldier as promised. There was one difficulty. The Japanese were like wild chickens and wild birds. Once, three Japanese came to me but one drowned himself by running into the water. Thus, I could only send the remaining two to Penwegon.

We received information from Colonel Howell that the Japanese 56

---

Sergeant Moore and a W/T set arrived.

[131] Major Torry went to Rangoon to try and resolve the W/T situation caused by Sergeant Henney going AWOL.

[132] In July 1945, the remaining Japanese divisions trapped in Burma attempted to reach southern Burma to regroup. In what has been called the 'Battle of the Breakout', SOE decimated Japanese units as they tried to cross rivers and chaungs during the monsoon floods.

[133] Getting the chronology right here is tricky as the interviewee seems to skip back and forth through time. The Hyena Red report records Japanese captured by date and place, but it is hard to pin down the three POWs that are referred to here.

Div. was crossing Sittang River in the middle of July and they were ordered to kill themselves if they were not able to cross by 15 July. Therefore, we waited for the Japanese at the other bank of Sittang River. That night the rain was heavy and the water level rose. The Japanese were too many so we could not shoot all. There was no way out. Some ran into the houses and burnt the houses to escape. Some went into the village to steal some food. The villagers left the village and ran into the forest. We asked help from the Air Force but they came late and bombs and guns fell on empty houses. On 2nd September 1945, the Japanese surrendered and informed all the other Japanese to surrender also. It was hard to talk to them, because they didn't care about surrendering.

In the end, the Japanese got permission to retreat. After Captain Barron recovered from his injury in India, he came back to Yay Twin Kone with Colonel Howell.[134] We continued to our base at Nwar Chi Gone village. On the way back, we asked the villagers to build an airfield for the plane to land. Captain Barron ordered me to finish the work. When the plane landed in Kyaukkyi, we asked for dynamite to destroy guns, plaster and TNT from Captain Barron.

We threw all the collected weapons and bullets that we could not keep into the Sittang River. Captain Barron asked me to build a bamboo raft and dynamite all left over weapons. Major Torry left for Yangon. Captain Barron, Sergeant Moore and I went to Karen community organisation in Kyaukkyi and went for 1st Karen Rifles in Taungoo. We had a farewell party at Yay Twin Kone and Captain Barron left for India via Yangon. I also returned to Kyaukkyi from Yay Twin Kone. I gave up fighting. After four months, I received a British Empire Medal (BEM) and my father-in-law received an Order of British Empire (OBE). My father-in-law attended the ceremony but not me. After I quit from Force 136 and went to Taungoo to work with a recommendation letter from Captain Barron to find a job. He could not help me with anything so I came out from the office and thought "If you cannot help me, I will do everything for myself".

## Saw Fair Play

*Saw Fair Play had watched the RAF battle in the skies over Tenasserim before waiting for a boat to take him to Rangoon. The boat never came, so he had returned to Tavoy (Dawei):*

I crossed to Thailand with some friends and we constructed a road to

---

[134] Capt. Barron returned to operations by Lysander on 27 July 1945.

Narayetaw Kyauk Taung.[135] There was no bulldozer so we had to dig with our hands. It was a very hard time and there was insufficient food and clothes so we had to use gunny bags as clothes as well as blankets. The white lice on the gunny bags were bigger than the lice on the head and very painful when they bit. The skin got itchy and became ulcerous. Some said they came out from our skin. Sometimes we had to go to the streams where people came, undress and kill the white lice on our clothes. Thai men and women passed by but we could not be ashamed. Many people died of ulcers. Dutch prisoners of war also died of ulcers. They too had to use gunny bags due to insufficient clothes.

Later on, we knew that ships had come and took Chin Rifles from Ma Li Island. I received news from Major Mwar Si before I left Ma Li Island because we worked together. He asked me to wait with his adopted Burmese but I could not wait anymore. When both of them arrived at Ma Li Island, the ship had left. The Japanese and Burmese army heard that they were there and they searched thoroughly for them and tortured the villagers so both of them were killed by the villagers. Major Mwar Si gathered intelligence on the enemy from Burma and Mae Sot, Thailand border to Koh Thaung. He said he was from the Royal family. We worked for three years in Thailand.

## Saw Htaw Tha Heh (AKA Saw Kway Kwi)

*Saw Htaw Tha Hheh was still at school when the war started. He remembered feeling the ground shake from the bombing and the retreating British Army:*

After a few years, the Japanese army was falling back from upper Myanmar (Burma). At the same time, British planes came to drop bullets, fire arms, equipment, and supplies along with Major Torry, an English Captain, Captain Barron, an American Sergeant, Sergeant Moore at Ler Doh and Yay Dwin Gone villages.[136] They called for volunteers for the army, and a lot of Karen people signed up to be volunteers. A group of five soldiers were formed and given guns and supplies. Karen youth from Kaw Lo Klo village to villages in Papun such

---

[135] Although the Thai-Burma railway is well known, Japanese road building is less so. See 'Japan in Northwest Thailand During World War II' [online], https://www.lanna-ww2.com/frontpage.html; David Bogget, 'JAPAN'S "BURMA ROAD;" Reflections on Japanese Military Activities in Northern Thailand' [online], http://www.kyoto-seika.ac.jp/researchlab/wp/wp-content/uploads/kiyo/pdf-data/no18/David.pdf

[136] Sergeant Jack Moore was British.

as Tee To Loh, Paw Pi Der, Myet Ye, Wel Gyi, Lu Aa, Haw Kho Ghaw, Twa Ni Gone, Own Shat Gone, Yay Dwin Gone, Nant Thar Gone, Daw Moot, Taw Kyont Pot became levies to fight the Japanese army. Guns and supplies were dropped for the troops that were stationed by Pouk Pin Gone village and surrounding areas. Our Karen youth were tested and we satisfied the leaders so we were accepted to become levy fighters.

We took positions on the bank of Kaw Lo river bank, which is the fall back route of the Japanese army, where they usually fall back in the night.[137] They used boats, rafts and ferries to cross Kaw Lo River. There was no problem for us in the day time but at night time. Therefore, we tied bells with one string and placed it in the stream. We would hear the bells ringing when the Japanese came along the stream. We fired where the bells rang and killed some Japanese soldiers for sure. There was also air support for us and help with heavy fire. Therefore, there were only a few Japanese troops who escaped from the fall back route. Once, my friend and I were ordered to deliver a letter. We were warned to be careful on the way and save the bullets for survival. On our way there, we met a troop of Japanese which came by boat between Yaytwinkone and Pheh Tho village. We took position to fire at them and saw them raising their hands to throw hand grenades. But when they got closer we saw nothing in their hands. We shot all the Japanese until we finished all the bullets in our magazine as it was war time and they were our enemy there was no need to think of anything. The Japanese were brave men, because we saw grass in their stomach. In spite of them eating grass, I respected their fighting ability. We were youths so we did not care for anything and were only interested in fighting and killing.

The war ended while I was serving there. We were ordered to return our weapons. We had a farewell party before Major Torry, Captain Barron and Sergeant Moore left. I still remembered that we sang:

> "Goodbye, Goodbye, Dear Major, We aren't saying goodbye.
> Goodbye, Goodbye, Dear Captain, We aren't saying goodbye.
> Goodbye, Goodbye, Dear Sergeant, We aren't saying goodbye," at
> the farewell party. It was unforgettable memory for a 19 year old young man.

---

[137] The western and southern boundaries of Hyena White area were the Sittang River. Unable to find a River Kaw Lo, the assumption is that it is a tributary or chaung.

## Saw K'Hsaw

*Saw K'Hsaw had helped organise the retreat while employed by the Bombay Burmah Trading Company before returning to his village. There, he had cared for Private Leslie Cryer until he died:*

I stayed in Hti Yo Boe Htar village in Kyaukkyi Township, Taungoo District from 1942-1945. In the middle of 1945, I heard that Colonel Howell came to Ba Law Khi village near Hti Yo Boe Htar village. I went and saw him secretly. He told me to help his Wireless Operator Sergeant Roe by helping him in recording and reporting information. From that time, I served as Corporal at 136 Spider Force in Hyena area.[138]

In November 1945, Colonel Howell transferred me to Lipyekhi and assigned me to gather information on troop movements.[139] In December, I had to go to Rangoon by plane with Colonel Howell to present the information for which I was responsible. I discussed with my teacher Saw Sar Say to tell Colonel Howell about the dead Irish soldier Leslie Cryer while I was serving in Lipyekhi but he told me to keep quiet and I was not able to say anything about him till now.[140]

## Saw Kay Ray

*Saw Kay Ray, serving in the Burma Signals, had retreated to India and reached Dimapur:*

We moved to Ranchi and then we were sent to Hoshiarpur by train to rest and attend further training (Refresher Course). At that time, I was only an N.C.O (Corporal). We were under the command of the British Army. Four teams of Signallers were transferred to the North Kachin Levies after over two years stay in Hoshiarpur.[141] I was in charge of the four Signals

---

[138] For identification purposes, indigenous personnel fighting with SOE were given an armband with a spider on it, hence the reference to Spider Force.

[139] November seems a bit late. The airstrip at Lipyekhi was found by Captain Guthrie on 3 May and after making it safe for aircraft, the first Lysander landed on the strip on 23 May 1945. Hyena HQ moved to Lipyekhi on 2 September. *See* TNA, HS 7/106, 'REPORT ON OPERATION "HYENA" BY Lieutenant Colonel H.W. HOWELL', 17 November 1945, pp.26-27.

[140] Private Cryer was separated from his unit in 1942 and after falling ill, died in a Karen village while trying to retreat to India alone.

[141] For more on the North Kachin Levies, *see* Ian Fellowes-Gordon, *Amiable Assassins* (Panther: London, 1958).

teams. Lieutenant Colonel Ford was our Commander. After serving four or five months, we were transferred to Hoshiarpur as there was less work. I was under the command of Captain P.O.J Nicolson when I was in India. The Japanese army was not able to fight the Allied Armies. I was promoted to Sergeant.

We received orders from Headquarters to transfer to Yangon/Rangoon from Calcutta by ship as the Japanese had withdrawn and there were no enemies for the British Allied Forces. When our Signals unit arrived in Burma, we reformed as Burma Signals and had Headquarters in Maymyo, now Pyin Oo Lwin.

## Saw Bunny

*Saw Bunny had joined Captain Seagrim's guerrillas in the Karen Hills:*

Major Nimmo and five privates parachuted in Mu Theh plain in October 1943. In December 1943, Major McCrindle and four privates parachuted in Phar Gaw.

On 15 February 1944, Major Nimmo was killed near Kaw Mu Pwa Doh and at the end of February 1944, Major McCrindle was killed in Mawchi mine battle. Major Seagrim gave himself up to the Japanese near the hill of Mae Wah Doh village, ten miles from south Papun's mountain.[142] At that time, he wore Karen dress on top of the white shirt with brown Shan trousers and slung a red Karen bag. I heard that he was imprisoned in a new detention hall on Strand Road, Rangoon on 29 April 1944. On 1 September 1944, he and five Karen Soldiers were killed at Kyantaw Cemetery.[143]

After Major Seagrim gave himself up to the Japanese, in April 1944, we Karen youth came back to Papun which was Japanese territory. I heard the British came down to Phar Gaw Pu field in December 1944.[144]

In the middle of January 1945, we ran away from Japanese territory and came back and served as volunteers in Force 136.[145] Some of my

---

[142] For Karen testimonies signed and witnessed after the war, *see* Major Seagrim's SOE file, TNA, HS 9/1334/7.

[143] Seven Karen were sentenced to death on 2 September, with Seagrim, and were buried in what is now called Rangoon War Cemetery, looked after by the Commonwealth War Graves Commission.

[144] If by 'came down' he means British personnel parachuted into Burma during December 1944, it was not SOE and so was most likely SIS.

[145] Major Turrell's Hyena team parachuted into the Pyagawpu area on 20 February, and

friends followed Colonel Peacock and I followed Major Turrell. In the first week beginning 12 April 1945, our army marched to Lerdoh region and on 12 April, following Major Turrell's deviously good plan we made a dawn attack against the Japanese. We captured the Japanese Headquarters.[146]

I was transferred to Major Wilson's unit and served with the army at Say Mu Doh region until the war ended.[147]

## Saw San Aye
*Saw San Aye had served with 1 Burif, and taken part in an important rearguard action under the command of Captain Thompson on the Toungoo to Mawchi Road:*

Eight of us came back to Momeik. Four of us joined the Shan police and four of us including me came back to Maymyo along the Maungnge, Kyaukme, Sakanthar road. The Sawba of Momeik gave us twenty Rupees each. We stayed in Waykapar (Sinlaung) village when we got to Maymyo.[148]

In 1945, we joined the American Army when they got to Maymyo and we fought the Japanese Army up to Yatsauk, Southern Shan state. We fought against the Japanese army about twenty times. We received 300 rupees for driving out the Japanese army from Yatsauk and returned to Maymyo.

## Mr Peter Andrews
*Peter Andrews had managed to escape from Burma to India:*

In 1943, I joined the Royal Corps of Signals, Eastern Command, which had Headquarters in Barrackpore, India and attended Advanced Signals Training. In 1944, I joined No.33 Battalion Victory Force in Imphal, on the India border and fought in battles around Imphal. At that time, the Battalion Commander for V Force was Colonel Murray.

During 1944-45, I came back to Shillong, Assam, to make myself fit

---

Lieutenant Colonel Peacock's *Otter* team followed on 23 February 1945.

[146] Presumably this is a reference to the attack on Kyaukkyi carried out on 15 April, and the captured HQ was the Kempeitai house described by Saw Smile Paul above.

[147] Captain J.W. Wilson was in charge of Hyena area Orange.

[148] A road runs from Kauykme to Maymyo (Pyin Oo Lwin), but the other place names remain unidentified.

and strong and then attended Parachute Training at Jessore Royal Air Force Headquarters. After the training, I parachuted into a village near Mawchi town, Kayin State to serve with Guerrillas.[149] Later on, I transferred to serve at Z Force which was under the command of Colonel Peacock.[150] The duty of the Volunteer force was to distract and attack the enemy and to cut off communication routes while the planes of Allied Air Force were preparing to attack Toungoo which was 175 miles from Rangoon.

During 1945-46 I had returned to my original Battalion and the Japanese army surrendered and World War Two ended. I retired from the army on 22 September 1946. I was a Sergeant.

## Saw Maw Ler

*Saw Maw Ler had seen action in Tenasserim before escaping, first to Rangoon, and then to India. At Imphal, the Japanese had bombed and killed two of his friends:*

After a month [in Ranchi] our CO, Captain Thomas, told us that he want[ed] two wireless operators for a special duty. Two of us, Soe Maung and me, volunteer for this duty so we are sent to Calcutta, then to Barrackpore and stay with Royal Signals for a month. Then we are sent to Dingyan, an American airbase in Assam.[151] We are then sent to Putao, called also Fort Hertz, the northern most town of Burma. [After] [a]bout a week, a column of Gurkha Rifles from Assam arrived with two officers, Major Bridge and Major Leach.[152] The duty of this special Gurkha column is to go and contact Chinese 92nd Division which came down from north eastern border of Burma to help American Marauder column which came across from Ledo, Assam, to capture Myitkyina and then push east to China to open Ledo-China motor road for transport which

---

[149] A V Force group of 30 men parachuted into Burma on 4 May 1945, joining Force 136's Otter group on 7 May. Among those dropped was Captain Murray. *See* Peacock, Geraldine, *Life of a Jungle Walla* (Stockwell: Ilfracombe, 1958), p.118.

[150] Lieutenant Colonel Edgar Peacock was in charge of the Otter group of Operation Character, which was an SOE/Force 136 team, not Z Force.

[151] Also Dinjan, in Dibrugarh district of Assam.

[152] The earliest drop of Gurkha parachutists into Fort Hertz was in July 1942, codenamed Operation Puddle. Edmund Leach was an anthropologist, who knew the area very well from his pre-war work. He arrived at Fort Hertz about September 1942.

is most urgently needed.[153] The journey is quite hard due to very high mountain and very cold weather.

Finally, we met the 92 Division at the border, a place called Chittupa and ask the 92nd Division to withdraw and come down on the side of the Shweli River east of Myitkyina. Back and forth the mission take about a month and then we arrived back to Putao. Then I was called again for special duty. This time it was the intelligen[ce] service duty between Kachin Levy and American troops who came down from Ledo. Our duty is to pass military information for the two arm[ed] forces which try to occupy Myitkyina and contact Force 136 in Burma for military information and for air force to disrupt enemy line of communication. This mission is very interesting. After [the] fall of Myitkyina, [the] American Marauder column was [relieved] by another column called Dead End Kids and Marauders were put back to India for rest.[154] We are also sent back to India at Shillong for [a] rest.

After a month['s] rest in Shillong I was again have to come back again to Burma on special duty with [a] V Force column of Assam Gurkha Rifles. This time we entered Burma from Imphal – Tamu side, then to Kalewa, and then to Sagaing. The Japanese are withdrawing from northern Burma and make only little resistance. From Sagaing we are heading toward Meiktila. At Meiktila I meet with Major Seagrim who try to see us as he heard there are two Karen wireless operators among the V Force column.[155] I think he need Karen wireless operator for his [Force]136 special intelligen[ce] force. But we are unable to join him as V Force duty is urgent and most important. As [the] Rangoon Mandalay road is in our hands so they who are cut off are unable to join their Japanese army in the east so [the] army from [the] delta and Tharawaddy and Prome [area?] are tak[ing [the] jungle route through Pegu Yoma. V Force duty is to harass the withdrawing Japanese troops. We are divided

---

[153] Most likely Chinese 96 Division which retreated to India via Fort Hertz. Another division, the 93rd, was further southeast in the Shan states. The 'American Marauder column' referred to here is 'Merril's Marauders', officially 5307th Composite Unit, and also called *Galahad*. It was a US formation that was similar to the Chindits in its role.

[154] For more on the Dead End Kids, *see* Sergeant Dave Richardson (Yank, the Army Weekly British Edition Vol 3. No.3), July 2 1944 [online] http://www.marauder.org/yank27.htm

[155] This seems unlikely, given that Seagrim gave himself up in March 1944, and V Force didn't operate more than twenty miles beyond the frontline. *See* TNA, WO 203/2696 for more on the role of V Force.

into small groups of 12 men and given [an] area (grid) to find out Japanese retreating columns and inform air force at Meiktila to bomb and straff them.

[After] [a]bout a month, we are recall[ed] to Pyinmana and then given duty to attack withdrawing Japanese from Kalaw and Taunggyi in Karenni state. At Pyinmana our V Force was divided into 3 columns. No.1 column is to attack Japanese that withdraw from Kalaw at Pinlaung. The 2nd column is to attack the Japanese at Moebye. The 3rd column is to attack the Japanese at Bawlakai and Kemapyu. I was in No.1 column so our duty is to attack the Japanese at Pinlaung. It was 3rd August and we start moving from Pyinmana toward Pinlaung through hills and mountain of thick jungle from from Pyinmana to Lebyaunbya [further place names indecipherable]. It was about 6pm when we arrived Lebyaunbya. Everybody is dog-tired due to difficult route and so I open up my wireless set at 8pm and try to contact G.H.Q. As soon as contact was made the G.H.Q signals offered me an (OW) message which means 'Most Immediate'. I at once told Colonel Stanley, Major Spicer, Captain Wright and another major and a captain whom I forget the names.[156] Then Colonel Stanley said we are dog-tired so if the message tell us to move on, we won't be able to in night in this sort of jungle and weather. Well, whatever it is I thought we are going to sleep here and start moving in the morning only after having our breakfast.

Owing to the bad weather it took me two hours to receive that message. After decoding the message, in short it told me that "Japanese have surrender[ed], the war has come to an end. So when you see Japanese you must not shoot them. If you shoot them action will be taken against you. Stay where you are and await further order[s]." In the morning we received a message telling us that we must turn back to a village called Ywagyi and there make a 3 days Victory celebration and then return to Pyinmana. Now the heavy burden of World War Two has fall[en] from our shoulder[s]. Our V Force column was then sent to Shan State in Kengtung area to a Shan village on the northeast of Kengtung at China Shan border for security purpose to see if there any Japanese left behind there. After about a year V Force was recall[ed] and then I return

---

[156] Lieutenant Colonel 'Nicky' Stanley was in charge of 2 V Ops of V Force. In December 1944, he was pushing patrols across the Irrawaddy, supporting 19 Division. *See* John Bowen, *Undercover in the Jungle* (William Kimber: London 1978), especially pp.96-98. To date (2023), nobody has written a history of V Force.

to my Signals unit in Maymyo.[157] I served the signals to the day of Burma independen[ce].

*It is interesting to compare this written account with Saw Maw Ler's interview, translated here:*

I had to come back to Burma in late 1942 for a special assignment. I was attached to 92 Company which was camped in Nantamine District, China border, Northern Putao and I passed through the mountains of Northern Kachin State. The reason I went there was to inform the Chinese army that the British army would march along the Shweli river, on the Chinese border with the object of capturing Myitkyina. The main reason was that the Americans were constructing the Ledo-China road for them and to help the American Marauder battalion which was coming from Assam. In early 1944, Major Bridge and Major Leach supervised this operation. The columns were Mahindra Dal Regiment from Assam Special Rifles.[158]

After a month's rest in Putao, I was transferred to the Kachin Levy in Laaung-ga between Putao and Sumprabum. I went with Major Coffey and my duty was to communicate with Force 136 which was operating in the Mountains of Northern Kachin State.[159] We had to undertake the duties of cutting off the communication system and deciphering Japanese army's signal code. Later on, I was assigned to communicate with the Marauder American battalion to capture Myitkyina.

After capturing Myitkyina, Dead-end-Hills battalion changed duty with the Marauder battalion which returned to Assam to rest. I was allowed to rest in Shillong in Assam. After resting over a month, I was assigned to a special duty in Burma with the Gurkha Special Volunteer army which was based in Assam. My duty was to clear the Japanese army which was harassing and deploying around Tu Mountain, Bago. When the assigned duty finished, the unit was assigned to fight the Japanese troops from East Pyinmana to Karenni borders.

---

[157] V Force was deployed in the Shan States well into 1946.

[158] The Mahindra Dal was one of three Nepalese battalions that deployed to India and Burma during the Second World War after an agreement was signed between the British government and Maharaja Juddha in December 1939. *See* Singh, S.B. 'Nepal and the World War II', *Proceedings of the Indian History Congress*, vol.53, 1992, pp.580 – 585; [online] www.jstor.org/stable/44142873.

[159] Major Coffey was northern Burma's intelligence officer.

While we were stationed in Kanpyuout region between Pyinmana and Pinlaung on 7 August 1945 we heard on the radio that the Japanese had surrendered and the war had ended. There was no need to fight the Japanese anymore. We received the order to go to Ywagyi village for the ceremony on victory day and came back to Pyinmana after the ceremony.

The officers of Volunteer Company were Colonel Stanley, Major Spicer, Captain Wright, Captain H. Hackson and I do not remember the names of the other two officers.

### Mel Du AKA Pu Hla Kyi Pa
*Mel Du had been helping to hide Captain Seagrim after the Japanese overran Burma:*

Later on, the Japanese received information that Karen people were helping British soldiers so they summoned village headman, including Mel Du from Lerwetkhi village, Thra Gaw Thu from Taku village, Grandfather P'doe Dtot from Kaypu village, and others, to the court in Lerdoh. When Village Headman Mel Du arrived at the court in Lerdoh, he was tied with rope and beaten and interrogated. Two Japanese soldiers put him between them and hit him on the cheeks with their iron boot studs. He was then released with his both eyes bleeding and a swollen and bruised face. Lerdoh villagers, where he had a lot of Karen and Burmese friends and his family, came to meet him and carried him back to his village. He was tortured so badly that both his eyes were badly damaged and he was now blind. The distance between Lerdoh town and Lerwetkhi village was about six hours by foot.

The villagers had to run and hide in the jungle as the Japanese came to Lerwetkhi village and destroyed houses, barns, rice and animals. Due to a shortage of food and insufficient clothing, the villagers suffered from disease and diarrhoea and many died including Headman Mel Du's parents. There was no one except Saw Maw Lay and two uncles at the funeral service. There was not even a small mat to cover the body. Saw Mel Du could not go to the funeral as he could not see. As he could not walk, he had to stay with his Uncle, Aunty, wife and children who took care of him.

He could only touch his children and remember the voices of the people who visited him 2-3 or more times. The two children took care of him when they grew up. His wife took the responsibility of taking care of him and the house. His wife suffered from asthma. One day she had an asthma attack while the children were out and he cuddled her with a blanket holding her to his chest. He did not know that his wife died in his hands. He only knew he was hugging his dead wife when his neighbour visited him.

He cried heart broken when they told him that his wife was dead.

## Saw Daniel Tun Baw
*Saw Daniel had joined the Navy in 1942:*

He attended Basic Military Training for three months as a new soldier. He could attend Instructor Training Class due to his education so he attended for another six months. He could manage work well and was appointed as Instructor in charge on a navy ship. He was well organized and a good manager, so after three months he was a navy signals officer. During his service, their ship visited India three or four times.

## Saw Baw Nay
*Saw Baw Nay had commented on the tense relations between Burmans and Karen when the Japanese invaded:*

When the Japanese combined with the Burmese to govern the country, it was much worse than under the British. The Burmese would say "A present devil is worse than the devil we knew" or "being frightened of tiger worship is worse than being frightened of the tiger." The poverty of the local people increased, employment and daily life was so difficult that people had to soften bark and use it to cover their body as clothing.[160] The Japanese governed the citizens cruelly. Due to some of the Burmese agitation Saw Baw Nay was beaten badly by the Japanese because his father had worked under the British. He could not forget that. At that time, he was a simple honest farmer.

At the end of 1943, he married Naw Lel Dar and after two years of marriage, the British governed Burma again.

*Although the war had been over since 15 August, many SOE personnel had to stay in the field as late as November 1945, filling the gap between the end of hostilities and the return of civil affairs officers. During this time, the Karen and their British friends held various victory parades and celebrations of peace which evidently included welcoming speeches by Karen*

---

[160] There was an acute shortage of all things, including clothing. Parachute silk used to resupply operations became highly sought after.

*leaders. Transcripts of some of these occasions have survived in the private papers of various officers. Major Ian Abbey had been in charge of Operation Nutshell in the south of Burma, in the Kawkareik area. The following address was kept by Captain Tony Bennett, a V Force officer seconded to Force 136 who served on Operation Nutshell, Team Antelope, dated 17 September 1945:*

Welcome address of the Karens of Kya-in village and those of the Village Tracts in Kyain Township, Amherst District, to the British Parachute Intelligence Organization, headed by Major I. Abbey, and which is intended to serve through the Organization as a representation on behalf of the Karen race in the Amherst District, and also in the whole of Burma, to authorities concerned ending in the British Parliament and the King Emperor, London.

..........................................0.......................................

# Address by Karen Leaders to Force 136 Officers and Men, Kya-in Village, September 1945

**Major I. Abbey, British Officers and Men**
On behalf of the Karen people of Kya-in and the neighbouring village tracts, I extend to you our heartiest welcome to our village. We are well aware of your hazardous mission for which you are commissioned and feel the trying and thrilling experience you have undergone as we believe you would equally do about our bitter experience and untold hardship for about three years and eight months of the duration of the war in Burma. Our thanks are due to Providence and the Allies who have brought the war to a victorious and unexpected conclusion giving us once again a sigh of relief. You, Sirs, as British Officers, we look up to you as symbols of freedom, strength and inspiration and offer to you our heartfelt gratitude for the part you have valiantly and nobly played for the sake of peace and humanity. From the bottom of our hearts we unreservedly extend to you our hearths and home for your rest and recuperation.

Sirs, permit me to say a few things relevant to this occasion. Throughout the period of war, Burma has literally been thrown into darkness and we, in this part of the country have become a benighted people. We have been dearly paid for our unswerving loyalty to the benign British Crown, especially the Christian section of our community, has been continuously under suspicion and surveillance of the Japanese, our erst-while enemy. A few incidents of interest in our trying experience may fittingly be related:

> As soon as the British armies withdrew from this country and the Japanese poured into this District, the Burman Thakin political element in collaboration with the Japanese, took the long awaited opportunity of seizing the rein of government. They carried with them the Burman masses and the whole country under their heels. In pursuance of their works of loot, pillage and butchering and giving vent to their pent up ill feelings they attempted to ransack this village, but they were somehow palmed off just before a bloody clash with our villagers took place.

Some time afterwards through back biting of the Burman, a company of the Japanese force, alleging that we harboured fleeing British officers and men besieged our village to be court-marshalled. However, nothing incriminating was discovered and the village was let off.

Later, Japanese Military, on account of intrigue and machinations of the Burman, arrested detained and persecuted leaders and elders of this village for alleged secretion of arms and ammunitions to hatch a rebellion against them and also for their loyalty to the British sovereign and their attachment and yearning for the Americans. Ultimately they exacted a toll of licensed fire-arms by confiscating them.

Forced labour:- Men, bulls, carts and elephants were commandeered by the Japanese for the construction of the Burma-Thailand Railway and Road as well as for the antimony mine and timber extraction. Two Japanese officers who were tyrants over labour, were shot dead and for this very incident, several Karens were beheaded and three promising young men of this and a nearby village were cruelly burnt alive.

In the rains of 1942, four intrepid Dutch war prisoners, one Captain and three Subalterns, escaped from a detention camp on the Burmo-Thailand railway. They roamed the dense forests heading for Singapore and came upon a Christian Karen's taungya hut who fed and guided them to a Karen Christian village, whose concerted effort, transported them camouflage, to Kya-in village under the vigilant eyes of the Japanese. The Kya-in people harboured them for a long time till the Burman suspicion and intrigue terminated this adventurous episode in their dramatic re-arrest in July 1944. For this deed of good samaritan, one villager of a neighbouring village who was the chief guardian over the Dutch war prisoners, was executed not before the villagers were harassed and persecuted.

[undecipherable] to prisoners-of-war, a recent exploit just before the end of war, is worthy of mention. A Karen levy, Saw Maung Ket of Shwedo[?] village was detailed to get out war prisoners from the Japanese camp. He cleverly set about his task and weaned away Saw Ba Min, a Karen Camp officer, under Japanese employ. Both moved about cautiously in the neighbourhood of Aplon. Their plans and movement were suspec[?] by the Japanese ambushed and killed one of them, Saw Ba Min.

Pages would not suffice to record genuine incidents of horror and gruesome tales of woe during the painful era of face-slapping, intimidation and servitude. An able artist would paint a better picture of the Japanese works of devastation and provide you with a graphic and vivid account of attendant rapine, pestilence and mounted death-rolls of both labour and war prisoners and would also spread before you a canvas depicting naked humanities. For this persistent campaign of resistance, lists of names can be furnished, of people like Saw Ah Toe and his colleagues, who have played prominent roles and those who acted behind the s[c]reen. We assume, Sirs, that you have been apprised of and are well aware of the general situation of the Province and we would not weary you any more with facts other than those necessary for our interest.

Kindly allow me to state that, throughout the period of war two outstanding features emerged, namely:

Burman open hostility towards the Karen race, and
Overt herculean efforts of the Burman to live out-side the British Commonwealth. The former has its sequel in the massacres of the Karens by the Burmans at Myaungmya and Papun, in the first phase of the war, and the latter, in its establishment of a crooked government headed by Ba Maw. These two facts, must, in our submission serve as food for thought for the British Parliament to review the previous Constitution of Burma in shaping its future destiny. We make bold to state that we have come to a parting of the ways with the Burmans, whence we prefer to prepare our own destiny in the British Commonwealth of Nations. As a minority, our political union with the Burman in the past under the guise of democracy had not been a safe, satisfactory and happy one. History repeats itself. Centuries ago, before the advent of British rule, our ancestors had continuously suffered persecution at the hands of the Burmans and no sooner had the British left this shore fr war strategy, then the tell-tale temperament of the Burman made itself felt on the Karen masses as narrated above. We venture to enquire if ever, a leopard could change its spot. Once a traitor always a traitor. A Burman's palm-in-glove with the Japanese against the British today is a slap on the Japanese face tomorrow. You could imagine, Sirs, what risk of life you would have run had you descended near a Burman village for your secret service. In faltering terms, news of your descent in the distant hills some while ago, was in relay, whispered into our ears. The damp and suppressed spirit was again

tuned up and yet we were wondering if fiction would not still be stronger than facts, till our hero Saw Ku's effort had made your presence in our neighbourhood, a fact and realization. We are heartened and gratified to know that you have reposed in us confidence for your difficult task and we on our part reciprocated it at our own risk also. News about our compatriots' tragic deaths at Kawkareik performed by the Japanese at the instigation of the Burmans, following the wake of your mission, was conveyed to us at the moment. Prominent among them, is Saw Sunday, Pastor of Kawkareik Karen Church. We crave your indulgence to imagine what calamity would have be-fallen us at the hands of the Japanese had not the war been ended abruptly after the exposure of the Metta-lar incident where your camp was discovered and burnt. Nevertheless, that incident afforded our young men a welcome brush with the Japanese where not a few casualties were inflicted on them at none of our expense. It may be recalled that a similar scuffle had taken place two summers ago at Hlaing Gyi Oke where Japanese and Burman military combined were tenaciously resisted by a village of ya-in, Saw Thin Gyaw Paw, Jemadar of the 2nd. Garrison, heading a handful of men, resulting in fairly heavy toll of deaths on their side as against one casualty on ours. We hereby, pay homage to his revered memory. All these bear testimony to our lonely revolt against the Japanese and Burman subjugation though reeling under their heels. We now, bemoan the loss of long awaited chance to play manly parts worthy of our race, as finishing touches to the final scene for the war and as contributions towards our liberation from the Japanese yoke.

One thing we are earnest to know is, whether or not the culprits who had personally perpetrated crimes of various kinds and in various degrees or through their instrumentality had brought about troubles and miseries to the Karens as well as others, would not be brought to book and adequately punished.

We strongly appeal through you Sir, to authorities concerned that the Karens be allotted a certain part of Burma where we could, under the guidance and care of the British Government, in the instance administer ourselves free from the Burman.

Sir, kindly pardon me for this long address. In conclusion, I once more say that you are all heartily welcome to our midst and during your sojourn here, I wish you to be quite at home.

I am,
Sir,
Yours cordially,
[signed, indecipherable]
Representative of Leaders
and Elders of Kya-in Village,
Kya-in Township,
Amherst District,
Burma

# Address by Karen Leaders to Force 136 Officers and Men, Mewaing, October 1945

*The following address by an unnamed Karen leader is dated 21 October 1945:*

### A PEACE CELEBRATION ADDRESS TO THE ENGLISH OFFICERS CONCERNED IN MEWAING FIELD

Dear Lt.Colonel King and Major Hood. We, the Karen people of Salween District, are grateful to you and to all other English officers, who come and rule over us. Our hearty thanks towards you and your people cannot be expressed by the human tongue. Before I continue my speech please allow me to relate a few words of the History of Burma.

During the time of the Burmese King our forefathers were put under heavy yokes. They were forced to build pagodas, to construct roads, to dig tanks (in Upper Burma) etc for the Burmese Kings. In doing so people had no time to work for their families. But at that time there was a saying, which was common among the Karen people and which said that their White Brothers would come and deliver them from the heavy yokes. They believed in this saying and looked forward to the days when the said Brothers would come. But they did not know who they were and from where they would come. As they were waiting some how or other war between the English and the Burmese broke out. The war lasted only for a few months and the Burmese King was defeated and overthrown. Then, there reigned the English King over Burma and only then that the Karen people had a happy time. As the English are white in complexion, the Karen people came to know that what was meant by their White Brothers. Their white brothers brought them peace and prosperity.

Alas this state of peaceful life went on only for a number of years, when, in 1941, the Japanese invasion took place and as the English retreated to India, we were left helplessly at the mercy of the dacoits and the Japs. They attacked us in towns, sometimes the dacoits and sometimes the Japs. The Japs were very cruel. They took away pigs, fowls, ducks, cattle, etc from us by force. Sometimes they paid for them with their cheap notes, but sometimes they didn't. So many innocent people lost their lives in their hands. They burnt up some of the villages and so many people are homeless now. When we were in such a condition we were longing for the return of the English, and for that we prayed, day and night. There are expert soothsayers among the Karens who predicted that at the end the Japanese would lose in the war, and the English would come back, but when, none of them could tell. We eagerly waited for their arrival but in 1942 there was no sign of them in Burma, in 1943 the same, only in 1944 that, good news came saying that the English were within Burma, and not long after that Rangoon was reoccupied. Few months later Lt. Colonel Critchley, whose arrival was expected appeared among us and we were ever glad to receive and help him. As soon as he arrived he formed the Karen Levies, the Home Guard among the people here, and so many young men joined them. He was the one who successfully drove out the Japs from Papun. After his successful attempt in Papun, he returned to Mewaing and prepared the Air Strip. He put a full zeal to his work and throughout his career over here, he was always successful. We are sorry he cannot be with us in this day of celebration. However, the Air Strip and other things reveal his good and honest work. We all wish him to be happy in England among his relatives.

And, Major Hood, you are worthy of praise. We, admire your good work, and the hardship you endure under the burning sun. When there is much work to be done, you always tuck up your longyi and you then look very much like a Burman Boxar. You are so hardworking and painstaking in your work that sometimes you forget to shave your beard. We cannot remain without mentioning your help you extended to us. We, the Karens here suffered very much in the hands of the Japs. They ate away our rice and sometimes destroyed our paddy in the barns. We were forced to construct roads for the Japs without being paid. Property were looted from us including clothes. We were about to be naked and starved, ha! When, we are in such a helpless condition rice and clothes were distributed among us. Medical help, also, come. Major Hood dear, we can never forget the gratitude you have done to us. When you go back to England, bear it in your mind that, the Karen people love you.

And Lt. Colonel King, too, we thank you very much for the trouble you have taken, to be with us today. Though we do not know very much about you, we are sure that you are trying your level best to help the Karen people here. God bless you in your work.

In conclusion I may say that the Karen people in Salween District wish the extensive British Empire, to be peaceful and prosperous, and last for ever and ever.

**PEACE CELEBRATION PROGRAMME AT MEWAING**
Oh Papun District – by Walaw Choir
Sword display – By two Shans
Karen drum with its complements - By Karens
Mixed Quartette "Juanita" – By Mrs Willie Saw and Party
A fight with swords – By the Shans
Karen Bugle - By the Karen
Karens playing between clashing bamboos – By Karens
A Peace Celebration Address to the British Officers in Mewaing – By Thare Po Pe
……..
The British Officers response
God Save the King – By All

# Address of Welcome by Saw Po Htin

**Major Hood, ladies and gentlemen,**
Today is a great occasion for every one of us who are present here to celebrate the victory of the Allied Nations over the enemy who were ruthless to the karens, and to commemorate the success of the British arms and the Karen levies led by British officers who are in our midst. We are grateful to them for making it possible within a short period of their operation for us to live once more in our homes, free from want and free from fear. Our children will never forget this when we are once more free from the rule of the Japanese for the last three years.

    We Karen are proud to say that we have been always loyal to the British. Every Karen knows through our traditions that the British are the only people who can look after us and help us to raise ourselves to a standard which will enable us Karens to take our place in the British Commonwealth of Nations. In the old days the Karens said of themselves that they had to live like jungle fowls and pheasants, having to move from place to place in order to exist. Thanks to the British government those days are gone. In this alone we shall ever be grateful. Compared with other nations our literacy rate is low and we suffer from a lack of school and medical help. This is a great setback and a problem confronting the Karen leaders, but we are resolved with the help of the British to do our utmost to overcome these difficulties. It will take some time but as sure as the sun sets we shall prevail.

    All we Karens looked forward to your return and to your ultimate victory in this great war, never doubting that you would leave us under the Japanese bondage. We know, and our sons and grandsons will know, and many of you British officers here today know how much we have suffered. Amongst you here today are men who had been tortured by the Japanese - all of us are proud of you. Trouble, fear, anxiety, and want have touched all classes, rich and poor, educated and uneducated, the old and the suckling alike. We have a proverb which says "clear water sweeps muddy water away" How true it has been in this conflict!

*If there was any more to this speech, then it has been lost over time for only this page exists. It is perhaps fitting, however, that the final paragraph mentions the torture endured by the Karen at the hands of the Japanese. As mentioned by Saw Smile Paul, the Japanese imprisoned, tortured and murdered many Karen people in their attempt to gain information. Here are some excerpts of sworn statements taken during 1945 and 1946 by the Allied War Crimes Investigators.*

*Kyaw Po was arrested in November 1942. He wrote his testimony, addressed to the Field Security Service (FSS) on 18 September 1945:*

Sir,

For the interest of posterity and of the public at large and the desirability of the victorious allies for the trial of the war criminals for the atrocities committed by them, I beg to state as follows:-

On Saturday Nov 1942, I was visited by SAIJOE and his Burman Clerk, whose name I do not know, but whom I can easily identify. There were outside the house on the road waiting, TUN MYAT and SOE MYINT (Burman J.M.P). At that time I was living in SAW E MAUNG's house in MOGAUNG, East Bank, TOUNGOO. SAIJOE said that the P.S.O. BA CHOE, wanted to see me in connection with a motor car case (which was a deliberate lie to get me to the Police station). I asked him whether it was in connection with my car and he said "No", but that I was wanted in connection with another motor car – I told him I don't know anything about another car, as I do not go anywhere. He would not have that and he compelled me to ride at the back of his motor cycle and took me to the Police station. There to my surprise he locked me up in a cell together with dacoits, robbers, thieves, smugglers and murderers. I could not get any Police officer to inform the D.S.P. and my friends about my arrest. In the evening my servant bought my dinner, which I could not eat, a young S.I.P. whose name I do not know, told me to send any message to anybody I like and that he would take the responsibility. I told my servant to inform U. Hla Pe, agent B.B.T.C.L., U. Pho Choe, Head clerk D.S.P's office and others. The next morning, (Sunday) SAIJOE came to the Police station very early at 6 a.m. and took me out of the cell and said "SAIJOE got one face – not two face", he then told the police constable to take me to the J.M.P. office and to tell him if anybody speaks to me on the way – then he said 'No – no – no – don't hit him, but write down the name of the person to whom I should speak'. We got to the J.M.P's office within half an hour and there I was kept waiting for about an hour till SAIJOE arrived. I was taken up to the office (upstairs) when SAIJOE arrived. I was given a seat at the table and was then asked by SAIJOE whether I went to Court on a certain date in October and when I told him that I did not go to Court, as I was not practising, he struck me a hard blow with a thick stick with knobs - he again repeated the question and as my answer was the same, he gave me another hard blow. He was boiling with rage when he started questioning me and his temper became worse and uncontrollable, when he could not get the desired answer. He blurted out in temper that NAZARETH told him everything about me and that he also learnt about me from my neighbours. He told me to get up and then tied my hands at my back and strung me up and struck me on my back with the same stick till he was entirely exhausted and could hit no more. He went away and left me suspended. He came back after lunch and released me. I slumped on to the ground. He dragged me to the cell downstairs and locked me up after taking away my longyi. I had to spend the remainder of the day and the whole night on the cold cement floor, half naked. The next day (Monday) I was taken upstairs at about 9a.m. and was further questioned. My condition was very bad and I was losing consciousness off and on. I asked him to allow me to go home, as I was feeling very bad and that he could question me later. He said that I will have to stay another 4 or 5 days more. Soon after Capt MURAKAMY, head of the J.M.P. TOUNGOO, came up and started shouting at SAIJOE in Japanese. He saw me spitting blood and after asking me some more questions about my food, he ordered SAIJOE to take me home in the car at once. When I arrived home, my condition became worse and Dr PAL was sent for. Dr PAL, came hurriedly and gave me injections. Nobody expected that I would survive the night. I had to sleep sitting down for days, as I could not lie down through pain. I think my lungs are still affected as I get pains at times. While I was in custody, I was informed that my house was searched by SAIJOE, TUN MRA and others. Even after my ill-treatment SOE MYINT, APPA and another S.I.P. came several times to torment me.

> I have the honour to be,
> Sir,
> Your most obedient servant,
> sd/- Kyaw Po
> Higher Grade Pleader.
> MOGAUNG.
> 18-9-45

# Sworn Statements of Kyaw Po, Jemadar Toe Kin and U Tun Baw

*An explanatory few lines after the testimony explain why 'Nazareths' and others were 'against' Kyaw Po. It seems that these people were taking the opportunity to settle their own scores, for example Kyaw Po had sent a notice to a Dr DWE on behalf of a client which was to prosecute him 'for cheating and misapprehension.'*

*While Kyaw Po's testimony provides insight into the ill treatment of Karens, seemingly to settle personal vendettas or grievances, the following testimony is from a soldier who served with SOE. Jemadar Saw Toe Kin, whose statement was sworn and witnessed on 15 February 1946, was working with the Operation Harlington team. The first all Karen advance party had parachuted into the Karen Hills in February 1943, and was followed by Major Jimmy Nimmo in October 1943. Knowing that there were parachutists in the area, in early 1944 the Japanese brought a Kempeitai unit up from Rangoon and began to hunt down the Harlington team:*

The Japanese Kimpe [Kempeitai] raided the village, arrested the elders and tortured suspected persons. On account of the Japanese raids, work in the villages was stopped, agriculture was destroyed and villagers were harassed. Some were even killed. Saw Heby [Saw He Be] and Saw pe were arrested on the spot on 15 FEB 1944 and Major Nimore [Major Jimmy Nimmo] was killed in the incident. The rest of us decided to surrender. Our reasons being if we did not villagers would be constantly tortured and ill-treated by the Japanese. We were all locked up in the Kempeitai Office. The Japanese Kimpe OKURA, ARKISTA and KANAMURA, beat every one of us to get the confession about our activities. Every one of us was taken out from the cell to the Office where we were questioned and beaten. Each of us got not less than 100 hits on the day we were tried. We 6 were put in the cell which was 8'x8' together with 10 civilian victims, when 8 slept the other 8 had to keep awake.

Beating all over the body, kicking the chest, ribs, stomach and head with boots on, were very common to every one and every day. Saw Tun Lin who was one of the 4 killed in Rangoon, was tied up to a bar with rope, with his feet just clear of the ground and was beaten to answer their questions.[161]

*One of the Karen officers who parachuted into Burma as part of the Karen advance party in February 1943 for Operation Harlington was Lieutenant Saw Ba Gyaw. Ba Gyaw was executed in Rangoon in September 1944, along with six other Karen comrades and Major Seagrim. After the war, his father-in-law, U Tun Baw, gave the following statement:*

I am an elderly Karen of 59 years of age with 4 grown ups sons and 4 grown up daughters and a lawyer of 38 years' standing at Toungoo, Burma. My eldest daughter Violet married an Army Officer, one Subedar Ba Gyaw of the Burma Rifles in May 1941, a few months before the Japanese war broke out. As the invading Japanese troops were getting near to Toungoo in March 1942, I and my family took refuge at the Shwenayungbin hills, some 21 miles to the east of Toungoo, staying at first at the Seventh Day Adventist Mission quarter and later on at the the Woodbrand bungalow servant quarter.

On the outbreak of the Japanese war, Ba Gyaw saw service in some frontier parts of Burma, but finally retreated to India along with the Army. Meanwhile none of us heard or learnt anything about him. Information or rumour was that sometime in 1942, Ba Gyaw landed as a parachutist in a certain place in Papun district and that he came in contact with Major Seagrim and other Officers and men of the Army in the Papun Karen Hill tracts.

On the 16th March 1944, a Japanese Military Officer, name, unknown coming in a motor car from Thandaung and I was going in opposite direction met me on the Toungoo-Thandaung road at the 20th Mile 6th furlong mile stone and he enquired of me whether one Saw Ba Gyaw was my son-in-law. I admitted having a son-in-law named Ba Gyaw, but said that there were also some Ba Gyaws in the Army. Whereupon the Japanese officer told me that in connection with Ba Gyaw's affairs, I, my wife (Mrs.E Tun Baw) and my daughter Mrs. Violet Ba Gyaw were required to proceed to the office of the J.M.P. (Kampetaai), Toungoo.

Accordingly all of us, including Peggy then aged 1 year 10 months daughter of Mrs. Ba Gyaw, in the early morning of 17th March 1944 left Shwenayungbin and proceeded to Toungoo and we put up in a place at Toungoo specified by the J.M.P. officer.

---

[161] TNA, WO 325/63, APPENDIX "A" PART II, ALFSEA War Crimes Instr No.1, FORM OF STATEMENT, Jemadar Toe Kin, 15 February 1946.

After detaining us for 4 days and on 20-3-44, another J.M.P. officer named Ocura took us in a motor truck to Thandaung. At Thandaung Okoora put us many questions about Ba Gyaw and subjected us to many humiliations. On 22nd March 1944, in broken or in most imperfect Burmese asked me about Ba Gyaw and ordered me to take to make a search of him. On the same day I went to the neighbouring village of Thandaung, namely Leikpyagale, Tawbyagyi and other localities and returned to Thandaung in the evening at 4p.m.

The J.M.P. Officer Okoora seeing me, called upon me to state where I had been and what I had been doing and I told him where I had been and the enquiries I made of my son-in-law Ba Gyaw. The J.M.P. Officer on a map spread before me, asked me to point out the places where I had been for the day and while searching to point them out, Okoora in a fit of rage and anger and in menacing mood, took out a big dah (knife) and with the blunt or back side of it, struck me several times on the whole body, the assault lasting for an hour.

After the assault, he ordered me to leave Thandaung forthwith with orders to search for Ba Gyaw and also directing me daughter Violet Ba Gyawor to write out a letter addressed to her husband to surrender himself, the search was to be made in the whole length and breadth of the Toungoo and Papun hill districts. Night was approaching, however I was to return to Shwenyaungbin at once, from whence I was to leave early the next day for searching, threatening me saying that he would come and look for me all the more.

In a very weak and painful condition and with night approaching at 6 p.m. I left Thandaung and had to feel my way through the pitch dark night which happened to be a stormy one and with great difficulty I managed to reached the S.D.A. quarter, Shwenyaingbin, a distance of 6 miles, at about 8 p.m. falling down 4 times on the way through exhaustion. My quarter was a mile further, but could not reach it.

After spending a sleepless night in the SD.A. mission quarter, early in the morning before dawn at 4 a.m. I left it and reached the Woodbrand bungalow servant quarter and after spending about an hour gathering a few belongings, at 6 A.M. on 23-3-44, I started on the long journey to search for Ba Gyaw, arriving at Kyettaik, the first halt on the same day.

From Kyettaik I proceeded onward covering at the daily rate of from 15 to 20 miles, touching and halting for the night at the various villages on the way. Though labouring under great pain from the effect of the Japanese assault, by God's help I managed to reach Papun on the 10th of April 1944 at noon after travelling for 18 days covering a distance of about 300 miles through plains, deep jungles, gorges, riverbeds and hill tops. At Papun the Township Officer, one Mr, Arthur Tabi told me that Ba Gyaw had been captured by the Japanese about ten days previously and after being subjected to searching examinations, most cruel torturings and ill treatments, he and other captured fellow prisoners had been taken and removed to Rangoon on the same day of my arrival in the morning at 6 a.m.

Information from the Karens of Papun hill tract was that the capturing of Ba Gyaw and others were effected by means of ill treatments, and torturing inflicted on many Karen villagers who happened to receive or accommodate the Allied soldiers and they were also under threat of death if they failed to surrender any of the Soldiers.

Regarding the ultimate fate of Ba Gyaw, during the month of July 1945, my daughter Mrs Violet Ba Gyaw received a letter from the Adjutant General of the Army Headquarter in India, Simla, while expressing deep regret, intimating her that her husband 2nd Lieutenant Ba Gyaw has been missing and is believed to be dead, the letter also mentioning that he has been executed by the Japanese on the 8th. September 1944. Reliable information from fellow prisoners who had been detained in the same jail Lock-up at Insein with Ba Gyaw and others, was that during September 1944, Ba Gyaw and other officers and men were taken away one morning in a motor truck by the Japanese and were never brought back to the Lock up and therefore the alleged execution by the Japanese was in effect a confirmation.

The Japanese Assault on me is still telling on my health, as certain part of my body are still paining, though the assault had taken place almost 2 years now. The J.M.P. Officer Okoora acted most wrongly and criminally in arresting me and my family and treating us in manners as mentioned above. My wife soon after her release got ill and was down with Typhoid, suffering for over one month which nearly cost her life, but for the medical treatment of a qualified doctor.

While narrating unpleasant experiences during the Japanese occupation, I must not forget to mention that with the return and reoccupation of Toungoo and Burma by the Allied Forces and with all the pleasant outlook and promises of a peaceful life in store for us, we feel that we owe a great debt of gratitude to the liberating forces which can never be repaid.

# Post War to Independence, October 1945–4 January 1948, Introduction

Japan surrendered on 15 August 1945, but the fighting in Burma, and across Southeast Asia, didn't just stop. Many of the Japanese refused to believe the leaflets dropped by the Allied air forces telling them that the war was over, dismissing them as propaganda. Clearing areas of stubborn Japanese soldiers and restoring order across the region was a massive undertaking. At the same time, nationalism across the Far East was now, as a result of the war, a much more powerful and pervasive force within colonial societies; it was pushing hard against a return to pre-war imperial subservience.

Burma, unlike countries such as Malaya, had been fought over twice. The devastation of infrastructure was significant, and the availability of staple resources such as rice, oil, salt, and clothing was minimal. In a rush to restore the Burma government after its three year exile in India, military control of Burma was transferred to civil authorities. This probably prolonged the economic reconstruction of Burma, thus exacerbating nationalist demands, since the military on the spot were much better able to bring in supplies than a distant colonial office in London.[162] Post-war lawlessness in Burma was widespread and prevalent. The country was awash with weapons, and since the emphasis was on repatriation of British soldiers and a policy of returning West African and Indian troops to their respective countries as soon as possible was applied, the forces of law and order were unable to cope.[163] In a country that is infamous for dacoity, in May 1947, in an audacious attack, around 200 armed thieves held up a train and stole about 27 tonnes of food.[164]

It was in these circumstances that the British tried to build a new, ethnically inclusive Burma Army, which absorbed Aung San's Patriotic Burmese Forces (PBF). The PBF was the name that the Burma National

---

[162] TNA, CAB 129/3, 'Developments in Burma', Memorandum by Secretary of State (Pethick Lawrence), 6 October 1945.

[163] John McEnery, *Epilogue in Burma, 1945 - 1948* (Spellmount: Tunbridge Wells, 1990), pp.29-35.

[164] George Appleton, 'Burma Two Years After Liberation', *International Affairs*, 23, 4 (Oct., 1947), p.513.

Army had taken in June 1945. Meetings with the PBF to discuss the military future of Burma's soldiers began as early as September 1945. The PBF was thought to consist of approximately 9000 troops, and it was agreed that 5500 of these could join an army which would have a ceiling of 15,000. An officer training school was established to address the shortage of officers, but the prediction was that the Burma Army was at 'grave risk of administrative breakdown' and would fail when British and Indian units left. From the beginning, political divisions within the army were also recognised, not just between the different races, but within ethnic groups.[165] Before independence, a Karen, Smith Dun, was made General Officer Commanding the Burma Army, but this did not prevent the turmoil which was to follow independence.[166]

In Britain, meanwhile, the Labour Party, under Clement Attlee, won a landslide electoral victory in July 1945. British parliamentary convention holds that no Parliament is beholden to the last, meaning that any promises that may have been made by the wartime government, or any White Papers such as the May White Paper on Burma Policy, didn't necessarily have to be kept.[167] Preoccupied with colonial affairs in Palestine and India, not to mention post-war reconstruction at home and the emerging Cold War, the policy of the Labour government was to court Burmese nationalist aspirations through Aung San. The hopes of many Karen, including some of the interviewees here, were dashed in 1946 when a Karen delegation to London was stonewalled, and later by the creation of a Union of Burma that placed the various ethnic groups of Burma under majority Burman political control.[168] Aung San was not to lead the new Burma, however, being assassinated in July 1947. Aung San continues to be revered in Burma, but from 4 January 1948 it was U Nu who was in charge until a military coup in 1962 brought General Ne Win and the military to power.

---

[165] Ibid, pp.3-5.

[166] *See* Smith Dun, *Memoirs of the Four-Foot Colonel*, (Cornell University: New York, 1980), pp50-1.

[167] TNA, CAB 66/65/40, White Paper on Burma Policy, 8 May 1945.

[168] B.L., IOR M/4/3023, P.G.E. Nash to Sir Gilbert Laithwaite, 12 August 1946.

# Post War to Independence, October 1945–4 January 1948

### Saw Johnny Htoo
*Saw Johnny Htoo had parachuted into Burma on Special Operations and been captured by the Japanese. He had later escaped, and joined SOE's Operation Character during 1945:*

After World War Two, I went back and served with the 3$^{rd}$ Burma Rifles and then I joined 2$^{nd}$ Karen Rifles which was under the command of Colonel Galbraith.[169] In 1946, I got an opportunity to attend Officer Cadet training and I attended at Artillery Batch (3) training class. I was promoted to Lieutenant after the training course. I was transferred to B.O.A.T.S (Burma Officer Army Training School) and promoted to Captain. I was sent to the War Office and attended Q course.[170] When I passed Q course I was assigned as a Lecturer at Burma Officer Army Training School. I had to teach three subjects. I hoped I would be the best person to be honoured at this Training School. Before the next class started, all the Karen soldiers were interned. From that time onwards, I received neither salary nor pension.

### Saw Michael Shwe
*Saw Michael Shwe had received further signals training before first joining the North Kachin Levies, and then going on a mission with the Secret Intelligence Service (SIS):*

I married Nant Julie Myint on 5 June 1947. I was awarded the 1939-45 Star and Burma Star medals.

---

[169] Lieutenant Colonel Percy Hardie Murray Galbraith was the last British officer in charge of 2 Karen Burif, 1946-1948. *See* Darryl Lundy, 'The Peerage' [online] http://www.thepeerage.com/p58596.htm#i585956 and Steve Rothwell, '1st Battalion, the Burma Regiment' [online], https://homepages.force9.net/rothwell/burmaweb/1stburma1.htm

[170] 'Q' is stores and supplies in the Army.

## Saw Aye Kyaw

*Saw Aye Kyaw had taken part in the Imphal battle, and then joined the American OSS going on operations in eastern Burma:*

We came back to Bago and slept one night and headed to Rangoon. We were given documents to collect our salary and they asked us "Will you continue serving here, if so we will send you somewhere suitable?" but we replied that we would like to go back to our village. When we were leaving, one of my old friends told me that the British Navy was recruiting new sailors for RNVR [Royal Navy Volunteer Reserve] Burma in St. Paul's school compound. When I went there, I met with new people from Pathein. After we had a medical check-up, we were accepted. At that time, some of the Karen leaders such as Saw Jack, Raymond Tun Myine, Shwe Thee, and Magsi Po Thing, were there.[171] I had to serve on gun-ship HDML [Harbour Defence Motor Launch] several times for up to two months.[172] When I was not on board I was sometimes assigned at Government House. I was at St. Paul's when Major General Aung San was assassinated [19 July 1947]. The people came and told me but I did not know the whole situation. After the British gave Independence to Myanmar [4 January 1948], I quit the navy like my friends did. Then I was working at BBTCL [Bombay Burmah Trading Company Ltd] Sawmill when I stayed in Botahtaung. I met with Mr. James, Mr. Brown, Mr. Rees and the owners of Pyinmana Sawmill and they said they would like to have three Karen people for the timber business in British North Borneo.[173] When we asked what we had to do, they answered "You have to check the logs, sleep, cook and eat in the forest and we will eat as you cook."

Three Karens, myself, Kyaw Shin, and Wah Maw went to Singapore

---

[171] Saw Jack was a naval officer, and he led the fighting at Pathein in January 1949.

[172] 'HDML' stands for Harbour Defence Motor Launch. There were eight of these 70ft vessels in service by the RNVR at this time. They were crewed by ten men, who could be accommodated onboard. *See* Sithu Kyaw Thein Lwin, 'The Navy's Most Important Ship' [online], http://frankstaylorfamilyandroyalnavyhistory.net/HMSScarabBurmaTheNavysMostImportantShip.html

[173] In January 1948, correspondence between Mr Gordon Hundley and the Foreign Office discussed the 'Problem of the Karen tribe in Burma', and suggested relocating them to North Borneo because there is work there and 'cultural similarities' between the Karen and Dyak. *See* TNA, FO 371/69509, especially the letter from Gordon Hundley to Secretary of State for the Colonies, A. Creech Jones, 2 January 1948.

via Penang on a BISN [British India Steam Navigation Company] ship from Rangoon and from there to Kuching, Sarawak's capital by another small ship. After a couple of days, we hired a ship which could carry up to thirty people and crossed the sea. We sailed along the river and we asked nearby villages to permit us to sleep there. Even if there were thirty or forty families they would stay together in a long house with separate rooms. They made steps out of logs and used them as a ladder which they would keep in the house at night and put out during the day. They looked Karen and weaved clothes themselves but their clothes had longer sleeves to ours. They do not wear any clothes when they are at home. Only when they go to town, they would wear their costume, including a turban with a bird's feather and the tusk of a wild boar. They would also decorate themselves with red and black paint on their neck, chest and back.

We arrived at Sandakan and started to work with the North Borneo Timber Company. They extended their work near Tawau town and built roads to bring the logs to the river. Then the logs were transported by small boats to the ocean where big ships waited to taken them to Hong Kong, Japan and Western countries.

Borneo, where I was staying, was a big island ruled by two nationalities, British and Dutch. I was staying at Kuching, the capital of Sarawak which was ruled by the British. I met the Dayak Iban ethnic group when I was there. The men had tusks of wild boars through their ears, and their chests and shoulders were painted red and black. After a one week stay, we hired a motor boat which could carry thirty people. We three Karen, three English, two government timber workers and ten Malay workers were in the boat and we followed along the coastline heading east. The whole way we could only see nipa palms along the coast line.[174] On arrival, we saw a tributary and went down stream. We arrived at a Dayak region and they too would stay together in a big house. It was a long house on stilts with two ladders. They hung human heads in front of the room and when we asked they said that their forefathers would fight and if they won they would hang the head of the loser outside their house. Even now, they would still hang the skull and hair in front of their rooms. The old customs were not strictly observed as time passed. We stayed together in the big house and carried water by dried gourd. We did not see any bamboo. The people there would be topless whether the climate was hot or not. It is the same for men and women. The maidens and teenagers were the same so we felt embarrassed

---

[174] The nipa palm, or mangrove palm, is native to southeast Asia.

seeing them, but we got used to it. One old lady asked me to say Ba, Bar, Barr, O, Ga in Chinese and Malay. At that time, I could not speak Malay. When arrived from Burma, these women did not dress, curl or dye their hair, but now, they are fully dressed. We arrived in 1949 and asked leave to come back to Burma in 1952 and continued working at Tawau North Borneo Timber Coy.

## Saw Ni K'mwe Paul AKA Lieutenant Saw Smile Paul
*Saw Ni K'mwe Paul had served with SOE on Operation Character's Hyena Red team:*

At that time, the Karen community formed the Karen Youth Organisation (KYO) in Yangon and I joined the KYO becoming a member in Toungoo. After Burma got Independence, the KYO got some chances and I was selected as Regional Officer.

## Saw Fair Play
*Saw Fair Play had spent three years in Thailand being forced to build roads for the Japanese:*

When World War Two ended, after the Japanese had surrendered, some of the soldiers from the Chin Burma Rifles and I went back to report to the British Army in Kanchanaburi [Thailand]. When we were planning to leave Htakanan, Kanchanaburi, some of the Thais said that the railway bridge was broken and stopped us and the boss also said not to leave as he could not give us any money. But we did not listen, we crossed Lel Gaw stream and waited for the train. After waiting for the whole day, a train came but there was one locomotive with only one coach. We could not get into the coach as it was filled with Japanese officers from when they governed Burma. However, we went up on the roof. One of the officers thought we were Gurkhas and reminded us to sit still and not to fall down.

    At that time, all the soldiers were being sent to their home country due to the war ending. After three days of reports, we were sent to Kao Din Camp, a Repatriation Camp (the camp where the soldiers were kept before sending them back to their country) where Major Roman was in command.[175] The Chin Burma Rifles soldiers returned to Burma by

---

[175] Possibly Kaorin, which was also known as Kao Din, on the Thai Burma Railway. *See* Ronnie Taylor, 'FEPOW Family' [online] http://www.britain-at-war.org.uk/WW2/Death_Railway/html/section_1.htm

train. Later on, I was sent to Tha Muang Camp where thousands of Japanese soldiers, thousands of Dutch soldiers, a few British soldiers and Indonesian soldiers were captured as prisoners of war.[176] The Administrator of this camp was Major Bame. The Indonesian soldiers were given sufficient clothes and food but were not allowed to carry weapons (guns) because at that time there was a rebellion against the Dutch in their country. About 3 or 4pm in the afternoon, thousands of people would go to Lel Gaw stream (River Kwai) for a bath and would bathe naked. The captured Japanese soldiers would have to bathe at the lower part of the stream while the Dutch soldiers bathed at the upper part of the stream. After the war ended, the Dutch soldiers who had been Japanese prisoners of war had to attend military training and join the battle in Indonesia. Dutch women, and children under twelve years old, were sent to a big camp in Thailand and kept under security. There were more than 10,000 at the camp. Dutch soldiers were not allowed to enter. I was allowed to enter once with Major Bame.

I was the only Karen there. Some British officers knew I was Karen once they saw me but some did not know. Major Bame asked me at his office when he first saw me:

Who are you?
I answered – I am a Karen.
Where do you come from?
I come from Burma.
So, you are Burmese?
I told him – I am not Burmese.

At that time, one Dutch clerk said while typing he knew the Karen race from when he was captured as as Japanese Prisoner of War and sent to Dawei to work for the Japanese and stayed at Mawro Karen High School.

After World War Two ended, the British kept Malaysian, Indonesian, Burmese and Singaporean people, who had worked on the construction of the Burma railway to connect Burma and Thailand, at a separate camp. Madrasi, Indians (Tamil) and Gurkhas were kept together. Major Debulie was the administrator. There were ten thousand Madrasi Indians but only 150 Gurkhas. There was a fight between these two races which we did not know the reason and forty Tamil were wounded as the

---

[176] Also a camp on the Thai Burma Railway. Remained occupied until 1947, see Ronnie Taylor, 'FEPOW Family' [online] http://www.britain-at-war.org.uk/WW2/Death_Railway/html/tha_muang.htm

Gurkhas attacked them with their Kukris. The Gurkhas were brave during battle therefore the British would favour them and they were allowed to have their Kukri. During the Korean War, they did not use guns but they cut the Koreans with their Kukri sword. Major Debulie could speak Tamil but not Hindustani so he wanted someone who could speak English and Hindustani. Gurkhas had their own language but all of them could speak Hindustani. I heard that Major Debulie told Major Roman that he needed a translator so I hid. But the Singapore Chinese clerk informed Major Roman that there was one who could speak both languages in this room so I was called. As I told Major Roman that I could only speak fairly, Major Debulie contacted Major Bourne via radio phone requesting him to call me but Major Bourne did not accept because he liked me. But Major Debulie came down with his own jeep and spoke to Major Bourne and asked me to pack up my bed roll and things and took me by jeep. I had to watch 150 Gurkhas. Later on, I came back to Kao Din Camp and stayed for nine months and then Major Debulie contacted me. He said he was going back to England but when he comes back he would go to Malaysia with Gurkha soldiers and asked me whether I could follow them. If I would go he would let me learn English and Malaysian language and mechanics and would give me leave if I wanted to go back to my parents. Captain Dr. Elliot for whom I was working as a translator at the hospital advised me to go back and serve with the Karen Rifles.

When the time came, the 150 Gurkhas and I waited at the train station to go to Malaysia. At that time, Dr. Elliot came and told us that Major Debulie was waiting for us at the Malaysia Station. But he pointed to four British officers and said that they were watching who was from which country to send them back to their own country and I explained this to the Gurkhas. The Gurkhas did not want to go back to Burma so most left the station. My younger brother Hto Day Day and Saya Daw Lay came to look for me and after thinking of our parents we headed to Burma by train.

When I came back to Burma I joined UMP – Union Military Police - and played football in Dawei. There were many servicemen in Dawei. There was the Royal Air Force, (C.T.M.B) and many other groups. After two weeks, D.Y.S.P [Deputy Superintendent Police] U San Thein came and reformed Southern Range Flying Squad of the Rangoon D.I.G [Deputy Inspector General] and twelve of us from Dawei had to go according to the leader's plan. There were forty members after the combination with U.M.P from Mawlamyine.

There were three Flying Squads – Southern Range, Northern Range and Western Range. The leader was an Indian and his rank was D.Y.S.P. We enquired about the enemy and if we could we fought, and if we could not, we waited for reinforcements but we could not fight as we did not have enough soldiers. Our duty was to get information on the enemy between Rangoon and Beik. According to the information, the communists had hidden twenty Japanese Officers and twenty soldiers in Tae Nan Taung which is a big village in Moe region.

At 5 in the morning, we surrounded the village and when we entered the village there were no men, and women and children were hiding under the house with bundles. When the officers asked "where are the men?" they answered "we don't know" and when asked "why did you pack up the bundles?" they answered "because we were afraid." The Communists got pre-information so we could not find them. We walked the whole night starting from four in the evening. Some of the Gurkha soldiers fell down because of giddiness, hence the British officers had to carry their guns and it was difficult for the jeeps to come and take them. When we got to Moe, our Flying Squad ate our fill at a shop which was for one Kyats because we did not eat for one day and one night. But all the rice and curry had run out so we were not full. After that, we came back to Taungoo by car.

D.Y.S.P U San Thein was a bad leader therefore all the officers and U.M.P from Mawlamyine who were under him returned to their mother unit. They had to reinforce Thaton U.M.P. He was very bad so after a month, we left with weapons to Pyu to return to D.I.G Office in Rangoon. We did not listen even though he apologised. It was already dark when we got to Pyu so we rested at the railway station. At that time, he said he telegrammed the D.Y.S.P Office in Rangoon saying that his group of men was tired and far from their family so they came to Pyu to have a rest. But we did not listen to him so he contacted D.Y.S.P Office in Pyu. Phyu D.Y.S.P came to meet us and said that he would not like the town people to get frightened as we had weapons and it is already night time and the Karen revolution had started. He told us to stay at a Police Station in Pyu town for a moment and he would seek advice. He told us to go to Taungoo first due to Taungoo's territory. We sent two men to Taungoo and they arrived safely. After a few days, the D.C [District Commissioner] of Taungoo came and checked the situation. After a month, the British official from D.I.G came and checked by himself and D.Y.S.P U San Thein admitted his misdeed/fault and then D.I.G returned to Rangoon.

After a week, a friend came and told me while I was going for a walk that we had to go to Rangoon as we had received a telegram. I could not think of the reason. Four of us took a Bren, a Sten and two Rifles and a Karen Sub Inspector Police – SIP – took a revolver. When the train arrived, there was no place as there were so many people and it was crowded. It was an important matter so we requested the engine driver allow us to ride on the coal carriage. The train left at night and we arrived in Rangoon in the morning, our bodies dark with coal dust. We hired a horse cart and the SIP said his niece was living nearby therefore we asked him to send us there. It took a long time for us to find the place. We looked dirty so the Burmese from Rangoon looked at us with strangeness. We had a bath, had a meal and took our weapons and walked to the office. We did not know that even British soldiers were not allowed to carry weapons in Rangoon. However, when we got to the office where General Aung San was assassinated we showed the telegram to the four officers who were guards at the gate. They explained that we had to leave our weapons and one could wait so I stayed behind with the weapons. My four friends went up to the office.

They did not come back even though three hours had passed and I was not sure what to do. Soon after, they came back with Burmese SIP Saw Mar. We greeted him with joy and he said all of us were smart and brave therefore D.Y.S.P U San Thein was suspended. A new D.Y.S.P was appointed for our army. The D.Y.S.P from Pyu who persuaded us to stay with him in Pyu for a while thought all of us were in jail. D.Y.S.P U San Thein shot at his lesser wife and children because he was suspended for his faults though his lesser wife was not shot, one of his sons died. After that he went back to his first wife and shot himself dead.

### Saw Kay Ray
*Saw Kay Ray had joined the North Kachin Levies before sailing into Rangoon in May 1945:*

After ten years service as a Signaller in the Army I was ordered to retire on 16 June 1947. I became a School Teacher after retiring from the army on 16 June 1947.

### Saw Bunny
*Saw Bunny had served with Major Seagrim on SOE's Operation Harlington, and later on Operation Character:*

After the war, Force 136 was disbanded. After that I joined Burma Army Signals in Maymyo and my regimental number was W/1118 with rank of Corporal. Major Carlyn was our Battalion Commander. I transferred to the Burma Army after Burma got independence and retired on 12 April 1953. I worked as a lecturer and instructor of Musical Instrument at Theology School after I retired from the army.

## Saw San Aye
*Saw San Aye had fought with the Americans in the Shan States:*

They were calling the veterans to Maymyo and I registered at No.3 Register Department. Colonel Tucker gave me a new regimental number, 75780.[177] After serving in Mandalay for five months, I was transferred to 1st Karen Rifles in Taungoo.

## Saw Htoo Mar
*Saw Htoo Mar had helped his parents as a teenager during the war years:*

In 1946, at the age of 20, he joined the British army in Beik due to his interest in fighting and to continue studying. The time he joined was when they were giving military training so he attended the training for six months. After, he was assigned to a place in Beik. He was interested in work and was obedient so the officers loved and trusted him and he was gradually promoted. He was promoted to the rank of Corporal (Section Commander). Sometimes, he would have to serve at Ye and Dawei.

## Saw Baw Nay
*Saw Baw Nay had farmed during the war, but even so, the Japanese had still beaten him:*

Saw Baw Nay had been interested in being a soldier since he was young. As soon as he heard that the British were recruiting soldiers in early 1946, he joined as a new soldier in Dawei (Tavoy). He attended military training for six months in Dawei. After the training, he was transferred from one place to another. The places he was assigned to were Kanpauk,

---

[177] Most likely John Darley Tucker, who had served with various Burif battalions since 1918. See Steve Rothwell, '14th (Shan States) Battalion, The Burma Rifles, Burma Territorial Force' [online] http://www.rothwell.force9.co.uk/burmaweb/14th_burma_rifles.htm

Lawloe, Yephyu, Mawtar and Thayetchaung.[178] He was active and clever so all the superior officers trusted him and was promoted step by step to Sergeant. Soon after he became Sergeant, he was sent to Mawlamyine to attend Intelligence Training. When he finished Intelligence Training he came back to Dawei and was assigned to supervise the arsenal. He was assigned this duty as he was trusted.

*One of the arguments that has continued through the decades since the Second World War is whether or not the Karen people had been promised independence by British officers and colonial officials. No substantial archival evidence of a promise has been found, although the May 1945 White Paper on policy for Burma after the war has been used to show that commitments were not kept. The White Paper stated that areas such as Karenni would remain the responsibility of His Majesty's Government 'until such time as their inhabitants signify their desire' to join a Union of Burma.[179] Only a few short months after this White Paper, from August 1945, the optimistic Karens witnessed their aspirations being put aside by a new British government led by Clement Attlee. In hope, Karen leaders penned long petitions setting out their case, which were sent to the Secretary of State for India and Burma. From August 1945 until April 1947 this was Lord Pethick-Lawrence:*

## The Humble Memorial of the Karens of Burma

To His Britannic Majesty's Secretary of State for Burma.

Sir,

May it please Your Honour that your Memorialists, the Karens of Burma, at this Momentous time, have great cause to be very much concerned about the future of the Karens in this transitional stage of the much promised Constitutional Progress pledged to the Burmese people to full self government as soon as may prove possible. Our National Identity, Jealously preserved as the Karens of Burma, and our National Virtue and National Morals, anxiously nurtured during the long trying centuries, appear at last to be recognised, though formerly we felt that only the baby who cried the most got the most attention, the Karens have faithfully and loyally followed the flag they vowed to fight for the distant lands, and not merely as evacuees. We realise that in the past many of our interests have been overlooked, because we failed to make adequate representation of our needs, but now, if the majority could

---

[178] These places, or names similar to them, are in the Tavoy [Dawei] area.

[179] TNA, CAB 66/65/40, White Paper on Burma Policy, 8 May 1945.

possibly merit Constitutional Progress to full self Government, we the Karens of Burma do deserve a double claim to British consideration. The Karens are known to have lived in Burma long before the advent of the Tibeto-Burmans into Burma. The Tibeto-Burmans in their advent pressed out the Karens southward to the Delta Areas, and eastward to the mountainous fringes bordering Thailand, Yes, even into Thailand and Indo-China. However much they were pressed during these long centuries, they unlike the Pyus, the Thet, the Kanyans and the Mons, did never succumb as a race to the evil influence of their neighbours. They kept aloof as a race, jealously preserved their National Identity, and anxiously nurtured their National Virtue and National Morals untarnished and unsoiled by contamination with their neighbours.

*After further explanation of what life was like under the Burmese Kings, the 'Memorial' continues:*

Then came the British, not only as a Liberator, but also as a Guardian Angel, maintaining Law and Order, and preserving Peace and giving Protection. Under such a benign Government, the Karens began to thrive, but still with great difficulty. There was no more physical torture, but the mental torture still had to be endured. The Burmese still treated the Karens with contempt socially. They still imposed on the Karens in business. They crowded out the minority races in official posts. In every sphere of life the Burmese took the best. Success was the situation. But in 1942, no sooner was the back of the British turned. No sooner was the Liberator and Guardian Angel taken away then reoccured both the mental and the physical torture in a manner unequalled in the whole history of Burma. This unfortunate, uncalled for and unprovoked series of bloodshed and persecution has turned the clock back a century in our relationships. The Karens, therefore, have come to feel very strongly that they must strike out on a course of their own to preserve their national Ideals and develop into a progressive and useful state of Burma in the British Commonwealth of Nations.

The Karens have unreservedly rendered military aid to the British Crown and Empire in all crises ever since the British annexation of Lower Burma. In the early stage of the British occupation crime, plunder and risings were very rampant in the country and the Karens under the leadership of Pioneer Missionaries helped considerably in suppressing crime and petty revolutions. Later on when the Karens were given opportunities to serve in the Burma Military Police, the Burma Sappers and Miners and the Burma Rifles, they readily responded, and from time to time helped considerably in maintaining Law and Order and suppressing risings such as the Chin Hills rising. The Shwebo rising, the San Pe rising, the crime waves of 1925-27 and the Burma Rebellion of 1930-32. In which not only Karens of the regular services, but also Leaders, Elders and the Karen Irregulars played prominent parts, Again in the Great World War I, the Burma Sappers and Miners, the Burma mechanical Transport and the Burma Rifles acquitted themselves with credit. Here again in this Great World War II. The Karens occupy no second place in Burma both in numbers, integrity and daring achievement.

*The point is pushed home that many 'young Karens [...] gladly sacrificed their noble lives in the valley of Death for their King and country.' The text then goes on to describe some of the details of what happened to the Karens once the British withdrew to India in 1942:*

While Burma was under the military administration of Burma Independence Army they branded the Karens as rebels, and persecuted and tortured them in all possible ways and in certain District resorted to whole sale massacre not even leaving babies, and set the Karen village on fire. In Myaungmya District alone, the Official Report reveals that about 400 villages were set on fire in this way, and more than 1,800 Karens were slaughtered, including a Karen Judicial Minister of the British Burma Government and his whole family. Karens of the Salween Hill District, Papun, fared worse. All the leading men were slaughtered, and their wives and daughters, before being massacred, were subjected to immoral degradation in the presence of their husbands and fathers. Other of our fair women hood were forced to live in shameful submission to the B.I.A. soldiers. Their mission stations were looted and set on fire. Two of their Missionaries, Father Calmon and Father Loizean, were arrested, and their faith [sic] up to now is unknown. Taking advantage of the Military Administration, the Burmese did all in their craftiness to brand the Karens with a bad name, and caused them thus to be put to death. Many died the death of Christian martyrs under horrible conditions. At that time no influential Burmese Leader raised his hands and called a halt to such a senseless massacre. Were it not for the timely intervention of the Nippon Imperial armies, we could not imagine how far the matter would have gone. General Aung San, who was head of the Burma Independence Army, was known to have tendered his sincere apology to the Karens, but that was when the 14th Army of the Allies had captured Mandalay.

The National Policies of the Karens are all broadly based on holding high British honour and Prestige and to imbibe all that is finest in British Ideals. The event of this war, both at home and abroad have made us stronger in these believes [sic], and the Karens are, therefore, more determined to achieve their National Ideals, for these again affect our future security as a Nation. The pressing problem before us is to secure for ourselves a future security and safeguards in order that we may peacefully develop as a separate individual people in our homeland Burma.[180]

*Getting desperate for answers, in August 1946, a Karen delegation set out to persuade the British of their case by travelling to London. They called themselves the 'Karen Goodwill Mission', and they hoped to 'persuade the British Government and public that the Karen had a legitimate claim to an autonomous state within the Commonwealth.'[181] By then the Attlee government had moved on, and the Karen delegation returned to Burma disappointed - but unwilling to give up their cause. Various local Karen Associations were created, and the lobbying continued. The reasons why a majority of Karen wanted to remain 'under the direct control of the Governor' were set out by the Shwegyin Karen Association in 1947, and sent to the governor in Rangoon:*

To
His Excellency,
The Governor of Burma,
Rangoon.

Subject: Hill Karens Wish To Be Under The Direct Control Of The Governor.

Herewith attached the resolutions passed by the Shwegyin Karen Association which met at Medaingdaw Village, Kyaukkyi Township on the 7th March 1947. The Karens of this area wish to be a distinct

---

[180] From the private collection of papers kept by Major F. Milner, with thanks to David Mattey the current custodian. This document was written before the Karen delegation went to London in August 1946.

[181] Mikael Gravers, 'The Karen Making of a Nation' in *Asian Forms of the Nation*, edited by Stein Tonneson and Hans Antlov (Routledge: London, 2003), p.243.

Territory under the direct control of the Governor because of the following amongst other reasons:

> That 95% of the Karens in this Area are still illiterate, at least 90% of whom do not even understand Burmese to an appreciable extent; the bulk of the population knows nothing about democracy and dictatorship, about communism and fascism, about Dominion Status and Independence; they realise only that they owe everything to the British and the Allies for their present liberation; at present they acknowledge no other master except the British and they still wish to be under the control of the British at least for an indefinite period.
> That the Karens of this Area do not want to live among their neighbours who are by nature turbulent and rebellious, who never hesitate to commit robbery and dacoity, to carry on strikes and sedition, and who are prone to resort to rowdyism and hooliganism; whereas the Karens want to live in a place where there is orderly administration with good discipline in all of the services and that it is their conviction that two peoples of different temperaments and characteristics, and different moral conceptions and ethical principles cannot be paired together under the same yoke of equal weighting.
> That in the history of the Karens, this part of the land, particularly Part I and Part II areas, was never conquered by the Talaings and Burmese Kings; they had never paid tributes and taxes to outside monarchs except their own chiefs called "S'kawa" and the British later on. Thus they refuse to be included in Burma Proper to accept the same system of administration.
> That the present Burmese leaders have no plans and schemes whatever, not to say of concrete pecuniary help or otherwise, for the development of Part I and Part II Areas educationally, industrially, hygienically and so on. Such leaders with no plans prepared ahead are unfit to look after the interest of a backward people.
> That if a separate Area is given to the Karens with provincial autonomy in their hands they will prove that they can excel other districts in Burma in the maintenance of law and order, peace and personal security, and in the upkeep of the high tradition of discipline and morals, if not in other respects. In these respects Salween District with only 6 Burmans residing in Papun is leading a clean record of no dacoity and serious crimes. The Karens want to live in such a place.

That during the darkest moments of the Japanese occupation when there was no hope of the reconquest of Burma, the Karens in this Area fanatically threw in their lot with Major Seagrim, D.S.O., by doing everything in their power to form a formidable Spy Ring and powerful organisation behind the lines. The Karens valued and thought a great deal of the following letter from General Auchinleck which was read out and translate to them on the 11th December 1943, in the presence of the late Major Seagrim, D.S.O., the late Nimo, and the late Captain McCrindle:

New Delhi,
The 17th November, '43.

"The loyal attitude of the Karens has been reported to me by my officers. Loyalty through so long a time in your difficult and dangerous circumstances is worthy of the highest praise. I know that many of you have borne arms in defence of your country and will bear them again to ensure victory. In the meantime my officers and I do not forget the loyalty of the Karenni."

Sd / Auchinleck
General,
Commander in Chief,
India.

(A similar letter from Lord Louis Mountbatten was also read out at that meeting. Unfortunately it could not be preserved.)

The Karens had fought and died, had sacrificed themselves and imprisoned, scores of them were punished and tortured, and some of them were executed and sent to penal servitude. They feel very bitter to learn eventually that the contents of the above letter are meaningless and such other assurances are empty.

And that the Karens of this Area went through a series of bitter experiences during the war attributable to the treachery of their crafty neighbours. They shall not forgive and forget the atrocities and rape committed at Papun in April and May 1942, they shall not forget hateful measures of religious intolerance and highhandedness and barbarism committed in certain parts of the Area during the

Japanese Occupation. Experience has taught them to be cautious and their best safeguard is to establish a Territory of their own where they are given the powers to look after their own interests and manage their own affairs with the option to remain in the British Empire.

These hillmen intuitively realise that a United Burma with 17 millions inhabitants is helpless and hopeless against foreign aggression. Instinct of self-preservation has urged them to clinch to the British Commonwealth of Nations.

The Karens are bewildered to learn that the British have ignored their promises given during the war and have let them down by delegating power to a leading party to shape their future destiny during such time when their racial existence is seriously threatened. If the British government have any conscience at all they shall not allow a favoured few who are biased and prejudiced already to dictate terms to an unwilling people.

Under the circumstances the Karens in this Area firmly claim their right of self-determination be recognised by the concession of a separate Colony for the Karens. If the British fail to honour this great responsibility of theirs the Karens should not be blamed if they think of alternatives to achieve their legitimate objectives.

Sd.
President,
Shwegyin Karen Association,
SHWEGYIN
10-3-47.[182]

*By June 1947, the Karens were thinking 'of alternatives', as this letter to the Governor Of Burma, Hubert Rance, reveals:*

Your Excellency,
Kindly permit me to present the following fact before you for your information.

It is rather known by all Karens that the Burmese intend to disarm them and are completely at their mercy. Virtual Government by the Burmese over the last few months has not led the Karens to believe in

---

[182] From the private collection of papers kept by Major F. Milner.

their good faith, sincerity and honesty.

The Karens have a certain number of weapons that they used against the Japanese on behalf of Force 136. With painful memories of Myaungmya atrocities and other Burmese persecutions first in mind <u>they are not willing to give up</u> these arms for any pretext whatsoever to be left at the mercilessness of the Burmese.

Your Excellency must understand that the Karens in the areas concerned, as they have shown so far, are quite capable of maintaining their own law and order. They have neither been a party to any dacoities going on or have they lost their arms to the dacoits. There is no pretext whatsoever under which these law-abiding and peace-loving people can be legitimately disarmed whilst such complete lawlessness prevails in the country.

Any untoward incident caused by attempts of the Burmese to take away these weapons that the Karens are entitled to, for their own protection will not be the fault of the Karens but of those who attempt to disarm them.

May I have your Excellency's assurance that this representation has been sent to the Secretary of State, the Prime Minister, and the Leader of the Opposition.

I beg to remain,
Your Excellency's
Most obedient servant,
Saw Marshall Shwin[183]

---

[183] Saw Marshall Shwin to His Excellency the Governor of Burma, 'Arms in the Possession of Karens of Ex-Force 136', 29 June 1947. From the private collection of papers kept by Major F. Milner.

# After Independence, Introduction

On 4 January 1948, Burma became an independent country, remaining outside of the British Commonwealth. The British Labour government could not, however, simply sever all ties. As part of the Anglo-Burmese Treaty conferring independence, a Defence Agreement was signed which committed Britain to three years of Armed Services cooperation from the day of independence.[184] Under the terms of this treaty, a British Services Mission was deployed in Burma, which in June 1948 consisted of '96 Military, two Naval and seven Air Force officers.'[185]

By April 1948, there was a rapidly developing threat to the Government of the Union of Burma. Although it was recognised that the Burmese communists were 'not necessarily Moscow inspired', it was not in the British government's interest for Burma to have a successful Communist coup, and so the government and its military were supported.[186] The political fractures in the Burma Army burst open in April 1948 with desertions and arrests, and, according to General Smith Dun, 1st Burma Rifles deserted entirely 'in sympathy with the Communists.'[187] The Karen were, in the main however, hostile to Communism, and most Karen units fought against the Communists and 1 Burif alongside a Kachin battalion to retake Prome. The Prime Minister of Burma, U Nu, appealed to Britain for military equipment, from Spitfires and bombers to ammunition in order to suppress the Communist insurgency. Under the defence agreement, Britain was

---

[184] 'Treaty between the Government of the United Kingdom and the Provisional Government of Burma' (London: HMSO, 17 October 1947) [online], https://www.cvce.eu/en/obj/anglo_burmese_treaty_on_the_independence_of_burma_london_17_october_1947-en-cd1357f8-0e15-41a7-ae41-f39aa1a6db9b.html

[185] Hansard, House of Commons Debate, 21 June 1948, vol 452 cc931-2 [online], https://api.parliament.uk/historic-hansard/commons/1948/jun/21/anglo-burmese-treaty

[186] TNA, FO 371/694881, Report of General Bourne for HMG and the Burma Government, 9 February 1948, p.5.

[187] TNA, FO 371/694881, Report of General Bourne for HMG and the Burma Government, 9 February 1948; Smith Dun, *Memoirs of the Four-Foot Colonel*, (Cornell University: New York, 1980), p.1.

'bound to assist her in obtaining arms' so 'the most generous allocation to Burma which our resources permitted' was agreed.[188] By June, the Burma Government was not expected to hold, causing a dilemma over whether the SS Kindat, due to arrive in July with three million rounds of ammunition on board, should be diverted.[189]

The Karen fought against the enemy of the Government of the Union of Burma, 'not from love of the party in power but from dislike of Communism and also from the tradition of loyalty to the Government as a Government.' The same Foreign Office research paper also argues that 'it was largely the Karens who checked the movement and saved Rangoon.'[190] Once the Communist threat had been checked in August, it was not long before conflict between the government and the Karen re-emerged. Tensions had been simmering through 1947, when the Karen National Defence Organisation had been formed, and in February 1948 the British ambassador to Burma, James Bowker, wrote 'it would be deplorable if internal dissension were to break out in Burma so soon after the transfer of power.' He was also worried about the Karens expecting to receive British help in their fight for an independent Karen state, and assured U Nu, the Burmese Prime Minister, that this would not happen.[191] By the end of the month, however, the first rumours of former Force 136 men helping the Karen reached the Foreign Office. This was a persistent rumour over the next four years or so, and became the subject of attention again in the 1990s with the release of files to the British National Archives. Those files showed the Foreign Office knew that Lieutenant Colonel Cromarty Tulloch, former commander of the Walrus area of Operation Character, was actively supporting a proposed Karen coup.[192]

Tensions heightened through the remaining months of 1948, fueled

---

[188] TNA, FO 371/69482, Appendix B of a letter from Defence Minister A.V. Alexander to Foreign Secretary, Ernest Bevin, 1 June 1948.

[189] TNA, FO 371/69482, Draft letter from 'S/S' to Minister of Defence, A.V. Alexander, 7 June 1948.

[190] TNA, FO 371/83110, 'The Karens of Burma', Research Department, Foreign Office, 19 January 1950, p.6.

[191] TNA, FO 371/69509, Cypher 'From Rangoon to Foreign Office', 9 February 1948.

[192] See TNA files FO 371/69509 to 69513; *Forgotten Allies*, BBC 'Timewatch', 1997; Aldrich, Richard, 'Legacies of Secret Service: Renegade SOE & the Karen Struggle in Burma 1948 – 1950', *Intelligence and National Security*, 14, 4, (1999), pp.130-48; *see* also Richard Duckett, *The Special Operations Executive in Burma*, Epilogue, pp.179-196.

by rumours of British connivance with the Karens which was widely reported in the press, and Communist incitement aimed at persuading the Karens to join them against the government. Then, during Christmas mass in 1948, Karen worshippers were murdered by Burmans. The Civil War began in 1949. That war persists until today, as predicted by a Burma government newspaper which, in June 1948, had advised on the 'futility' of violence between Karen and Burman because 'neither [...] would ever be able to destroy the other.'[193]

In March 1949, Saw Samson had his letter published in *The Telegraph*, where he explained why the Karens were fighting:

Dear Sir,
So much has been said against the Karen rising in Burma that I hope a few words of truth will find their way into your paper.

We have not risen. The Karen National Defence Organization was recognised by the present Government and allowed to carry arms to defend isolated Karen villages from dacoits.

Some dacoities were committed by private armies known as levies belonging to different political parties. Very little is heard of the Tavoy and Mergui incidents, where the A.U.M.P. another private army, massacred Karen men, women and children, burning down their villages.

The government, while talking about peace, was arming its private armies with up to date military equipment, quite unknown to its Supreme Commander, Gen. Smith Dun, a Karen who was properly hoodwinked. Finally, when things came to a head, he submitted his resignation.

On 31 January, the government forces surrounded two Karen quarters near Rangoon. One peacefully allowed their arms to be taken away. The result was that the whole quarter was set upon by the AUMP, plundered, burnt, and men, women and children slaughtered.

The second is at Insein, where I am writing this letter. We were wise. We refused to surrender to a private army. We are not fighting the Union of Burma. We are fighting a bunch of Fascists who call themselves anti-fascists, and under the name of the Union Govt. of Burma seem determined to wipe us off. We are not fighting for a separate Karen State. We are fighting for our women and children and our lives.

---

[193] TNA, FO 371/69509, James Bowker to Ernest Bevin, 19 June 1948.

I do not know if this letter will find its way out of this place and reach your office. But if it does, for the cause of justice let all know the truth.

Yours etc,
Saw Samson
Insein, March 1949.[194]

*The British and the Karens who had served alongside each other in the war, and even some who were posted to Burma after the war, formed some very close bonds of friendship. The British Government's handling of the Karens and the news out of Burma in the post war years, as referred to in Saw Samson's letter, was evidently very distressing; Leslie Glass wrote 'I have been stopped on the street by men who fought with the Karens in the war [...] with tears in their eyes.'[195] In the private collections of relatives of Burma veterans, there are often letters of correspondence dating through the decades into the 1990s, as well as letters petitioning politicians to do something to help the Karens and other minority races in Burma. On 1 September 1949, Saw Ohn Pe,[196] MBE, MC, wrote to Major Dennis Ford, latterly of Force 136:*

## KYOWAING

1st September, 1949.
My Dear Major Ford,
It will give you much surprise to see this letter of mine, since I received your letter of the 29th April 1948. Your letter and the snaps [photos] are still with me whenever I moved about during these troublesome days. You might have heard in the broadcast news about the unrest in Burma. Since the 31st August 1948 when the K.N.D.O. (Karen National Defence Organisation) have overpowered the Govt in Thatin [sic: Thaton] District, I was selected by the Karen leaders of the District to organise our boys and lead them for better understanding between the Govt in Rangoon and K.N.D.O. in this District.

---

[194] Saw Samson, letter to *The Telegraph*, March 1949, in the private collection of both Martin Smith and Lt.Col. Sam Pope.

[195] Leslie Glass was in the Burma Civil Service from 1934 to 1947. *See* his memoir, *The Changing of the Kings* (Peter Owen: London, 1985).

[196] *Opposite right* photo courtesy of Lt.Col. Sam Pope.

Brigadier Ohn Pe, standing on the right with two unknown Karen.

The administration in this District was run as a parallel Govt. Major Butler was posted as D.C. about the beginning of 1948.[197] I was controlling the K.N.D.O. assisted by Willie Saw as O.C. for Salween District with SATAKI as his Adjutant.[198] It was a great strain on my nerves to run such a difficult show. I have to deal very tactfully with the Force Commander of the Union Force who happened to be 2nd Kachin Rifles and Commissioner of Tenasserim Division as Chief Administrator. I have done my level best to lead my people who are clamouring for fair play, yet the Officials of the Union Govt of Burma are still adamant to accede to the wishes of my people to give a separate state like they have given to the Shans, Kachins and Chins. The matter was brought to a head when GHQ of our K.N.D.O. declared a state of resistance to the Union Govt by open fight at Insein Area. Our boys have stood the onslaught from 28th January 1949 until the 23rd May 1949 when Insein was evacuated by our Force. In Thaton we have taken full control from the 21st April 1949. There was negotiation for amicable settlement of the question of surrender. The terms imposed on us are so drastic and humiliating resulting in our refusal. The Kachins combined with Burma Territorial Force (Burman) attacked us on 21st June 1949. Our boys have resisted braverly [sic] but we were short of ammo, and heavy equipment such as LMG and Mortars so I have to give an order for organised withdrawal to the North. The experience gained by me in the last world war give me a point to adopt a guerilla fighting for the whole area.

In the meantime our leaders at Toungoo have declared a de facto Govt. of KAWTHOOLEI KAREN STATE from 14th June 1949 with Toungoo as the HQ. We have established a broadcasting station and is still going strong. I was appointed a Brigadier being promoted from my last War Substantive Rank of a Captain. There are altogether

---

[197] Major Saw Butler MC served with both SIS and SOE during the war. He was well educated and well respected by the British. He served with SOE's Operation Character in 1945.

[198] Saw Willie Saw was one of Major Seagrim' first recruits in 1942. Before the war he worked in the forestry business. Major Ford described him as an 'almost legendary character' and that his 'advice is sought after' by Karens in the Papun area. Saw Sataki was a Headman, and he served SOE/Major Ford as a Home Guard leader and in an intelligence capacity. He apparently 'suffered very badly' under Burma National Army and Japanese torture.

4 Battalions of Infantry under this command at present. Each battalion is approximately 750 strong. Our friend Willie Saw is now a Lt. Colonel in charge of Salween Battalion. All our boys in Force 136 have practically joined up and some of them have distinguished themselves in the field. Saw Po Htin of KYOWAING is very enthusiastic about our resistance and is trying to collect arms and ammo., wherever possible.[199] Union Govt., forces are trying to suppress us, but they cannot do that. The fire of freedom is burning steadily in the rank and file of our KAWTHOOLEI ARMY.

This letter is written as an appeal to all and every British Officer who have been amongst the Karens during the last day of resistance against the Japanese Army and who had lead the life of guerilla warriors to come to the aid of the Karens in Burma. We do not want to eliminate the Burmans but to bring them to their senses to grant us freedom which we Karens wanted for so long since the British Govt., left us in the lurch and at the mercy of Burmese Politicians. We want arms and ammo., very badly. If any foreign firms can smuggle us such necessities we are prepared to repay them in honest sweat and toil. We can beat the Burmese socialists party who runs the Govt. at their own fancy. We are determined to fight for the right cause and trust that God Almighty will shower His Blessings on every Karen who are still alive to fight until freedom is achieved.

As the Burmese Govt., is trying their best to block us as far as possible I was unable to write to the outside world. Even to my folks at Bassein I am unable to do so. We have W/T sets to communicate amongst our unit HQ. Our forces have operated in all the Districts in Burma where the Karens are predominant. In Thatin [sic] at present we still hold the whole of KYAIKTO and PAAN sub. Division and the country East of the Sittang right up to Toungoo. In the Delta we have parts of Bassein, Myaurgmyo, Maubin and Pyapon. A few weeks ago our troops have occupied Taunggyi to help our Shan sympathisers who dislike Burmese troops in their area. Some Kachin troops are also helping us in Toungoo District. We have a tough time with the Kachin Troops in our area because the O.C. of 2nd Kachin Rifles now fighting against us have been bought over by

---

[199] Major Ford said of Saw Po Htin: 'The uncrowned King of the Papun District - no timber is moved, no elephant is cradled, and no labour is hired unless Po Htin gives the word. He is Buddhist, suffers from diabetes and was, even in 1945, one of the richest Sgaw Karens. Fanatically pro-British, he gave every possible kind of assistance to the Allied Cause'.

the Burmese Politicians with bribes and given quick promotion. He was just a mere Jemadar during the last war and remained behind in Burma.

This letter is posted through a friend of mine who goes out of Burma to a foreign country and do trust that it will reach you at home address. By this time I expect you would return from Austria.

Please do convey our needs to all other friends in Great Britain. Papun is my HQ where we have a landing ground. We are using B2 sets.[200]

God is with us always.
With Best Wishes,
Yours Sincerely.
O.P.[201]

*In January 1950, Ohn Pe again wrote to Major Ford.[202] He began with 'due remembrance and our friendship during the war days' before giving news of the Karen struggle against the Government of U Nu. He was sure that, if they were somehow supplied with enough ammunition, 'the present struggle will be over very quickly.' The appeal was specifically to 'our old friends in Force 136'. By this point, the help that might have been coming had come to an ignominious end. At least two ex-Force 136 men, Lt.Col. John Cromarty Tulloch and Major Alex Campbell, had been conspiring to supply weapons to the Karens, but Campbell had been arrested in Rangoon in September 1948 after the Burmese government was alerted to his plotting. Campbell had entrusted an air steward as a courier with a letter for Tulloch in Calcutta. The air steward, suspicions alerted and sensing a profit, opened the letter and upon reading its contents, decided not to deliver to Tulloch. He instead handed it over to the Burmese embassy in Karachi. The plot thus exposed, Tulloch was forced out of India by the authorities there and back to the UK. Tulloch continued to support the Karen struggle*

---

[200] This is the radio set that they were trained on and used with SOE.

[201] Letter from Ohn Pe from the private collection of papers held by Col. (retired) Sam Pope. Captain Ohn Pe served with both SIS and SOE. Before the war he was a Government Assistant Inspector of Timber. He was Ford's Intelligence Officer in 1945, having joined Operation Character from the Kachin Hill Tracts where he had worked for SIS.

[202] Letter from Ohn Pe to Major Dennis Ford from the private collection of papers held by Col. (retired) Sam Pope, 16 January 1950.

until September 1952 when he was sentenced to eighteen months in prison for allegedly embezzling funds intended for Karen scholarships in Britain. In his defence in court, Tulloch said the real purpose of the money being sent to him was to organise arms and ammunition, but 'the judge called his defence "humbug"'.[203] Private correspondence provides some more insight, with one letter asserting that 'they might have brought off a coup had they not trusted Alec [sic] Campbell' who had been 'idiotic enough to trust a BOAC steward with the plan'.[204] There was no support for the Karens from His Majesty's Government, as official policy was to support the Union of Burma, even if that meant supplying weapons that would be used by the Union Government against Britain's wartime allies, the Karens.[205] How much Saw Ohn Pe knew about all this is unknown, but his next letter is dated 1 March 1951:

> My Dear Dennis,
> Thanks so much for your affectionate air mail letter posted on 22/11/50. It was received at Bilin within the first week of December 1950. Since that date there was a lot of changes for us, those who are in this present struggle. The enemy have launched a big scale offensive on our front in Thaton district and we have to withdraw up the road to Natkyi and my central front have to move back to Mindwin area, the DZ for Giraffe in Force 136 days.[206] Paan front not affected. By

---

[203] Arnold Latcham, 'Gun-runner Colonel Spent £150 A Week', *Daily Express*, 25 September 1952, cutting in TNA, KV 2/3869.

[204] Letter to Tony Stonor from Colin Mackenzie, 21 January 1985. From the private collection of Martin Smith. Stonor arrived in Burma in 1946 as a nineteen year old officer with the Royal Welch; Mackenzie was head of SOE's Force 136 for the duration of the war.

[205] For different interpretations of the conspiracy to arm Karens against the government of the Union of Burma, see Richard Duckett, *The Special Operations Executive in Burma*, pp.190-95; Richard Aldrich, Legacies of Secret Service: Renegade SOE and the Karen Struggle in Burma, 1948-50', *Intelligence and National Security*, 14, 4 (1999), pp.130-48; 'Forgotten Allies', *BBC Timewatch*, 1997; Giulia Garbagni, 'The Friends of the Burma Hill People': Lieutenant Colonel John Cromarty Tulloch and the British Support to the Karen Independence Movement, 1947 – 1952, *Journal of Burma Studies*, Volume 21, Number 2, December 2017, pp. 263-298.

[206] Giraffe was the codename of a Force 136 team that was part of Operation Nation, working with the Burmese Nationalists during 1945.

16th December 1950 we in Thaton district have suffered reverses. Again in January 1951 Kyawkkyi and Shwegyin have fallen to the enemy. However, we are not dismayed. Fortunes of war are such a thing that KING BRUCE of SCOTLAND have become fugitives for sometime, but by strong determination and perseverance have overcome his enemies again and drove them out of his kingdom. Our morale is still good and the only handicap for us is short of arms and ammo. Yet, God is so gracious, that we as yet did not suffer any irreparable losses as may be broadcasted to the world by our enemy.

Please do raise up our heart to hear some news from your country and I do trust that almighty God will not suffer us the least amongst the nations to be annihilated. Our determination to achieve our freedom as a NATION is very strong.

Please remember us to all friends in Great Britain.

Yours sincerely,
Ohn Pe[207]

*Later in 1951, Ohn Pe wrote again to Major Ford. It seems Ford had become a father and made Ohn Pe Godfather to his daughter, Nicola Jocelyn Maw Eh. He sent best wishes and prayers that she would grow up 'free from all troubles'. He also hoped that the Labour Party would lose the forthcoming snap election in Britain that had been called for 25 October: 'when the Conservatives return to power, foreign policy of the UK will change and we do hope it will be for the better towards our Karens to free themselves from the domination of the Burmese.'*

*Ohn Pe was also keen that Ford told his 'friends back in UK or in the Common Wealth that the KARENS will never be communists. We will fight on the ticket of DEMOCRACIES. Britons and Americans have opened our eyes to Christianity and they must come again and help us in order that God blessings may be showered on them. Otherwise, if they neglect, the little ones like us, some of us imagine they will go the way of Great Kingdoms like, Egypt, Babylon, Greece and Roman Empires before them.'*

*In this letter, Ohn Pe described how it was to be smuggled out of Burma with the help of Saw Johnny Htoo, now a Brigadier commanding a Karen brigade in Amherst district.*

---

[207] Letter from Ohn Pe to Major Dennis Ford from the private collection of papers held by Col. (retired) Sam Pope, 1 March 1951.

# After Independence

### Saw Johnny Htoo
*Saw Johnny Htoo had been an instructor at the officer training school until he was interned:*

In April 1949, I joined the Revolutionary Army and served for fifteen years. I did not get any leave during my service so the Chief of Staff, Saw Bo Mya, gave me two months leave.[208] At that time, I was Divisional commander of 6 Division KNLA (Karen National Liberation Army). While I was staying at a house on a hill during my two months leave, one of the villagers informed on me and showed the Burmese Army the house where I stayed. I was captured by Major Thaung Kyi of the Burmese army based in Mawlamyine. Thaung Kyi worked together with me while we were attending B.A.O.T.S [Burma Army Officer Training School]. He invited me to come and work for the Burmese government but I refused and later he released me. After that, I attended special classes at Burma Divinity (Myanmar Institute of Theology) for one year.

I was offered a position of Pastor in Taunggyi before I finished my studies. I accepted the offer and become a pastor from 16 April 1967 until 1973; I was ordained in 1973 and served as an Ordained Priest until 1989. While Burma was agitating for democracy, I returned to Karen revolutionary territory and served as Mission Advisor. Now, I am 81 years old and still serving the Lord and praying and hoping for Myanmar to have peace and independence and to get help from the British.

(Saw Johnny Htoo died on 25 April 1995, and as his beloved wife I prayed for the kind British, who were kind to us and especially for all the Karen veterans, and wish may God bless you all abundantly).

### Saw Aye Kyaw
*Saw Aye Kyaw had joined the navy until independence, and then gone to North Borneo to work in forestry:*

---

[208] General Bo Mya was a leader of the the Karen National Army for over fifty years. He died in 2006. See obituary, for example, 'Myanmar Rebel Leader Dies After Long Illness', *Reuters* [online], https://www.reuters.com/article/us-myanmar-rebels-leader/myanmar-rebel-leader-dies-after-long-illness-idUSBKK2996520061224

I started working in 1949 and returned to my homeland in 1952 but there was nothing I could do. I was not able to carry weapons for the soldiers due to my old age. Lieutenant Salmon asked me to follow him. I had a broken leg and occasional pain, so it was not easy for me. Therefore, Pu A Gyi, Pu Ta Ru, QMG asked me if I could work with Rev. Robert Htwe. I had to help in the grocery shop at Mae Tha Waw. Soon, Pu Lel Wah sent me to officer Htee Moo. When the war started, Officer Hteh Nar ordered all the men and women who were working at Headquarters to live at Baw Naw Hta camp.

I asked leave to visit Mergui/Tavoy while staying with Phoo Pae Du. I handed over my duties to Phoo Pae Du. I stayed behind at Mae Th'mee Hta, Mergui/Tavoy. I went to KRC, Mae Sot with Rev. Robert. I then went to Thay Baw Boe to grow sweetcorn and after harvesting sweetcorn we grew teak. P'doh Tha Taw, from the KNU Forestry Department arranged it. After a year, I got malaria several times, so returned to Rev. Robert.

P'doh Be Baw Yu Paw and P'doh Htoo Htoo Lay took me to Three Pagodas Pass after the Mon and Karen started fighting. While staying with P'doh Mhan Kyaw Min in Three Pagoda Pass the enemy came so we moved to Sangklaburi. Not very long after, Th'Nay Maw camp was established together with refugees and I stayed there. Then I returned to Sangkhlaburi to be in charge of the refugee's food supply together with P'doh Marshall until 2004. In May 2004, the doctor told me to take a rest due to my old age so the Karen Women's Organisation of Sangkhlaburi arranged a place in the compound of Thramu Say Paw where other elderly men and women were staying.

Later, the doctor asked my age and I said 84 years old so he wanted me to stay near friends as I did not have anyone to look after me when I retired. P'doh Marshall said he would take care of me if I wished to stay in the camp so I did. I believe that it is a blessing from God. I am really grateful for that. Some invited me to go abroad. It is not my wish but the willing and preparation of God. Some of the Karen refugees have left to go abroad. For me only 1% go abroad and 99% stay here and it is in the hands of God. Those who have left were believers so the Karen people would know how and why they left.

### Saw Ni K'mwe Paul AKA Lieutenant Saw Smile Paul

*Saw Ni K'mwe Paul had joined the Karen Youth Organisation becoming a regional officer:*
When Colonel Nay Win took over the government [1962], I joined the KNU [Karen National Union].

## Saw Fair Play

*Saw Fair Play had worked in the camps along the Burma-Thai border until finally returning to Burma and joining the Union Police:*

After serving for a year with the new D.Y.S.P, my friend Saw Phar Lar and I submitted a letter to transfer to the Karen Rifles. The D.Y.S.P approved willingly and told us to be good. We went to Mandalay and showed our documents and the 3rd Karen Rifles accepted us well. The time we got there was recruiting time so there were about 200 people. We could not join immediately as ex-soldiers. We had to stay separately for a week and had to do a medical check-up, vaccinations and only then we became 3rd Karen Rifles soldiers and could stay with the old soldiers. We attended six months military training and had to take an oath on a Bible and the flag that we would serve the army faithfully.

After a year, our company had to go to the headquarters in Maymyo where the ex-officers attended training. During their training, their stars were taken off and only the badge was put on. They all had their own company and section. There were about 200. There, Regimental Sergeant Major (RSM) Saw Tun Tin trained us to line up and parade and a Burmese Sergeant and a Gurkha Sergeant trained us for physical training. We played football with officers. An officer from A.Company chose six of my friends and me, altogether seven of us to attend Burma Army Officer Training School (BAOTS). The first two weeks started with physical training and not even after the two weeks, orders came from Headquarters and our commanding officer, Lieutenant Colonel De Htoo, had to go for security duties for the families of 2nd Karen Rifles from Meiktila. He said that Lieutenant General Smith Dun got a higher rank than Major General Ne Win. Smith Dun was a Karen.[209] We came down to Meiktila by train as ordered. By the time we arrived at headquarters of 2nd Karen Rifles in Meiktila, there were no soldiers, just a family was there. But we could not go to their place. After waiting for three days, the car came. Our section got in to the car but did not know where to go or what to do. We passed Yi Na Chaung and slept in Magwe, on the bank of Irrawaddy. We saw many Karen Rifles, Chin Rifles and Gurkha soldiers doing patrols along the road. In the morning, we got in the car and continued. At four in the evening, we met with sentries from 2nd Karen Rifles who were watching each side of the road. It was drizzling

---

[209] General Smith Dun was made first Commander in Chief of independent Burma's Armed Forces from 4 January 1948. *See* Smith Dun, *Memoirs of the Four-Foot Colonel* (Cornell University: New York, 1980). Ne Win was Second in Command.

and we knew there would be a battle soon. We got to 2nd Karen HQ after passing the sentries two miles later. Platoon Commander. Lieutenant Jolly asked us to follow him as we got down and he took us to the forest saying this is the battlefield. He then left us and went back to headquarters.

The Burma Rifles had left Mingaladon headquarters, Rangoon, and when they got to Pyay they said to the soldiers that they were no longer under the government and were now communist. After that they came back to Rangoon but there was a rebellion so they moved to Upper Burma near Aunglan and 2nd Karen Rifles was ordered to fight the Communist army. The 2nd Karen Rifles could defeat the first defence but not more than that so we 3rd Karen Rifles came to help with the arrangement of the British Army. We stayed there for three days and again fought the next morning about 9am. The battle took the whole day and until 4pm in the evening they would not withdraw so as ordered we launched an offensive with fixed bayonets and then they withdrew.[210]

The withdrawal took only five minutes, therefore we attacked and charged them the whole day. In the evening when we got near Aunglan town, a District Commissioner went past on a bicycle, so we captured him and questioned him. He said he was Deputy Commissioner of Aunglan town and not to fire when we entered town, as the Burma Rifles unit which became Communist was not in Aunglan town as they had left. The officer of the Karen Rifles had known the situation and told us to go to Aunglan the next day. At 5pm, we arrived at Aunglan and there was no battle as Burma Rifle communists had left the town. The D.C gave us help as promised and we stayed in Aunglan for a week to get information on the enemy.

Later, we got information that the Communists had waited for us to attack at the hillside and to destroy Bwe Gyi Bridge with mines and they still waited there to attack us. The water level of the river near Bwe Gyi Bridge was rising and falling and a man could sink below even at the time of river level falling.

When the time came, we Karen Rifles left Aunglan town and only a Union Military Police U.M.P section remained. We arrived near Bwe Gyi Bridge and camped along the river which was difficult to cross because the Communists had destroyed the bridge. Then, we prepared mortars and machine guns and the Communists waited with mortars and

---

[210] Before the Karen fought against the Union of Burma government, they fought against Burmese Communist forces, helping to save Rangoon and the Union government from falling under Communist control.

machine guns as well. During the battle the Communists fired at the camp using mortars and caused serious damage.

Later on, our Platoon Commander Lieutenant Jolly said he would attack and called No.1 section and attacked. We slung our guns on our backs and, holding the rails of the bridge, we crossed over to the other side. After that No.2 section climbed behind and I was there. While we were crossing, the Communists saw us and fired with machine guns. The troops behind helped and fired at the enemy with heavy weapons. The battle started and both sides were attacking and our unit was between the bullets from the enemy and the troops behind us. As ordered by our superior, we crossed over to the other bank from the bridge. The Engineers Platoon with their guns slung on their backs were trying to repair the bridge during the battle. There was no time to fire at the enemy. Finally, the battalion and our section were on the other bank and climbed the hillside and attacked the enemy. While two privates were trying to get down from the bridge they got stuck in mud and could not move. The battle was four hours long and the enemy withdrew at 5pm. Only then could we pull the stuck men up with ropes. We could carry artillery and mortars across when the bridge had been repaired. The two armies attacked in turns daily and then arrived in Pyay town. Pyay's D.C had made arrangements like the Aunglan D.C so there was no battle in the town. After capturing Pyay town, we had to follow the enemy and attack them along the Ayeyarwady bank. After capturing Pyay town, the Communist captured Aunglan town where only one UMP section was, therefore we had to recapture it with two Karen Rifles companies.

Though there was a war, there was post. We would get letters from home and could also write home. One soldier got letters from his two girlfriends/sweethearts at the same time, so he was quite happy. We also got a salary. During the war, there was a battle every day for one month.

After a week, we got an order that soldiers from our 3rd Karen Rifles battalion could go back to 3rd Karen Headquarters which was in Mandalay Palace. We left Pyay and slept a night in Thayarwaddy and continued our journey the next morning and slept at Mingaladon for a night. The Communists harassed us on our way back. The next morning, we departed with forty armoured cars and arrived at Taungoo at 5pm and slept there one night. Taungoo was 1st Karen Headquarters.

We continued our journey the next morning and arrived in Meiktila. We were ordered to stop in Meiktila but did not know the reason. The Burmese Rifles and Chin Rifles asked us to surrender but nobody surrendered. Our company only had 150 people. The people who surrounded us were about 3,000. I had to stay at Rifle Court and in the afternoon I had to retain the weapons. In the night, the soldiers took the weapons and I could not do anything. The Burmese officers tried day and night to make us surrender but it did not happen. After a week, three of our captains were told to come up to Maymyo. When the three of them came back, we all had to parade and give up our weapons. It was because when they went to Maymyo they saw all the Karen armed forces had surrendered their weapons and were captured with their families. The leaders from Maymyo were worried about our army which was under their control, so therefore we were asked to surrender our weapons. We all lined up and there was admonishment from 6 to 12pm and we surrendered the weapons. In the morning, all of us were captured and sent to Maymyo together with other Karen armed forces and UMP, altogether about 200 people. There were guards at all the railway stations.[211]

When we got to Maymyo, the armoured cars were waiting and after we got down from the train, we were lined up and then we had to go to the cars. A Burmese officer and one of our officers checked our shirts, trousers, and backpacks one by one as we got on the cars. Each car would leave when full. Once the car started, the soldiers sang "Ya Ta Mu Lar Ah Khaw Hti". When we got to the place where they would imprison us, those already captured said, "Brothers, this is jail". At that time, there were about 1000 to 3000 prisoners in the town. They would give us salary and food but we were not allowed to hold weapons. We were always in a state of readiness. Our C Company was still in Myin Chan and Pakokku, therefore a Major from the Burmese Army called one of our officers to go along with him to Myin Chan and Pakokku, but the soldiers were not allowed to go. The Burmese Major said if he got to Myin Chan and Pakokku and he could see that our C Company is serving well, he would allow us to hold weapons again. Our officer decided to go with him and if he was asked to surrender he would rebel. They had gone to Myin Chan and Pakokku and like before they asked C Company to surrender, so there was a battle and the Burmese Major was wounded seriously. In Karenni State, while the Officer of B Company went on a patrol, the Burmese officer brought them all and asked them to surrender, therefore B Company commander went to the mountains and at once went underground. The Burmese Army could not do anything.

After a week, two planes passed over our place and at 1pm a man came

---

[211] Towards the end of January 1949, the 3rd Karen Rifles in the Mandalay and Maymyo area were all interned by pro-government troops.

with a jeep to our camp and asked us to come out. Our leaders had stopped us but he was attempting to call us out, therefore many of us went out passing the guards. There were only about forty guards so they were weaker than us. We did not answer when they asked why. The forty guards were watching where we were detained. Among the guards, there were people from the Shan Rifles and the place was fenced with two layers of barbed wire. The height of the first layer was ten feet high and another layer was five feet wide and four feet high.

After we got out from there and got to the main road, a Kachin Officer, Naw Shal came and called us along and said to go quickly but we did not know where we were going. Finally, we got to Rifle Court where they had the armoury and asked us to destroy the fence. He brought the Company Commander and his wife, an English woman, to the Rifle Court and made them sit because they were not doing as he asked. It was about ten miles from Maymyo Airport. He landed his plane and organised the Kachin Rifles and Gurkha Rifles and all were his followers. When he came to Maymyo, he left about sixty Kachin Rifles and Karen Rifles who had come with his plane at the airport and some at the Rifle Court. There were many Kachin soldiers from Northern Burma and now at Rifle Court he could organise them.

We broke open the locks and took the weapons and came back to the place where we had been imprisoned. All the officers led their own companies into position and ordered us to attack immediately. We started firing at the Chin Rifles near there. At that time, the British officers who were left in Maymyo raised their hands to stop the firing and made the Chin Rifles surrender. After the Chin Rifles surrendered their weapons they were taken and were imprisoned. We went forward to the place where our soldiers were held and we let them go. They took up weapons and fought against the Kachin Rifles and Gurkha Rifles and within a few hours we could capture Maymyo. We captured thirty Burmese officers.

The 1$^{st}$ Karen Rifles and KNDO captured Taungoo town and fought in Meiktila and they stopped two British planes and made all the passengers get out and go to Maymyo with thirty Karen Rifles and thirty Kachin Rifles.[212] We became Kawthoolei soldiers from that time.[213]

One of the Burmese officers out of the thirty and one of our officers

---

[212] Karen insurgents apparently targeted aircraft. *See* Jonah Fisher, 'The man who carried out one of the world's earliest hijackings', BBC, 27 June 2014 [online], https://www.bbc.co.uk/news/magazine-28014394

[213] Kawthoolei is the name given to the Karen state they are fighting for.

went to Mandalay to tell the Burmese troops to surrender but both came back after they had refused. That night, the Burmese troops entered the town secretly and took position in the houses so the fight occurred again. The whole town was razed by fire and the battle went on day and night. We wanted to rest, but we had to hide in the buildings. The leaders gathered 500 soldiers to clear the town from the start to end starting from morning but some of the Burmese soldiers still hid in the houses and the battle had not ended. Finally, we gathered again and cleared from one end of town to the other and cleared all the houses and only then the battle ended. Each day the soldiers who were killed and injured were not less than fifty.

The British took photographs by raising flags during the battle. They were not frightened of anything. The troops from Meiktila and Maymyo came to Mandalay and fought for three days and captured Mandalay. The battles in Nyaunglebin were severe so most of the troops went to Nyaunglebin and only 300 troops from the Karen Rifles and Kachin Rifles were left in Mandalay. The Burmese troops tried to destroy the gate of the palace with a train so we had to fire often to make them retreat. They fired on us with 3" mortars from U Khan Ti Mountain. After one week, we left by opening the town gate on the Maymyo side in the morning putting all the rations, ammunition and all the important things on a truck as it was difficult to stay. Half of the way Burmese troops attacked and all 300 of us got down from the truck to fire at them to retreat and continued to Maymyo after that. We camped in Htoe Phaw Mountain.

After two weeks, one of the Kachin Rifles men who had not joined us came to ask to join us but we were careful. The Kachin Rifles which fought together with us explained that troops came to make us surrender and we need to fight them and said if we did not fight they will fight against their own race. But unexpectedly they came as they really wanted to join with us and they did not fire a shot. We watched them and when they came in, we asked the Kachin Rifles to surrender. The Kachin Rifles which fought with us went back to Kachin State and went on operations. Some of the Karen officers were included in that plan. The troops which were at the Mandalay battle did not know about this matter therefore the troops from Maymyo came down by truck to inform us of what happened. We gathered manpower and put all the necessary things on the truck and went to the jungle via the jungle route outside the town. When we got to the place where the car could not go and it was getting dark, we left taking the guns and bullets and as much as we could carry.

The strong men would take two guns each but no food was brought and heavy weapons and many bullets were left on the car as the things were not in order and we had to do it quickly.

The officers looked at the map and went down to Shan State. It took 25 days by the jungle route. The only food was drinking stream water when we passed. There was no fruit that we could eat. But the 300 soldiers and officers were without sickness. When we got to Ho Pone (Taunggyi) region, our people from Thailand came and gave us food and only then could we eat. We were not allowed to enter the town when we got to Ho Pone because ten soldiers had gone to the town and had noodles at the noodle shop and were killed there. We came down to Karenni region after one or two days. Kayah and Padaung people captured Kayah State except Moe Pyal and Phal Khone. Kayah and Padaung could read and speak Sgaw Karen. We walked on foot from Ho Pone to Loikaw for many days. At that time, Company Commander Johnny Htoo and 80 people left Shan State along the jungle route so they could not take many weapons.[214] Later, we met with the woman leader Ma May. When we asked "how many guns could you all bring?" she said "everyone could bring a gun each except me."

After a week's rest, we combined with the Kachin Rifles, and Karenni which came from Taungoo and captured Moe Byal and Phal Khone. We again combined with Karenni and Kachin Rifles and captured Taunggyi without firing a bullet. It could be because we went there at night time with many cars which scared them. About a month later, Burmese troops attacked us mostly from Shan State and the battle was severe and we withdrew to Loikaw.

We heard that the houses from Beik and Dawei (Tavoy) were burned due to insufficient weapons and difficulties in defending there, therefore Lieutenant Saw Nu and I planned to go back to our region as we were from Beik, Dawei. Lieutenant Saw Nu married a Padaung woman while staying in Loikaw and worked together with Karenni Leader Saw Shwe. Lieutenant Saw Nu left earlier than me and I waited because the Kachin Rifles, under the command of Lieutenant Naw Shal, were planning to come. But Padoh Phoe Nyaw planned to go up to Kachin State so Kachin Rifles were not coming and I came back with seven soldiers from the Delta. When we got to Kyar Inn, we met Lieutenant Saw Nu via Phar Saung, Papun, Kawkareik, Ka Ma Maung, Hlaing Bwe, Hpa-An, Htee Gu Thaw and combined with seventy other troops. The soldiers, some were from Beik, Dawei people, some were from the Insein battle, some

---

[214] Possibly the Saw Johnny Htoo included in this volume.

were from the Taungoo Battle, some were UMP and some were Karen soldiers. We came down to Ye and arrived at Maukkanay where a Mon Leader asked for our help. While we were assisting the attack, eighty young people from Beik and Dawei went to Taungoo to take the weapons, but Taungoo Kawthoolei Headquarters was captured by the enemy and they could not go. Therefore, we gave military training to them and trained them at the battlefield without weapons as there was not sufficient arms. After a month, Lieutenant Saw Nu told us to come down to Beik, Dawei. We went to Beik, Dawei passing by the Yar Pu, Law Thal, Pa Saw Law, Wah Paw, Ka Maw Thwe, May Tar villages. From there to Sint Ku, Lal Tar Pu, Maw Thwe Khwar, Phaw Taw, Kanal Hkaw, Tar Mae Htar, Maw Ma Tru, Kah Taw Ni, Htu Ler, Hkaw Hti and climbed Sin Pyain Mountain and arrived at Per Khee.

When we got to Tar Lay Kho village, the villagers and leaders made a plan and circled Pa Lout town. After a week of battle, Lieutenant Saw Nu ordered us to capture Pa Lout town as the enemy had not retreated. When the fixed time of 4pm came, all of us attacked in force on four sides of Pa Lout town and captured it. We captured some weapons and discovered ten enemy corpses. After capturing Pa Lout town, we organised a brigade with the adults, youth, and women who participated. There were 1000 soldiers. According the administration system, there was a group in each village, a leader for each group, a women's association leader in every village, village chairman, woman army medical officer and 100 men. The doctor was Doctor Bar Thaw from Thaton. Moreover, we discussed building schools with school teachers and education officers. At Beik and Dawei, we held a meeting once a year at every village and everyone attended.

The eighty young people who went to Taungoo to take weapons became military officers and instructors. We captured from Dawei to Wah Yet, Kyoe Daw. When we attacked Tanissary town, Lieutenant Fregie was sent to wait for a ship from Beik. He took four women, forty villagers and soldiers and a D.C to Beik. A battle occurred and the D.C and Lieutenant Fregie was killed. Only seven out of the forty returned. The English who had a shipping business asked to go back to Rangoon and it was allowed. A week after they left, seven warships came and there were forty coastguards in each ship which we could not defend against and had to retreat to Ta Phoe Htar. It could be assumed that it was a British plan. The name of the D.C who died at the bank was Htait Tin Dwin and he was one of the last generations of the Burmese King.

After two years of holding Pali, Burmese troops captured it with the

Navy. We also re-captured Pali again, and then, the Burmese troop recaptured it once more and we had to retreat from one village to another and establish our Headquarters in Toe Ye town, Tanawthayee River. I went to Papun Headquarters from Dawei two or three times to meet with the leaders. We had to walk from Maymyo to Dawei/Beik. We did not rest on the way.

I was 27 during the war and I got married. The village I got married in was Sandi Win village. My wife's name was Naw Daphne who is 5 years younger than me. She passed her Matriculation exam from Mawro Karen High School, Pa Nar Mee village. At that time, the Pa Nar Mee village had been burnt down. When we got married, my father-in-law gave us two elephants but my wife sold them as we did not know how to keep the elephants and had no time. I could not give anything to my wife from the time I married her. I could only give her a thin longyi which Lieutenant Saw Nu gave me.

I received a letter from the Lieutenant after the third day of marriage: "A lot of Burmese troops are coming and it is not possible without you" therefore, I had to plan things immediately and went down to Ta Phoe Tar to attack Tanintharyi town.

When General Ne Win was in control, he held peace talks with all armed groups over many years but only got peace with part of the KNU. We came back with over 3000 soldiers and among them 300 were from Dawei. After two years, the Burmese army arrested sixty of us including me in Thaton. Other troops ran away to the border after hearing this. Ten out of sixty, including me, who were arrested were sent to Insein jail. They sent us by special train with a troop of guards. Our hands were tied with rope and everyone was placed far from each other. The soldiers were ready to shoot and two of them watched each of us.

When we got to Rangoon Station, two Burmese captains came up and covered our eyes with cloth. They asked us to get down from the train and then put us in a car and asked us not to speak and drove away. We did not know where we were going. After an hour, the car stopped and we were asked to get out, sent to another place, untied and the cloth was removed but I could not see any of my friends. There was only me. The jailer opened the bedroll, gave me some clothes to change into and kept my other things. He kept my ring, watch and money.

The doctor came, questioned me and examined my health. Another person came and asked whether I ate fish, beef, mutton, pork and duck egg and if not they would give me a vegetable dish without meat. They asked what kind of cheroot I smoked and gave me a blanket, a pillow and a bed. The water could be opened from 7am to 5pm in the evening if needed. They gave tea in the morning at 6am, rice at 9am, tea at 12 noon, and rice at 4pm.

Once a week, they would buy what we ordered if we had money. I could only send 50 to my house a month. They cut my hair twice a month and if sick I told the guard and they would call the doctor. If the lights went out, we had to call the guard and only then he would come and repair it. After staying alone for three months, they put three people in the cell. After staying with three people for a week, they added ten people and moved to us Building 3 where many people were. That building length was 150 yards and a two story building. There were long rooms, narrow rooms with a partition and ten of us had to stay in a long room. There were eight buildings and one building was destroyed by a bomb by the British during World War Two.

At that time, the ground was vibrating and the building was locked with keys so we could not run away and it was so terrifying. That jail was over a hundred years old. There were seven locks from the wicket gate to our building and at night big dogs were on watch. The army and jailer were watching us from around the fence. There were ten of us and after six months, they gave us a Burmese newspaper to read. We could send home Bible, Burmese books and English books. But nobody knew where we were.

After two years, they allowed us to write to home, but only in Burmese and English. At first, they allowed only two and then four and then nine to write home. Among us Major Phoe Wai was not allowed to write home until we were released. The letter got to his house a month after he wrote it. They allowed us to read letters from home.

I got a letter from home "Father, I received the letter you wrote and am now replying. There will be good news and bad news while you are reading this letter. When your letter came, mother is not here anymore. Mother died." I could not continue reading anymore. I could not speak. I was very hurt. My other friends were happy reading their letters. When they came and asked, I could not answer I just gave them the letter to read.

Later, they divided two each out of ten and sent us to other rooms where many people were. Then, they combined four of us and moved us to another place, after two weeks, we were combined with six and moved to another place. But we were in the same compound so we could see them going around the compound. After eight years, they allowed guests to come and see us. My brother and young niece came and visited but were allowed only fifteen minutes to talk. On visiting day, many people were there talking and it looked like we were in a noisy market. When time was up, they let the guests leave first, and covered our faces and took us back. The jailer would bring the food the guests brought for us later.

After nine years of staying, one day at 4pm, they asked us to pack and called ten of us to the living room. A Colonel had a chat with us and asked me "Where are you going back to?" "Dawei" I answered. "You cannot go back to Dawei, if you go there, the people from the jungle will ask you to work again and they will kill you if you refuse" he said. "I do not know what to do in Rangoon" I replied. Then, he left us after talking for an hour.

After that, all of us were sent to the place we had to stay by car. They did not torture us during the nine years in prison. They returned all the money, watch, ring and mat they had taken when we first arrived. When we got to Rangoon, we met with Muso Kawkasa Hunter Tha Mwe. At that time, General Ne Win had the highest authority. The people who stayed in Rangoon asked for houses, cars and they got it. The people from Thaton, Mawlamyine, Dawei, we did not know what to ask for so they advised to ask for machines. Machines could pump water, plough fields, light the house and grind paddy. But we did not get them and could not take them as the place was too far away. After staying for a couple of days in Rangoon, we returned to Thaton by train. I queued up for a long time to get a ticket but I could not get a seat and travelled all the way standing. We were all captains but now like the villagers we had to stand on the train, said one captain.

While staying in Thaton, a Burmese soldier invited us for a meal and we ate and chatted and they sent us back. In the morning, Captain Colwin made a new Registration Card and within an hour and General Oh Pe had a prayer meeting at his house for us and Captain Phar Khat and I came back to Dawei by plane the next morning. When I arrived in Dawei, my son, Saw Say Kya Wal was an adolescent now and he was taller than me. He was a bit shy when he first saw me. He was Grade 8 studying at school in Dawei where his aunty and uncle lived since his mother died. I went to Panarmee village by sea and slept on Ma Li Island for one night on the way and got to Pu Law town.

I met with my wife's siblings at Panarmee village and came back to Beik by boat. When I got to Beik, I met with my brother-in-law Captain Thein Maung and my daughter Naw Ah Si. She passed 8 grade and was now a teacher at Done Pa Lel Au. She was getting married. I attended her wedding and I planted 1000 coconut trees, 1000 banana trees, 1000 betel trees, and durian and mango trees. I did it myself without hiring people. There were many fruits. And then, I went back to Dawei and then to Panarmee, the villagers and Sayar were making a match for me to get married again. But I refused as I did not need a wife and had never seen her.

I got married again and my wife's name was Naw May Nar, she was schooled up to 7 Grade at Mawro Karen High School in Dawei. She was 16 years younger than me and I had 3 children with her. In 1988 the situation was not stable and the Navy called and questioned me again and again, therefore I called my wife and children and came back to Panarmee as I was afraid I would say something wrong. On 16 February 1997, the Burmese army attacked Dawei and Beik so we moved to Thailand and are now staying at Bongti village on the Thai-Myanmar border. Now, I am 82 years old and my birthday is 22 October. This is all about my life from the time I was born and till my 80s. I do not know what will happen in the future but I am still living by the Grace of God.

## Saw San Aye
*Saw San Aye had joined the 1st Karen Rifles in Toungoo:*

> There again, we had to fight the Communists. When I joined the First Karen Rifles
> Battalion Commander – Lieutenant Colonel Starmon
> Second Battalion Commander – Major Steach
> Adjutant – Capt. Donny (Karen)
> Company Commander – Capt. Min Maung (Karen)
> Company Commander – Capt. Telmadge.

At that time, I was a Corporal. In 1949, our battalion was under the command of Burma Army (during Burma's independence all the battalions were under the command of Burma Army). The Karens revolted for independence. We were based at Mawchi and formed a battalion and the Battalion Commander was Lieutenant Colonel Min Maung (who later became KNLA General).

## Saw Maw Ler
*Saw Maw Ler had served in the army as a signaller until independence:*

During independent era I joined the KNU [Karen National Union] and all my privileges are lost. From 1943 to 1947 I was always on special duty on front line and my more than four years pay were lost because I was a deserter. According to yearly backpay slip my backpay was more than 5000 Kyats. In those days with 5000 Kyats you can do some little business. So the end.

*And the separate interview:*

In 1963, I joined KNU so the British thought that I was a traitor and I did not get any benefits for my service from 1943-47.

## Mel Du AKA Pu Hla Kyi Pa
*Mel Du had been tortured by the Japanese, which left him blind. Later, his wife had died in his arms after suffering an asthma attack:*

During 1972-74, the Burmese government had the Four Cuts campaign, so the villagers in the mountains on the outskirts of Lerdoh town had to move to P'na village.[215] At that time, his

son died so he continued staying with his daughter and son-in-law. His daughter died in 1976, so his youngest brother called him to his house and he died in 1978. He was known and respected and loved by everyone. He was 72 years old when he died.

## Saw Daniel Tun Baw
*Saw Daniel Tun Baw had been doing well in the navy:*

In 1947 when the Karen revolution started, the leader Saw Ba U Gyi organised the Karen soldiers who were serving in the Army and Navy. That's why Daniel Tun Baw and friends quit from the British Navy and joined the Karen revolution for the independence of the Karen people. He had to serve as a signaller as he had in the British Army. His place of

---

[215] The 'Four Cuts ' policy is a strategy employed by the Tatmadaw to sever links between insurgents and the population which sustains them. The 'four cuts' are food, funds, information, and recruits. *See* Kevin Woods, The Commercialisation of Counterinsurgency' in Mandy Sadan (ed.) *War and Peace in the Borderlands of Myanmar* (Copenhagen: Nias, 2016), pp.120-22.

duty was Thaton Township. Soon the battle of Insein started and they had to go there. They lost and had to withdraw. He was back in Thaton in 1950. After serving one year in Thaton, the Burma army put forward a proposal to the Karen revolutionaries for a ceasefire and cooperation for peace in the country. If they didn't the Burma Army would capture and jail them. Some hid on the mountains and forest reserves as they did not want to unite with the Burmese.

Papun became headquarters for the Karen and Karen leaders would meet there. He was the mechanic of the headquarters so he had to transfer to Papun. He served as a mechanic for the leaders. He would lead in discussions and meetings as he was an intelligent man.

He had to travel from one place to another. He met and fell in love with Thra Mu Daphne in 1953. They married on 5 June 1954. They married at Katalti region, Karen territory. After seven months of marriage, he went to Kawlo bank to build a house where his parents' owned paddy fields. The reason for building a house there was so that his wife could teach and it was a good place for him to work for his people. He would work willingly and enthusiastically. He would work to his satisfaction even if it was tiresome.

After two or three days of working very hard, he could do no more as he was exhausted. There was blood when he coughed due to his weariness. They called a doctor from the Communist territory on the other bank to see him. At that time, the Communist Headquarters was on the other bank of Kawlo River. After checking, they knew that he had tuberculosis. The doctor advised him to go to Rangoon General Hospital. He thought that this happened due to him a catching cold and drinking alcohol during his service at sea with the British Navy. He stopped drinking when he joined the revolution. When they X-rayed him, both his lungs were infected with many lesions. After he knew he had tuberculosis he noted that if he could live it was God's will for him to live. He decided to serve God if his disease was cured. He was sent to a special TB Hospital in Mawlamyine. He was cured after two years of treatment in the Mawlamyine Mission Hospital. He returned to his wife after being discharged from hospital in 1956.

At that time, his wife was working in Syriam. She was working as a teacher in St. George's Diocesan High School. They had their first son on 4 May 1957. He did not do any work but stayed at home helping to look after the child. As he decided he would serve God if his disease was cured, he attended Myanmar Institute of Theology, Insein in 1959. He would go and see his family in Syriam once a month during the time of attending Theological School.

They had a second son on 21 September 1960 while he was studying. He passed in March 1963 after studying four years at the Theological School. In 1964, he was appointed as a pastor in Nam Kham Dr. Gordon Seagrave Hospital. He delivered good news to the people in Northern Shan State while taking care of the parish. Due to his unremitting effort to look after the parish and preaching the good news of Christ, he was ordained as a Minister in 1973.

In April 1974, he went to Meiktila for a Baptist Convention and then to Taungoo. On the way to Taungoo, he suffered from stomach pain so he was sent to Pyinmana Hospital. He got better after three days in the hospital. The doctor gave him vitamin injections as he was weak. Within a few minutes after the injection, he had a fit and died. After he died, the doctor examined and found out that he had diabetes.

The vitamins he injected did not agree with diabetes so he got a shock and died immediately. The two nurses who worked in Pyinmana Hospital studied medicine in Nam Kham Hospital so they knew Saya very well.[216] They sent a telegram to his wife and children about his death. He was buried with a fitting funeral service.

## Saw Htoo Mar
*Saw Htoo Mar had joined the army in 1946:*

In 1949, when the Karen revolution started, he was at the battle of Insein. He served as a British soldier from 1946 – 1949.

The Karen lost to the Burmese at Insein and withdrew. He returned to Beik, Dawei after the battle. He returned to his parents and helped them. In 1952, he married Naw Shar Day, the youngest daughter of U Kar Lu. The Karen people from Dawei contacted the Karen revolution leaders and formed the Kawthoolei army. At that time, the Karens from the revolutionary party came and requested him to fight for a Karen independent state so he joined the revolution. It was Karen 6th Brigade in Beik and Dawei. The Brigade commander was Lieutenant Johnny Htoo.[217] He assigned Saw Htoo Mar as a Company Commander. He served loyally for the revolution and was promoted step by step to Battalion Commander of Beik, Dawei. He did not look for personal gain but for independence for the Karen people. He sacrificed himself for the revolution. While he was serving, he would go to enemy territory to

---

[216] 'Saya' is a term of respect for male elders and means 'teacher'.

[217] The rank is too low for that of a Brigade Commander.

organise and often faced difficulties not being able to eat for three or four days to one week while hiding but he would serve responsibly without being discouraged.

In 1972, during a battle he was shot and it was difficult to take out the bullet so he was taken to a hospital in Thailand. He was taken to Suangpung Hospital (Thailand) but it was too late and he died. His body was brought back to Burma and he was buried at Naw Phoe Thay. His wife and children neither saw his body nor could attend the funeral service. He had left his beloved family and the Karen revolution.

## Saw Baw Nay
*Saw Baw Nay had joined the army in 1946 and been promoted to sergeant:*

In 1948, the British gave Burma independence and gradually withdrew the army. After independence, there was conflict between Karens and Burmese and the Karen started their revolution. At that time, some Karen who served with the British Army and continued to serve with the Burma Army were Saw Baw Nay, Saw Kyarken, Thra Unapo, Thra Phoe Khin and Thra Sar Lu. As soon as they heard that Saw Ba U Gyi started to revolt against the Burmese, the five of them secretly met and decided to occupy the arsenal. They set a date and drew up the stages of a plan. At that time, Saw Baw Nay held the keys of the arsenal. As planned, they informed the Karen people from the villages of Maytar, Kawpor, Klerpu and Klawmawsoe School.

Saw Baw Nay took out lots of boxes of weapons from the arsenal as assigned and hid some at his house and some in barns.

Before the planned time, the five of them met and discussed again. At that meeting, Thra U Na Po raised the question who would they appoint as a leader if they won. Saw Baw Nay proposed to appoint Thra Sar Lu as a leader. Everybody agreed but Thra U Na Po did not say anything, but had a sad face.

The villagers from May Tar, Kawpor and Klerpu village came to Dawei to take the weapons before the planned day. There, Thra U Na Po told the villagers who were on their way up that the plan was cancelled (actually the plan was still active). There was misunderstanding among the people. The Burmese army noticed and they sent some trusted Karen soldiers to enquire about the Karens and learnt about the planned revolution. When the Burmese troops knew that Saw Baw Nay had hid the weapons, they issued orders to arrest him. One Burmese who was respected and loved him and was worried told him about the orders.

He called some trusted Karen youths and took the hidden weapons and ammunition and left Paycha region the same night. The Burmese troops went to Mawlamyine to arrest him. The Burmese troops arrested Saw Kor Htoo who looked like him and killed him thinking he was Saw Baw Nay. When he arrived at Paycha, he told the people that Saw Ba U Gyi had started the revolution against the Burmese and the Karens from Beik and Dawei drew up plans. But he was here because the original plan was cancelled. He explained that Karen people should not stay like this and need to prepare to confront the Burmese. He gathered healthy youths, gave them weapons and trained them. From that time, that village was prepared for any eventuality. The Burmese had the attitude of being a superior race and oppressed them. The Burmese troops came from one village to another and finally got to Paycha village. The Burmese troops came in by military trucks. The villagers shot the Burmese troops first as they had prior information and were prepared. A lot of Burmese soldiers died, and only two or three Burmese soldiers escaped as they did not stop the trucks.

Saw Baw Nay contacted the Karen leaders from Upper Myanmar. He was called to Tanintharyi River (Tenasserim River) and went to join KNU headquarters.

He served with Kawthoolei leaders at Hteemoepawar for three years and served back in his village Paycha and around the Palaw region. In 1956, he participated actively on the frontline. In 1974, the Burmese government started the Four Cuts campaign so it was difficult to operate so he returned to Mergui/Tavoy District Headquarters (Kaymarhtar). He served with the KNU [Karen National Union] for about five years and retired due to old age. After retirement, he lived with each of his children in their respective houses. He died of old age on 1 February 1992.

# Part Two

# Interviews by Raymond Brown

Saw Thu Po Mu, 2002

*Raymond was Sally McLean's son in law. He died in April 2002. The transcript was supplied by Sally who was with her son in law when the interviews took place.*

### Saw Thu Po Mu, age 95

*I live at Ma Ka Sa La camp near Mae Sariang, and I am 95 years old. I enlisted on the 3rd September 1930. My personnel no. was 42, and No.477 was the number of my gun. I was in the Salween District Armed police and worked at the British District Commission. The names of the people in charge there were Mr Ray who was no. 2 and Mr Fritz who was no. 1.*

**Interviewer**: "What were your duties?"

**Saw Thu Po Mu**: "I was a rifleman in the armed police. I had to look after the two horses of the district commissioner."

**Interviewer**: "Did you fight the Japanese?"

**Saw Thu Po Mu:** "When I had served for eleven years the Japanese attacked Burma. I fought the Japanese at Moulmein. The Japanese forces were very strong and we had to withdraw up the Salween river to Papun district and then to Taungoo. I worked with Major Seagrim. When he was in Papun district I met with Seagrim."

"The Burmese are rebelling against the British and I am helping to start a campaign to stop this. I will be needing a lot of soldiers from the Karen," is what he said.

I was serving at a border village when Seagrim sent a message for serving soldiers to meet with him. I was afraid because martial law had been declared by the Japanese and people were killed without trial. I was wondering what I had done wrong that Seagrim had called me. However I went and when I reached Papun my friend told me that tomorrow I would have to go for selection. At 7.00 in the morning he showed me the secret place where I was to meet with Seagrim. It was in the forest. When I met with him, he said, "you worked for the British people and we are going to ask you to help us. I am going to start something." But the Americans said that he was a mad man. He was a tall, thin man. He was dressed in a simple vest and short pants.

> He said, "Now I am going to start something. The Burmese have rebelled, so I am going to start something to repress this. I want you to help me with recruiting Karen soldiers."
>
> Beginning that day I was made a recruiting officer with one star.
>
> Seagrim said, "You are the recruiting officer for me. I am going to start something, but the Americans say that I am a madman."
> This happened in 1941. He said that the British would withdraw to India and in 1943 they would come back and then we will start something. He added "that if they were not able to come back in '43 then by '45 they would definitely come back."
>
> **Interviewer**: "Do you still have your medals?"
>
> **Saw Thu Po Mu:** "They were all destroyed by the Japanese. I received medals and a gold certificate, but they were all destroyed. I had to fight with [against?] the BIA [Burmese Independence Army] and they all got lost."
>
> **Interviewer**: "Do you remember the British giving you a shield to say that they will not forget you?"
>
> **Saw Thu Po Mu:** "I remember Major Seagrim saying, Now I am fighting together with you, I won't be going back to England. After the war, I will stay and work in order that the Karen will have a country of their own. That is what Seagrim told me."

I did not receive a shield because I was not in a leadership position.

**Interviewer**: "How do you feel about the British not keeping their promise?"

**Saw Thu Po Mu**: "They said, you will get your freedom after the war." It was not the fault of the British but of the Burmese. We should be their brothers but they acted like the British towards us.

**Interviewer:** "Would you like the British to come back and help you?"

**Saw Thu Po Mu**: "I am still hoping. Assessing our situation I would say that, we have been struggling for self determination for 50 years. We still have not achieved that. We are partly to blame because we are not an efficient people. We hope that the British will come to help us to achieve self determination."

I would like to add a little. At that time the Burmese knew that they would not be given independence from Britain without the support of the ethnic nationalities. So they organised meetings between themselves and the ethnic nationalities and openly stated that they were all brothers and sisters and that all national wealth would be shared equally. They got independence on that basis and when they asked for independence from the British they promised that all ethnic people would have equality in Burma. So independence was achieved on 4$^{th}$ January 1948 but then the Burmese never considered giving ethnic people their own state.

Seagrim had said that he would be happy to die for the Karen, but the Burmese had a heart like seven fish hooks. I myself was very badly affected by what the Burmese did to the Karen after the British withdrew [in 1942]. We were considered the enemy and Karen wives and children left behind by soldiers who went with the British to fight in India were slaughtered by the Burmese Independence Army while they were absent fighting.

**Interviewer**: "Did the Karen teach the British how to use herbs from the jungle as medicine?"

**Saw Thu Po Mu:** "Yes we did show them. The only medicine against malaria was tree bark. It was bitter and contained natural quinine.

There was not much interest, as they were more interested in fighting at that time. When the British parachuted in, some were injured and were treated by Karen with herbal medicines. Two Karen medical men were quite efficient. They treated a British officer with a broken back and cured him."

**Interviewer**: "Have the British given you any money or help since the war?"

**Saw Thu Po Mu:** "I got back pay of 1400 rupees. After that I got six month pay from the Burmese government of 60 rupees a month. Then I found that the Burmese were not sincere and retired from the military."

**Interviewer**: "Did you get a pension?"

**Saw Thu Po Mu:** "No. In the last two years I have received first 4,000 Baht [around £63.00] and then the next year 3,200 Baht [around £51.00] from the British Commonwealth Ex Services League. That is all I have received. Can you tell me if there will be any more support in the future?"

**Interviewer**: "Thank you so much, your testimony will be very valuable and I hope that we will be able to get more help for you."

*Projects to support refugees from Burma gave Saw Thu Po Mu 3,000 Baht. He stood up and sang, "Stand up, stand up for Jesus, you soldiers of the Cross" in Karen.*

## Saw Mahler, age 80

*From the content of this interview, it is clear that Saw 'Mahler' here is the same 'Saw Maw Ler' above who was interviewed in 2001. It is interesting to have three interviews with the same soldier:*

Born 11 November 1921. Joined the Burma Army in 1941.

**Saw Mahler:** "My father said to me at the start of the war, "you are the eldest son, now our country is at war, as our oldest son you must defend our country.""

**Interviewer**: "Did you see much action?"

**Saw Mahler**: "So much fighting. As our Bible says, the valley of death", I ought to have died long ago. I was shot at by the Japanese.

"I fought with the British as well as the American army. I was sent to the American headquarters as liaison between the British and Americans to pass information about Japanese movements."

**Interviewer**: V Force?

**Saw Mahler**: V Force, yes. At that time I was shot down at [?]
The Chinese 92nd division came into Burma at that time to join the Americans, along with a column who fought with the "Marauders."[218]

**Interviewer**: "The Marauders?"

**Saw Mahler**: "Then we were given rest. As for the Kachin, they did not need me. I was to work with Major Coffey. Intelligence. Two majors, Major Bridge, and Major Leach. In pre war days [Leach was] a civil officer who spoke Kachin."[219]

**Interviewer**: "Can you describe the job that you did?"

**Saw Mahler:** "The job was to find out. We asked them to withdraw from the Lashio side. Population very thin. If you need some rice, no one can give. Came down from the Lashio side. That mission came down from Oh Dow. Major Seagrim was looking for me for wireless operation, but it was more important than what I was doing with V force."[220] Spearhead for main body for troops. Their

---

[218] 5307th Composite Unit, was unofficially called 'Merrill's Marauders' after its commander, Frank Merrill. It was an irregular American unit, also known as *Galahad*, and took part in the battle for Myitkyina in May 1944.

[219] Major Coffey was in charge of intelligence in the northern part of Burma; Major Bridge was in charge of the Kachin Levies; Captain Edmund Leach was an anthropologist who had worked in Kachin villages before the war.

[220] Major Seagrim surrendered to the Japanese in March 1944, so there appears to be an error with chronology here.

officer was Captain Wright [and] Colonel Stanley.

**Interviewer**: Can you remember a story that you would tell to your children?

**Saw Mahler:** From my childhood to my school days and through army service. Until Burma was given independence. When it was given independence then the Karen revolution started.

**Interviewer**: Do you remember fighting with the Americans?

**Saw Mahler:** The fighting was very very dangerous. The Japanese were a kind of suicide soldiers, they never retreated. I was never in the front line, but a little behind.

**Interviewer**: Thank God. Did you ever capture any Japanese?

**Saw Mahler:** No, when I worked with Major Coffey I tried to capture Japanese alive to get information. If you captured a Japanese alive you were given you 1,000 Kyats.

**Interviewer**: Did you ever get one?

**Saw Mahler:** "They got two and asked to send for an interpreter."

**Interviewer**: "Did you get any information? Did they commit hari kari?"

**Saw Mahler:** "No, when the Kachin got them, they tied their hands together behind their back, so they did not do it. We gave them rice, and chicken curry and pork curry."

When they were interrogated the officer said to them, "please tell me from what place you come from. Where is your company headquarters? We are not asking for much information."

They replied, "I came to Burma not to tell you where my company headquarters are, I came to Burma to fight you." The officer said, "Alright take him back. Fetch the other one." He tells the same story. "I came to Burma to fight you.etc." We tried, but we got nothing."

**Interviewer**: "If the Japanese had captured you, would they have done the same thing?"

**Saw Mahler:** "The Japanese would have cut our throats."

**Interviewer** The Karen fought very hard with the British. For almost four years?"

**Saw Mahler:** "Not for four years, but for almost twelve. Our leaders said, "If we fight like this the battle will never end.""

**Interviewer**: "Do you feel like you have fought with the British for so long and that they have deserted your country? Do you think that they should help you to get independence?"

**Saw Mahler:** "Now the Karen people have no home. But the Burmese would say, "This is our internal affairs.""

# Interviews at Mae La Camp, 18 January 2009

### Sein Aye, age 95

**Interviewer:** How long did you serve with the British Army?

**Sein Aye:** Three years.

**Interviewer:** Where were you?

**Sein Aye:** Papun District, Karen State, Takaw.

**Interviewer:** What kind of fighting were you doing? Counter insurgency? Hit and run?

**Sein Aye:** The first time, we were fighting against the Japanese at Oo Long for three days and three nights.

**Interviewer:** You were a guerrilla army essentially?

**Sein Aye:** Yes, hide and then attack.

**Interviewer:** How many were there in your group of fighters?

**Sein Aye:** Eight

**Interviewer:** Did you have any British soldiers with you?

**Sein Aye:** At that time we fought with the British. One of the officers died, he was shot. I was carrying the officer's body, and they shot me in the back.

**Interviewer:** When you were fighting, were you in the jungle? Where were you living?

**Sein Aye:** We were hiding in the jungle.

**Interviewer:** Did you ever see your family in the three years you were fighting?

**Sein Aye:** We met secretly.

**Interviewer:** The British Officer who died, do you remember his name?

**Sein Aye:** Captain Bonny.[221]

**Interviewer:** Did the officers make promises to you about Karen Independence?[222]

**Sein Aye:** They said, "Don't worry, we will help you."

**Interviewer:** Were you told why you were fighting? Why did you decide to fight the Japanese?

**Sein Aye:** When the Japanese came to Burma, they attacked the Karen. Therefore we took up arms against the Japanese. We captured a Japanese and took care of him for two years, and he lived in the same village and married a Karen.

**Interviewer:** What was the hardest thing; food, sleeping in the jungle?

**Sein Aye:** It was the Japanese stealing our harvest.

**Interviewer:** But what was the hardest thing?

---

[221] There is no 'Bonny' listed on the Commonwealth War Graves Commision. A 'Bonnie' is listed, but was a West African Private. CWGC [online], 'Find War Dead' https://www.cwgc.org/find/find-war-dead/results?lastName=bonny&country=Myanmar&war=2

[222] There has been lots of discussion over the years since the Second World War which has focused on whether or not the British made promises to the Karen that in return for their services in the war, they would be given independence. Certainly some British officers who served have said promises were made, but I have been unable to find any archival evidence to support the claims. **See** Richard Duckett, *The Special Operations Executive in Burma, 1941-1945* (IB Tauris: London, 2017), pp.183-85.

**Sein Aye:** One of the hardships was not having enough food. Also it was not being able to see older relatives.

**Interviewer:** When there was no food while you were living in the jungle, what did you eat?

**Sein Aye:** We ate fruit and nuts in the jungle, not very much.

**Interviewer:** When you were carrying the British soldier, what happened to him?

**Sein Aye:** My friends were far away from me, but I went and asked them to help me.

**Interviewer:** What kind of rifle did you have?

**Sein Aye:** Old fashioned, hand made rifle.

**Interviewer:** It's always raining in the jungle, how did you keep your ammunition dry?

**Sein Aye:** Carried it in a waterproof cover.

**Interviewer:** Did you receive a pension after the war?

**Sein Aye:** We got nothing from U Nu's government.[223] We got small payments from a charity. These payments dried up after three years. They stopped two years ago. I don't know why. It was 4,000TB [Thai Bhat] a year (note this was from when the Burma Forces Welfare Association who discontinued grants to those in the refugee camps saying they were well enough off and didn't need them).

**Interviewer:** How do you feel about that?

**Sein Aye:** I don't know.

**Interviewer:** What do you think about life in the camp?

---

[223] After the assassination of Aung San in July 1947 U Nu emerged as the first leader of independent Burma from 4 January 1948.

**Sein Aye:** I like it here. I'd like a car.

**Interviewer:** Before you started fighting, what were you doing?

**Sein Aye:** I was a farmer.

**Interviewer:** How did you get your military training?

**Sein Aye:** My grandmother wanted me to stay on at school, but when the Japanese came and persecuted the villagers, I decided to follow the British Army. I learnt by just watching the soldiers.

**Interviewer:** When you spoke to a British soldier, did you always have to salute?

Maung Sein

**Sein Aye:** Yes. The British said that if a Karen soldier saw a British Officer, they should salute.

**Interviewer:** What do you feel about the British now?

**Sein Aye:** I don't feel anything.

## Maung Sein, aged 92

**Interviewer:** How long did you fight the Japanese with the British?

**Maung Sein:** Three years in the jungle.

**Interviewer:** What was the most difficult at that time?

**Maung Sein:** Being away from my family, my mother and my sister.

**Interviewer:** What did you do before you were a soldier?

**Maung Sein:** I was a farmer.

**Interviewer:** And how did you know how to be a fighter?

**Maung Sein:** The British taught us, I had six months training.

**Interviewer:** When the fighting was happening, were there promises made?

**Maung Sein:** Yes, they promised that when there was independence the country would be split between the Karen and Aung San.

**Interviewer:** How do you feel about what happened?

**Maung Sein** I am very sad about that, but can do nothing.

**Interviewer:** When did you come here?

**Maung Sein:** In 1990.

**Interviewer:** Do you like living here?

**Maung Sein:** Yes because food is provided.

**Interviewer:** You and your fellow old soldiers have been receiving a small grant – do you still get it?

**Maung Sein:** It has stopped for the last two years.

**Interviewer:** What difference does that make? What hardships has that caused you?

**Maung Sein:** Everything here is sufficient, but we have no tea or coffee, we are sometimes hungry.

**Interviewer:** How do you feel about the British stopping your grant and not supporting you?

**Maung Sein:** I am angry about that, because they promised to help. Now the Karen are nothing.

**Interviewer:** How do you feel about your officers?

Saw Hla Tin

**Maung Sein:** I am angry and we haven't forgotten.

**Interviewer:** Have you heard of the Gurkas from Nepal?[224]

**Maung Sein:** No [NB people in the camps have no access to the internet, television or newspapers].

### Saw Hla Tin, aged 83

*Interviewers note: I understand this man fought with the Spider Group (SOE/Force 136):*[225]

**Saw Hla Tin:** I joined up when the Japanese came to fight with the Karen. It was the year 1303 on the Burmese calendar.

**Interviewer:** Who was Major Seagrim?

**Saw Hla Tin:** He was a great man. He first fought in Papun.[226]

**Interviewer:** Did you know Major Seagrim?

**Saw Hla Tin:** Yes

**Interviewer:** Who was your commanding officer?

**Saw Hla Tin:** Captain William[s].[227] When the Japanese came to

---

[224] Presumably asked because in 2008-09, British actress Joanna Lumley led a well-publicised and successful campaign to enable Gurkha veterans and their families to settle in Britain.

[225] *Armband illustrated above left* With thanks to David Mattey, proprietor of Arundel Antiques & Militaria, for allowing me to photograph Major Milner's effects, July 2021.

[226] Captain Seagrim arrived in Papun to organise Karen guerrillas at the end of January 1942.

[227] Possibly Captain John Philip Williams, who parachuted into Burma in 1945. *See* 'The Men of SOE Burma' [online], https://soeinburma.wordpress.com/the-men-of-soe-burma/

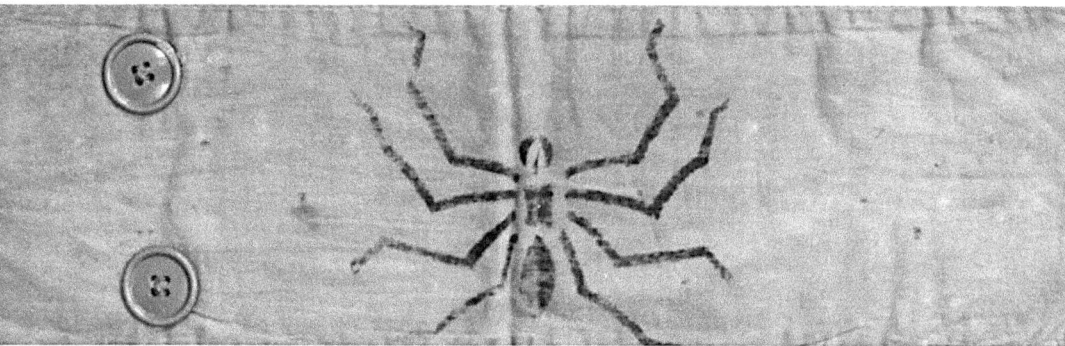

Armband worn by Karen levies who fought with Force 136, hence the occasional reference to 'Spider Group'. Photograph taken from the Major Milner collection.

Burma all the British soldiers moved to India. They left Major Seagrim. The soldiers were scattered. After two years the British soldiers came back to Burma. I was with Saw Ba U. Two years later the Japanese surrendered. The British came back for two years.

**Interviewer:** What was your job? What did you do?

**Saw Hla Tin:** I was a Sergeant – Bren gun.

**Interviewer:** How many years did you fight against the Japanese?

**Saw Hla Tin:** More than two years.

**Interviewer:** How do you feel about the British?

**Saw Hla Tin:** They promised to help me. But we can do nothing.

**Interviewer:** What is the situation with the money? Has your money been stopped? How do you feel, you fought with the British, now you don't get a pension?

**Saw Hla Tin:** I expected to get a pension.

**Interviewer:** How do you feel?

**Saw Hla Tin:** Very sad about that, because at that time, I worked

hard for that and now I have nothing.
**Interviewer:** Are you angry with the British?
**Saw Hla Tin:** If I get some support, I won't be angry.

**Interviewer:** Where did you meet Seagrim?
**Saw Hla Tin:** Two years later, I met him.
**Interviewer:** What did Seagrim say to you?

**Saw Hla Tin:** We believed him. After, he was captured by the Japanese.

**Interviewer:** You fought with the Spider group. What did they do?

**Saw Hla Tin:** I was in the camp, waiting for the Japanese, and then shooting at them.[228]

**Interviewer:** What do you think of the Japanese now?

**Saw Hla Tin:** They were ruling the country, not the Karen.

**Interviewer:** How long have you been here?

**Saw Hla Tin:** I have been in Mae La since 2000. I was in Ka Mow Mow before. My family is here, my wife is alive, I have two sons and two daughters. Two daughters have gone to the US, my sons are here. I want to stay.

**Interviewer:** How do you feel that you can't see your daughters?

**Saw Hla Tin:** I can get contact with them on the phone. I am not sad, I am pleased for them.

**Interviewer:** How often do you phone?

**Saw Hla Tin:** Twice a week, or once a week. They are in Texas.

---

[228] Presumably a 'static' levy then, as opposed to a 'mobile' levy. Static levies were trained and armed, with the expectation that they would stay in their village to protect it from any threats. Mobile levies were used on patrols and active guerrilla warfare. Also referred to as 'Home Guard' in some reports, *see* for example, TNA, HS 1/10, 'REPORT BY CAPT. C.H. SELL', 11 September 1945.

## Saw Percy, aged 81

**Saw Percy:** I was together with Maung Sein in the war.[229]

**Interviewer:** How much training did you have?

**Saw Percy:** Six months. I took care of the food and the camp.

**Interviewer:** Did you receive a pension?

**Saw Percy:** I never heard about that. I was working with the British Army. The Japanese came and killed and persecuted the villagers. That is why I joined the British army under Major Hoare. The British left, two years later the British came back.

Saw Percy

**Interviewer:** Did you get any money from the British?

**Saw Percy:** Since 2000 and then it stopped.

**Interviewer:** How do you feel now that you get no money?

**Saw Percy:** I don't care, at least I once got it.

**Interviewer:** Do you have any family?

**Saw Percy:** I have a wife and children. Three sons and three daughters. I have been here for 20 years.

**Interviewer:** Can you go outside?

**Saw Percy:** Never been outside in 20 years.

**Interviewer:** When you were a young man, you could travel where you wanted. How does that make you feel now?

---

[229] Maung Sein interviewed above.

Major Frederick Milner with his Karen guerrillas on victory parade in August 1945. Note the six Bren guns. Maybe Saw Dway Maung is in this photo. Photo courtesy of Simon Leney, son of Sergeant Roger Leney.

> **Saw Percy:** Here I can get food.
>
> **Interviewer:** What do you want the future to be like?
>
> **Saw Percy:** Peace in Karen State and in Burma.
>
> **Interviewer:** Do you hope to return to Karen State?
>
> **Saw Percy:** If there is peace or change in Burma, yes. But there is nothing that I can do about that from here.

### Saw Dway Maung, aged 87
*Very tall and strong looking still. Arrived late with a baseball cap on:*

> **Interviewer:** How long did you fight with the British?
>
> **Saw Dway Maung:** I joined in '41
>
> **Interviewer:** What unit were you fighting with?

**Saw Dway Maung:** Under Shwe Chen, near Mawchi.

**Interviewer:** Who was your officer?

**Saw Dway Maung:** Captain Brown and Major Milner.[230]

**Interviewer:** What were you doing?

**Saw Dway Maung:** Bren Platoons.

**Interviewer:** Were the Japanese good soldiers? (Saw Percy laughs)

**Saw Dway Maung:** Not very good. But Aung San called the Japanese to come to Burma.[231]

**Interviewer:** Did Britain make any promises?[232]

**Saw Dway Maung:** They promised the Karen that upper Burma would be for the Burmese, and the lowlands for the Karen. After peace there was no land for the Karen. Until now the Karen are fighting. If all the Karen blood that has been spilt were put together if would be like a stream and all the bones would be like a mountain. We were made promises by the British.

**Interviewer:** How does that make you feel?

[voices no answer]
**Interviewer:** When did you come to the camp?

---

[230] Major Frederick Milner was in charge of a Force 136 group code-named Mongoose White, from March 1945. This was part of Operation *Character*. There was no Captain Brown on this operation, but there was a Captain Bourne who served with Milner.

[231] Aung San led the Burma Independence Army, and had been trained by the Japanese. He marched into Burma from Thailand with the Japanese Army in 1942.

[232] The subject of 'promises' has been a point of contention for many years. What promises were made and at what level is difficult to discern, but the feeling of betrayal is one that has been voiced by both British personnel who served in Burma and Karen veterans since the war. *See* Duckett, *The Special Operations Executive in Burma,* pp.183-5.

**Saw Dway Maung:** Twelve years ago.

**Interviewer:** Why did you come?

**Saw Dway Maung:** The Burmese soldiers were persecuting the Karen. The Burmese soldiers tried to kill me because I fought with the British. The Burmese soldiers were specifically looking for soldiers who fought with the British. Also they looked for the KNLA soldiers [Karen National Liberation Army].
After the war I served with the police. In 1948 they took down the British flag and hoisted up the Burmese flag.

**Interviewer:** What happened to you after the British left?

**Saw Dway Maung:** I ran a small shop.

**Interviewer:** Do you think your grant has been stopped?

**Saw Dway Maung:** I don't know. I got a pension from the British from 2000 to 2008. I would like to say that after the war Captain Brown was in a Karen village but he had to go back to the UK and we had to say farewell to him. We wrote a song about it. The words say, "Why did you leave us? You said you would never leave us. How can we live without you?"

# Ban Surin Camp, November 2012

*Here are my reports on the three old soldiers we met.*

## Saw Harcher

Now 88 and deaf (Myeh Htoo had to write my questions down for him), Saw Harcher comes from Lerlewte, near Mawchi. In 1942-43, when the Japanese came, he was around fifteen years old. He signed up to become a rifleman in the Karen levies, and his commanding officer was Captain Peacock.[233]

Saw Harcher says he wanted to join up because things were "terrible" when the Japanese moved into the area, and some men fled to the jungle. The Japanese tortured and killed people, and some didn't have food to eat, "so when the British soldiers came, everyone wanted to help the British fight the Japanese". One of his uncles was tortured by the Japanese, who chained him up, lit fires in front of him and behind him, and beat him with a stick.

After the British came, things got a little better because some British soldiers supported them with food. Saw Harcher says he shot many Japanese soldiers, and once caught one alive and handed him over to a British soldier. The Briton was very happy, he said, and gave his new prisoner "a good meal of curry".

Saw Harcher says he worked mainly with younger British officers but he met Seagrim once, at Thawthikho Mountain, when supplies were parachuted in.

After the war, he joined "the revolution against the Burmese government", fighting with the Karenni National People's Party. On May 10, 1950, he was shot in the side, and after that he became a township leader in the Mawchi area. He was married twice and has six children.

He has been in the camp for fifteen years. His injury was very painful and his family told him that if he came to the camp he could get some 'ATX medicine', which helped with the pain. He asked if I could get some for him and I said I'd do what I could, but I'm really not sure what kind of medicine he was talking about.

"If I was strong I would fight for independence, but now I am very

---

[233] Lt.Col. Edgar Peacock arrived in the Karen Hills on 24 February 1945. He was in charge of the Otter area of Operation Character.

old I cannot do anything," Saw Harcher said to laughter from those in the room.

He doesn't want to go back to Burma until the Karenni people get independence, then he would go back. When I asked what he thought of the British, he said he would like to thank them for their support and he wishes them good luck.

## Saw Thart'gay

Saw Thart'gay, who has lived in the camp for twenty years, is 88 and blind. He was born in 1924 and comes from Sholo, near Mawchi. He has betel-stained teeth and is sharp, talkative and very likeable.

In 1936, the British came to make a road in his area, and in 1942 the Japanese arrived. In 1943-44 they opened a mine in Mawchi, so he went to work there for two or three months.[234] Then in 1945 he heard that the British soldiers had come again to Mount Thawthikho, so he volunteered and got two weeks' training, and was then sent out in the field. Saw Thart'gay says he never saw Seagrim but carried food for him to Geygouper village, where he was hiding. (This was the Anglicised spelling given to me by Myeh Htoo, though I can't find any reference to it).

The volunteers called themselves the Thawthikho soldiers, he says, after the nearby range of hills. He only fought for a short time before the Japanese left Burma, but in that six months he saw a lot of fighting - "so please help me see again", he joked.

He served under two officers – Montague, an Englishman, and Captain Maung Twesay, a Karen. I think Saw Thart'gay must have been referring to General Sir Montagu Stopford, later head of South East Asia Command, but I need to do more research to confirm this.[235]

Montagu was quite old, and "because he was English he was very tall and big – like you", Saw Thart'gay told me. Montagu gave Saw Thart'gay a prize on two occasions. Once, he asked him to deliver a letter to Thawthikho. It was usually an overnight journey, but Saw Thart'gay got there and back the same day, so Montagu gave him 10 Rupees as a

---

[234] The Mawchi mines produce wolfram and tin. They were put out of use as part of the British denial programme as they withdrew in 1942.

[235] It is more likely that Saw Thart'gay is referring to Captain John Cook Montague, who was in charge of the Green area of Otter, Operation Character. See 'The Men of SOE Burma' [online], https://soeinburma.wordpress.com/the-men-of-soe-burma/ Allowing for an incorrect spelling, there is no record of anyone close to the name of Maung Twesay in the records for Otter team.

reward. Another time, Montagu gave him 10 Rupees and a glass of whiskey for coming first in a shooting competition.

Once, the troops were fighting the Japanese in the hills and Saw Thart'gay didn't notice that all his comrades had retreated, leaving him the only one in his position. He shot six magazines from his Bren gun, until the bullets ran out, and then went back. Montagu congratulated him and carried his Bren gun, while he carried Montagu's lighter gun.

After the war, he said, Montagu wanted to take him to England, though he doesn't know why. He didn't go because he had a girlfriend in the village and was "deeply in love".

He fought in the Karenni revolution for two years, then got married and worked as a pastor's assistant. He had six children, but only two survive.

When he was a British soldier, Saw Thart'gay said, the Karen and Karenni people helped the British. Now the revolution has been going on for 64 years, and many people have come to the refugee camps. He wants the British government "to help them like they did before".

"Please go to tell your friends from the British government not to help the Burmese government. Please come to help the Karen people, we are very poor," he said, adding that he would like to ask British soldiers who fought in the war to support them. "Now I cannot do anything, just sitting in the camp."

He would like to go back to Burma every day but doesn't dare because "just here is a tiger" he said to laughter, referring to the Burmese government.

The next day, Saw Thart'gay came to the Bible School again and said he had something to show me. He and Myeh Htoo took me to a hut, and showed me a brass plaque mounted on a piece of wood, which had been presented by the British authorities after the war. Above it, inscribed in the wood, are the words 'Heaven's light our guide' and below, 'At the going down of the sun and in the morning, we will remember them.'

The plaque reads:
**'TO THE HONOUR AND GLORY OF THE KARENS OF THE OTTER AREA WHO LAID DOWN THEIR LIVES FOR KING AND COUNTRY IN THE FIGHT AGAINST TYRANNY AND AGGRESSION.'**

I was told that the plaque had been presented to Maung Hla Say, a Mawchi local government official, who in turn left it to General Aung Than Lay, who fought with the British and later became a leader of the Karenni people's armed movement, the KNPP. He died in the camp two years ago. His wife and daughter now keep it in their hut, and I was told that is only shown to British visitors – of whom they naturally see very few.

Saw Thart'gay touchingly told me that it showed the British people "are thinking about the Karen people". If the British government asked, he said, they could show the plaque to prove that they worked with the British before. They could also show it to younger Karen people, to explain how they had helped the British. "With this, you can be sure you are really with Karen people," he said.

The general's widow, Naw Ko Ree, 70, said the plaque was "very valuable for Karen people, so we have to take care of it from generation to generation".

## Saw Ba Kyaw

Saw Ba Kyaw, 84, is bent over almost double when he walks, but still gave me a proud military salute when we met.

He says he fought with the British because he was very young and wanted to be a soldier, and because the Japanese had caused problems for people in the area. He was only thirteen when he first started taking care of the stores for the guerilla forces, and after doing this for a couple of months he was chosen to act as a "postman", carrying messages between different guerilla units.[236]

He did this for six months, until the war finished. At that time, he was very small and couldn't carry a rifle so he was given a Sten gun and told to shoot if necessary. "When I was young, I wasn't afraid of anything," he said.

---

[236] It seems the British were not overly worried about recruiting children. In photos of the Mongoose area, a child named 'Maurice' is described as fifteen years old. *See A Most Irregular War: The Diaries of Major Trofimov*, (Devonshire Press: Devon, 2023); *see* also TNA, HS 7/107.

# HEAVEN'S LIGHT OUR GUIDE
## 1941 — 1945

To the honour and glory of the Karens of the Otter area who laid down their lives for King and Country in the fight against tyranny and aggression

Photo of the plaque, courtesy of Sally Mclean MBE, Help for Forgotten Allies.

There were two postmen at first, but one didn't work hard so they got rid of him, leaving Ba Kyaw the only one. But sometimes he didn't know the route to the villages, he said. Once, making his way back through the jungle at night, in heavy rain, he suddenly realised that he was surrounded by Japanese troops. In his bag he had a letter, and a British officer had told him: "If you die, it doesn't matter, but keep the letter safe."

So when he saw the Japanese, he threw the letter away and then hid under a tree until 5am. But as he made off he saw four Japanese soldiers nearby, so he shot them, emptying the magazine of his Sten gun. He heard later that three of them had died, and one survived. Five days later, he went back to the same place, found the letter he had thrown away and delivered it to Thawthikho.

Another time, the Japanese shot at him as he crossed a river. The bullet missed but he fell in the river and pretended to be dead, then ran away when no one came. And on another occasion, he "saw the leaves moving towards him" so he fired one magazine, and the next morning they found one dead Japanese soldier. All of this must have been very frightening for a boy of thirteen or fourteen!

Ba Kyaw served under Captain Butler, a Karen officer, and Captain Peacock.[237] Once, the Japanese shot Peacock, injuring his leg, and there was no one around to help him. Ba Kyaw went to help but he was very small and couldn't lift Peacock, saying the officer's leg alone was "as big as his body". So he went back and got a friend, and together they returned to help Peacock.

Ba Kyaw says he had heard about Seagrim, but never met him. After the war, he became a farmer in his village and served as a soldier with the Karenni revolutionary group for seven years. The Burmese soldiers shot at him twice while he was working in the rice fields. "Their hearts are not true," he said.

At 25, he married and had two kids. He came to the camp ten years ago. When I asked why, he said: "God chose me to come here." He is happy in the camp, and doesn't want to go back to Burma. He now lives alone in a wooden hut on stilts, with mats on the floor.

When I asked him what he thought of the British, he said they had good government. He would like the British to come and help the Burmese have good government, and to help the Karenni people.

---

[237] The Karen officer was Major Saw Butler, who served as liaison officer.

'Maurice', apparently aged 15, with Force 136's Operation Character, Mongoose area.

# VJ Day Interviews, 2015 by Mark Fenn[238]

**Tha Din, aged 91** (interviewed at Naw Jercy's house)
He says he served under Major Seagrim before the Japanese came and got him, then he ran away and joined Major Wilson.[239]

Seagrim came to his village and Tha Din decided to join him. At the time all his friends, the teenage boys, all joined as they wanted to be soldiers. They saw the guns that had been dropped by British planes and they wanted to fire them. He was 20 years old at the time.

"We always trusted them [the British]," he said. He got a gun and was "very happy to fight the Japanese".

He saw some very serious fighting, and his unit captured eight Japanese who surrendered. They ambushed the Japs and took them back to the village.

"Major Wilson gave the Japanese better food than me!" he said. "I only got one tin of milk but the Japanese got two tins."

He spent one year with Seagrim, and after Seagrim died the Japanese put him and three colleagues in jail in Kyautkyi.

He fought with Seagrim three or four times around Papun, and served as his bodyguard. "I loved him," he said of Seagrim.

Did he kill any Japanese? Yes, he laughs – around ten.

Why did he love Seagrim? "Because Seagrim came to our country. I loved him because Seagrim loved the Karen. He sometimes wore Karen clothes."[240]

He fought around Sosiko (Totiko?), which would have been in Lt-Col's Peacock's area.[241]

---

[238] Mark Fenn was a British journalist working out of Thailand until 2016, when he died suddenly at the age of 38. He worked with Sally Mclean and H4FA, who kindly provided these interview transcripts for this book.

[239] Major Seagrim gave himself up in early March 1944. The Character teams were dropped into the Karen Hills from February 1945. Major Roy Wilson was dropped to the Hyena team on 14 May 1945. Captain Frederick Wilson parachuted into Burma on 28 March 1945, as part of the Walrus team.

[240] When Seagrim surrendered, he was wearing a Karen longyi with an army shirt. A longyi is probably easiest described as a Burmese style of sarong.

[241] 'Sossisso' was where Otter set up their headquarters. It is above 7000 feet, and looks

After Seagrim was arrested, he ran away and joined Peacock in Operation Character, and then joined the American 101 battalion of the Office of Strategic Services (forerunner of the CIA).

In one battle, he took a bullet through his lower right arm. Major Wilson gave him 1,800 rupees after he was injured.

He remembers Lt-Col Peacock, saying "he was very kind to us", and mentioning the food rations he gave them.

After the war he became a police officer for a while, and then joined the Karen revolution and served time in jail. After his release he became a policeman again. He is a Christian, from Taungoo.

### Saw Ba Aye

Claims to have been born in Rangoon in 1909, and to be 106 years old. Also known as Saw Sa Paw.

He said he was President Thein Sein's teacher. He has traditional tattoos on his legs, head and arms to protect him and give him courage. He claims to be a wizard (perhaps shaman is a better word), who can cast spells, heal snake bites etc.

He joined the Burma Frontier Force [(BFF)] in 1936, and was given the regimental number 1759. After military training he became an instructor himself, and taught new recruits.

He was serving in the BFF when the Japanese invaded. They came three ways, and the middle way was through Kyautme [Kyaukme?] in Shan state. He spent ten days fighting the Japanese there, and was then sent back to Prome by train. At Prome, he spent another ten days fighting the Japanese, and then moved elsewhere. Each of these three battles lasted for ten days, he said.

A Colonel Alco? (possibly Alcock or Harcourt) then took him to Bombay by boat. He spent two years in Bombay and one year in Hyderabad, serving as the bodyguard of Colonel Alco.

After that, he was parachuted into Pegu division along with some African soldiers, in 1945, but the Japanese had already surrendered so he helped round them up.

He was a servant/bodyguard/batman to Colonel Alcock. He also remembers a Mr Ray, who was district superintendent of police.[242]

---

down on the Mawchi area.

[242] Probably Betram Langford Denis Rae, who was a policeman before and after the war. In 1945, he was District Superintendent of Police at Insein. *See* Claire Jordan's family research [online], http://members.madasafish.com/~cj_whitehound/family/Bertram_Langford_Denis_Rae_b1903.htm

He then sang Onward Christian Soldiers, partly in English and partly in Karen.

He loves English people "more than his parents", he says. "How can I love the Japanese? They slapped people's faces."

"God bless you."

### Tancy McDonald, aged 92[243]

Tancy was born in Mergui in 1923. His grandfather was an Irish artificer (a mechanic) who came over with a British army artillery unit during the Second Anglo-Burmese War in the 1850s.

His name was Michael McDonald and he was an Anglican, baptised in India, so Tancy thinks he was probably from what is now Northern Ireland. He married an Anglo-Burmese woman called Gladys Wells.

Tancy's father was Patrick Ernest McDonald, and his mother was Sarah-Jane Da Silva. Her parents were Mary Lee and George Da Silva, a Eurasian from Goa, then a Portuguese colony in India.

Patrick was a big boxing fan, and named his son after the Scottish boxer Tancy Lee, who was popular in the years just before he was born.

"I've had a lot of trouble with this name, people spelling it differently," Tancy said. "One friend of mine even called me Nancy!" But it's usually the adults who get it wrong, while children usually get it right, he said.

At first the family lived on King Island in the Mergui Archipelago, and then moved to an island called Kalatyun, where his parents owned a 30-acre rubber plantation and where Tancy grew up.[244]

He remembers his childhood in Mergui as a very happy time. It was lovely, with clear streams flowing into the river, he said. His father used to go shooting wild boar and green pigeons, as well as crocodiles "because

---

[243] Tancy McDonald featured in an article in an appeal for Help For Forgotten Allies: Philip Sherwell, 'Plea for the forgotten Burmese war heroes who secured British victory', *The Telegraph,* 26 October 2015 [online], http://www.h4fa.org.uk/images/documents/press_articles/telegraph_26-10-2015/Plea-for-the-forgotten-Burmese-war-heroes-who-secured-British-victory.html

[244] The Mergui Archipelago consists of over 800 islands, but finding one called 'Kalatyun' has proved elusive. Kanmaw Kyun Island, whose economy is almost entirely based on the rubber trade, was also known as Ketthayin Island during colonial times, so could be the island under discussion. For more on the rubber industry, *see* Voon Phin Keong, 'The Rubber Industry of Burma, 1876-1964', *Journal of Southeast Asian Studies,* 4,2 (September 1973), pp.216 – 28.

at that time there were lots of crocodiles on the island".

He remembers playing cricket, football, hockey and swimming, and going to the cinema occasionally. At his junior school they also staged concerts, though he didn't like to dance.

Growing up, "we were more British", he said, enjoying tea and cake and observing British traditions. "We sang God Save the King and we spoke in English. Some of our friends were Anglo-Burmese. There were a few Burmese, but very few."

Tancy remembers the racial discrimination, and that the Anglo-Burmese had to address the English and all Europeans as sir, "no matter who they were or where they worked".

But he didn't really mind, he said. Certain clubs, like the Gymkhanas in Rangoon and Moulmein, were only open to Europeans. But the Pegu Club, he said, was only open to higher salaried European men – "so they discriminated even among themselves!"

During the Great Depression, the price for rubber fell sharply so his father went to Yangon and took a job with a shipping company.

His mother didn't want to go back to the island, and one day someone came from Mergui and told his father he should do something about the plantation. So his father handed over all the documents and gave it to him as a gift, for free.

"It was a very lovely life," he says. "I was a boy, so I enjoyed it, but my mother was alone all the time while my father went to the rubber plantation."

When he was about six years old, Tancy was sent to school in Moulmein, where he studied until the seventh standard, then went to St John's High School in Rangoon. He was there when the Japanese invaded Burma in 1942.

His principal sent about six pupils, including Tancy, north to Shwebo, where there was an Anglican school.

"So my principal sent for us and said the British are withdrawing to India, so the best way you can go is to join a non-combatant unit, like the Royal Army Medical Corps," Tancy said.

Instead, he joined the Burma Auxiliary Force in March 1942, and joined an anti-aircraft gun unit in Mandalay. The Burma Auxiliary Force was all Anglo-Burmese, with a few Karen. It didn't take Burmese troops, Tancy said.[245]

---

[245] For details of the BAF Anti-Aircraft Regiment, *see* Steve Rothwell, '1sr Heavy Anti-Aircraft Regiment, R.A., B.A.F.' [online], http://www.rothwell.force9.co.uk/burmaweb/1st-HAA-Regiment-BAF.htm

After the order to withdraw, they were sent to a place near the Chindwin river, "and from there I trekked up to the border with Assam".

They were sent to the railhead at a place called Jasi. About 100 people started out with him on the trek, but it was a gradual withdrawal, the road was narrow, and people split up to make their own way to India. They couldn't take the anti-aircraft guns, so they blew them up.

It took about six days to get to Kalayway on a dirt-track.[246] "When we got there, they opened the stores and said take what you want," Tancy said. He took a pair of shorts and trousers, and of course a khaki shirt.

"They told us there would be three depots on the way, so I took ten packets of cigarettes although I didn't smoke. On the way, at the first stop, we did see a depot and they gave the four of us sardines and bread. Two men - the senior fellows - took the sardines and left the bread for the two of us."

After that, they continued walking and met the Indian mountain battery that had been next to them in Mandalay. They gave Tancy half a cup of tea and one chapati. Then he walked on alone, met the mountain battery again and they gave him the same thing, but on the third day he couldn't find them so he just slept on the roadside with nothing to eat.

"On the sixth day I met six Karen soldiers from the anti-aircraft battery. They had a small box of cooked rice, and there was a wild mango tree. They [the mangoes] were very small," he remembered.

The Karen managed to knock some of the mangoes down and called him to "come and join us", but "the rice they cooked was not sufficient for a full meal".

The next day, Tancy didn't meet anybody, but the following day he came to a quartermaster's store, where he was given a tin of salmon and a tin of jam.

He later reached a place called Tamu on the Assam border, "and I met some of our battery boys there. We had some rice, and I don't know what the curry was but it wasn't very good."

The following day, they were given a small bag of flour and some potatoes to share between fifteen people. Then they walked to a place in Assam, about twenty miles from Imphal, where all the British troops who had walked out of Burma were stationed.

"It was a staging camp. They gave us again half a cup of tea and a slice of bread, and the lunch was a little bit of bread and some bully beef. For dinner, we had two slices of bread and tea again. So two of our men went

---

[246] Kalayway might feasibly be Kalewa, which is on the Chindwin approximately 146km south of Tamu, referred to further on in the interview.

to a cookhouse and saw a British army unit cooking there."

The troops had to collect their water from downhill, so Tancy and his friends offered to carry their water for them in exchange for more food. They agreed and Tancy and his friends – eleven Anglo-Burmese – got an extra slice of bread each.

They stayed at the camp for about three days. The Indian troops a little further away had some chapatis and they sold them to Tancy and his friends. One chapati cost one Kyat.

Tancy had ten Kyats, silver coins, with him. "The others didn't have any cash - I was the richest man with ten Kyats," he said.

"When we were in the staging camp I had one tin of salmon and one tin of jam. We didn't have enough to eat, so one of our friends said 'what have you got'? I said 'jam and salmon'. So they took it and mixed it. We couldn't eat much, so we had to throw more than half of it away."

From there, Tancy and his colleagues went by truck to another camp past Imphal, and from there by truck to the railhead, where they met up with the officer staff of their battery.

There were then fifteen of them. At the railhead they were given another ten Kyats each and were put in a goods carriage. But by this time around half the unit had gone down with diarrhoea. From there they were taken to a place just outside Calcutta, and then to a place called Jangi, where there was another staging camp and they had to wait for all their troops.

"Half of us [including Tancy] were hospitalised with diarrhoea, but they gave us good food there."

After about two months, his battery was sent to a place called Mhow, where they waited for the other stragglers to come in.

"At Mhow we were properly organised. We had three meals a day - breakfast, lunch and dinner – and it was quite good," Tancy remembers.

But after about three months they still didn't have enough people to form a battery again, so they were joined by some infantrymen.

At Jhansi they had been given four 25-pounder guns for each battery. So they trained again on the guns, and after six months were seconded to the Burma Intelligence Corps. Tancy's unit was made up of Anglo-Burmese, with a few Karens.

Those who could speak Burmese properly formed three platoons, and Tancy was in 3 Platoon.[247] From there, they were sent to the Chindwin river. On the west bank were the British and on the east bank were the Japanese.

---

[247] For more on 3 Platoon, *see* Steve Rothwell, 'Platoons of the Burma Intelligence Corps' [online], http://www.rothwell.force9.co.uk/burmaweb/BICplatoons.htm

He was at the Chindwin front for six or seven months – "three of us were attached to 1 battalion" – and then the monsoons broke.

"While there we had to go across and do reconnaissance across the river. Sometimes the regiment went on fighting patrols, and sometimes just plain reconnaissance – six men, seven men - to find out where the Japs were."

After that, Tancy's unit withdrew to Imphal again when the battalions were changed. They stayed there for about four months and then went back to Mhow. Again, they had about three or four months of rest, and then they were sent for Chindit training.

Tancy took part in Orde Wingate's second Chindit expedition in 1944, because they were short of Burmese speakers.[248] Tancy was in column 34, a Gurkha unit. He was in 111 Brigade, and the men were flown into a jungle strip.[249] Half the brigade operated on the west bank and the other half, including Tancy, went across the Irrawaddy.[250] They operated there until May 1944, then were again sent back to HQ at Mhow.

"I saw Wingate once when he inspected us, and he was a short man. I was taller than him," Tancy said.

From there he was sent back again to a place just south of Imphal. Then in 1945 he had to go back to Imphal and fly into Burma.

There was supposed to be a third Chindit expedition and Tancy's unit was sent to a place in central India (he has forgotten its name) for training. But the third expedition was cancelled so they were sent back to the Chindwin front. They then went by road to Kaleymo (still on the Chindwin), and from there were flown into Meiktila, where Tancy was posted with the 17th Indian Division.

"Our Indian division had one Indian battalion, a Gurkha battalion and a British battalion. I was with the Gurkhas," he said.

---

[248] The second Chindit campaign was code-named Operation Thursday. The first Chindit offensive, in 1943, was code-named Longcloth.

[249] This is incorrect. 34 and 55 Columns were made up of 4th Battalion The Border Regiment, and part of 23 Brigade. The 111 Brigade, however, had 3rd Battalion 4th Gurkha Rifles as 30 Column. *See* Tony Redding, *War in the Wilderness: The Chindits in Burma 1943-1944* (Stroud: Spellmount, 2011), p.86.

[250] Tancy and the Gurkhas of 111 Brigade landed at an airstrip codenamed Chowringhee, while the British columns of the brigade landed west of the Irrawaddy at a landing site code-named Broadway. Chowringhee was in use from 6-10 March 1944. *See* Redding, *ibid,* pp.167-68.

He was attached to an infantry unit within the Gurkha battalion and stayed at Meiktila for two or three months.

The Japanese were still around Meiktila and would shell them every night.[251] So the next day they would go out on patrol to where they expected the guns to be, but the Japanese had moved elsewhere.

After two or three months they went down the Rangoon Road, and the next battle was at Pyawbwe.[252] That was a big battle, and over a thousand Japanese were killed.[253]

From there, the Japanese withdrew. Tancy's unit got to Pegu and was heading for Rangoon, but when they were 33 miles away they were stopped as the seaborne invasion from India had already started.[254]

They then went back to Pegu, and the seaborne troops occupied Yangon. There were no Japanese in Pegu but there were a lot of dacoits (bandits) in the area at the time.[255]

"We had to go out and find these fellows. But there were no more Japanese, they had all withdrawn. There were so many Japanese guns and the dacoits took them and went round the villages shooting, attacking and robbing. After about four months, the area was more or less rid of these people."

From Pegu, Tancy was transferred to Taunggyi. By then, some of the Japanese troops had already retreated to Thailand.[256] "So here again we

---

[251] In the middle of March 1945, the fighting around Meiktila was intense as the Japanese realised that they needed to deny 14 Army the airfield if they were to prevail. *See* Major-General S. Woodburn Kirby, *The War Against Japan: Vol.IV, The Reconquest of Burma* (Uckfield: Naval & Military Press, 2004), pp.306-311.

[252] The task of taking Pyawbwe was given to 17 Division, which it successfully executed by 12 April 1945. *See* Kirby, *ibid*, pp.357-61.

[253] Kirby gives the figure of 1,110 Japanese dead when the town was entered on 10 April. *See* Kirby, *ibid*, p.360.

[254] The seaborne invasion of Rangoon, code-named *Dracula*, ensured that the port of Rangoon was back in Allied hands by 3 May 1945. 14 Army had been held up by a stubborn Japanese defence around Pegu, which had to be held to allow the Japanese Army to escape south east towards southern Burma and Thailand.

[255] Dacoits were armed gangs of criminals who preyed on anyone for food or wealth. There was a particularly big problem with dacoits in Burma from this time until well after the re-establishment of British power. *See* for example John McEnery, *Epilogue in Burma 1945 – 48* (Tunbridge Wells: Spellmount, 1990), pp.97-99.

[256] From July, the 50,000 or so troops cut off in Burma attempted to break out to the

had to go and see if there were any Japs left, and we had to knock out the dacoits. We had a dual role," Tancy said.

And then on August 15, the war ended! Tancy was in Taunggyi on VJ Day, and says everybody was happy when they heard the news. "Everybody was quite happy and they started firing guns in the air, but I didn't." Tancy says he didn't fire any guns, but he was happy the war had ended.

He was involved in two big battles during the war, at Meiktila and Pyawbwe. He shot some Japanese, although he doesn't know if he killed any, and says the Burma Auxiliary Corps lost some men in those battles.

Tancy was demobilised in November 1945, and after that he joined the Netherlands Bank as a clerk, working there for fifteen years. He left in the early 1960s and spent two years trying to emigrate. Most of the Anglo-Burmese were going away, he says. "They realised that they had no prospects. They [the government] would only give to their own people."

In Ne Win's time, the highest rank Anglo-Burmese could attain in the armed forces was Colonel, then it was dropped to Major and now it's Captain. And they would favour Burmese people when they gave out business licences.

New Zealand said he didn't fit in with its quota system, so he tried Australia but at that time the embassy was temporarily closed. He then went to the British embassy, which accepted his papers, but there was a discrepancy between the age on his father's birth certificate and the one on his marriage certificate (his father had been orphaned at a very young age).

"At that time I got a bit ratty, you see. The man asked for a letter explaining it, but then I got ratty and said 'give it all back, I'll submit it again'." But he didn't. "New Zealand was a blank, Australia was a blank, and Britain was a blank." He got fed up and decided to stay in Burma instead - "So I just stayed at home looking for a job, but the pay was not attractive."

He was still toying with the idea of going abroad, but after a year his vicar, the Burma secretary of the Bible Churchmen's Missionary Society (BCMS), asked Tancy to help him out. At first he said no, but later joined as a part-time member of staff, helping with the accounts and typing letters.

---

south east. Coordination between the Army, Airforce and SOE (Force 136) succeeded in inflicting huge casualties on the Japanese into August. *See* Richard Duckett, *The Special Operations Executive in Burma* (London: IB Tauris, 2017), particularly Chapter 5, pp.127-150.

The following year, 1965, the government ordered all foreign missionaries to leave the country. Tancy was working as a liaison between the locals and the BCMS head office in London, with an office in the bishop's quarters, but "they were pushed out, so I had to work full-time".

He later took on a second role, as secretary of the provincial church office, before he retired in 1990 after 25 years with the BCMS. He was then 67, and a pensioner.

He married a Karen woman at 59, and they had three children [Note: I didn't ask him about this as I know his wife and two sons died, so I didn't want to upset him and we were pressed for time anyway. I'm sure Sarah can tell me more next time I see her.][257]

Tancy has no regrets about not emigrating, but says the Ne Win years were very tough. The press wasn't free and Ne Win had such a lot of power, he said. "Everybody was afraid of him. He spoiled the country."

Tancy's father died before the war, and his mother, brother and sister chose not to make 'the trek' out of Burma but stayed behind in Twante, a township in the Yangon area where they were then living. During the war, his brother - who was ten years older - worked under the Japanese, in "construction or something", so he could help their mother with some money.

Anglo-Burmese weren't discriminated against by the Japanese and were actually favoured, getting jobs more easily than the Burmese, he said. [Note: I'll have to check this as there is a discrepancy in my notes. He may have been saying the opposite, as I remember him saying that in the past.][258]

Tancy's family were safe but his sister died of tuberculosis during the war. "There was no medicine, nothing."

He is not sure how many Anglo-Burmese are left in Burma - maybe a few thousand, he says, but there are many who can't even speak English. They are just naturalised.

---

[257] Interviewer's note.

[258] Interviewer's note.

# Epilogue

In February 2021, the military again took over in the country now more often referred to as Myanmar than as Burma. Since then, there have been renewed offensives against the Karen, as well as the Kachin and the Chins in the far north of the country. In October 2022, airstrikes killed around 60 Kachin in Hpakant Township, Kachin State.[259] That same month, there were airstrikes on the Karens in the Kawkareik area after the Karen National Liberation Army 'killed several Myanmar army soldiers and police'.[260] According to the UN, 974,000 people have been displaced within Myanmar since the military coup, with an estimated 40,000 seeking sanctuary in neighbouring countries by June 2022. In the first half of 2022, humanitarian relief agencies reached a total of 3.1 million people.[261] Naw Bellay Htoo South, one of the interviewers of the veterans for this book, has been delivering aid to displaced Karen people.

**Brief Report from Naung Lin Bin 2022 Distribution**
As we all know the situation in Burma is pretty tense and unstable. It's a country where not safe to live in and we don't know when will ever be change again. We pray that the people in Burma to have a safe place and secure to live with no fear or danger. Every day, I receive messages from Facebook Messenger, friends and relatives mention that airplane fly over us 2-3 times a day. We don't sleep well and have nightmares because of airstrikes. We had to sleep in a hut or a ditch and it was very cold or wet for months. By hearing their news I feel stressful and very angry too.

The situation in NLB areas has gotten worse since June, many

---

[259] Oliver Holmes, 'Myanmar airstrike kills 60 people at concert, says Kachin sepaaratist group', *The Guardian*, 24 October 2022 [online], https://www.theguardian.com/world/2022/oct/24/myanmar-military-air-strike-kills-dozens-at-concert-says-kachin-separatist-group

[260] Linn Htin, 'Myanmar military bombs Karen State town from air as Karen resistance alliance strikes junta targets', *Myanmar Now*, 21 October 2022 [online], https://myanmar-now.org/en/news/myanmar-military-bombs-karen-state-town-from-air-as-karen-resistance-alliance-strikes-junta

[261] Myanmar Humanitarian Update No. 21, 2 September 2022, UN Office for the Coordination of Humanitarian Affairs (OCHA) [online], *https://reliefweb.int/report/myanmar/myanmar-humanitarian-update-no-21-2-september-2022*

villagers fled from Kyat Kyi and nearby villagers fled to NLB town and other towns as well. There are over 10,000 IDPs in the area alone. Regarding our WWII veterans and widows in NLB list, few live in conflict areas. The money distributors had to take much caution to travel and reach out, anyhow the distribution went well. Many of them are unwell and their health are deteriorating. Most of them are look after by their family. Some photos on the following pages.

We could take all the photos only some.

**TTT Trip Report**

I thank God for giving me strength and energy daily and most of all give me my family. I appreciate my husband for his support for my travels in a war zone. Furthermore, I thank the Karen leaders who allowed me to travel and assisted me in my trip. The trip was short but fun too. I finished the mission successfully by many of my friends' prayers.

Most of the trip involved travelling by car and boat for many hours to reach to the community high school. This is one of the KNU (KECD) high school. It is more important to provide education to children in the area after the 1st of February 2021 coup in Myanmar, as many government schools (actually, run by the SAC junta) are closed, and teachers and students on strike.

It was very bumpy, dangerous ride and the whole day sitting still down in the boat. On the way back, the boat engine broke down, so we lost two hours. It was dark by the time we reached our destination, and we didn't have a good spotlight to see the route so a few times we landed on the sand bank. It was scary but we helped each other and arrived safely. It was hot, but breeze with open air and occasionally spotting wild animals as we ride along such as monitor lizard, various bird, boars, monkeys, and fish. The beautiful mother river gives water to bath, swim, fish, drink, cook, laundry and cleaning. My meals are very delicious and free - healthier with organic food. It was great meeting old friends, new teachers, and students during the trip. Over 2 years ago, we had submitted the TTT Community High School building proposal to a few international organisations and donors, but no one would help us. However, the community was pleased to receive support and donation from H4FA and Karen people living abroad, to build more classrooms for students to have enough spaces to study.

During this trip we focused on helping build the school building. The school building is falling apart and cannot accommodate more students. The number of students at the school has almost doubled, to 320 children - with many new arrivals coming to KNU areas for protection and education, after the coup. The school building was crowded, and the classrooms are not big enough space for students. The township hall is used as teaching classrooms – but it has no divided walls so quite noisy while teaching and difficult for students to follow teachers' instructions. Therefore, the township personnel, education department officer, school committees, school principal and teachers form the school building committees and plan to re-build the high-school in coming year.

Karen friends in USA donated money for a meal (pork and venison curry, followed by traditional dessert) for all students and teachers to enjoy together. Everyone enjoyed the first feast together. We also delivered a specific donation towards the school and church to have piano (keyboard), guitar, microphones, and speakers. The community can glorify God in church as well as improve music skills for the young generation and occasionally ceremony entertainment. At the same time, seeds for vegetables donated for the student to grow. The students are very happy and thrilled to grow more vegetables by the stream. The only problem is they must carry water to water the plants. We hope that in the future we can help them with water pressure pump. With this exercise, I've seen the students are working in a group as a team together. Therefore, they can harvest organic vegetables to add nutrients to their meals. They take responsibility and work hard during their studying. They are thrived to learn and fulfil their dreams. They don't have any digital or technology to connect to the outside world and many live apart from the families to gain limited knowledge and education.

The community is very grateful for all the support, and it is very encouraging for those living in the unstable political crisis. Although transportation is very difficult, prices are rising and finding food is challenging, the community is always willing to help each other. In the area, some teachers have very little experiences, with limited teaching materials and resources, but they are dedicated to their work. Some teachers walked for 2 days with small infants and some a day bumpy dusty hilly motorbikes ride to get to the district headquarters for the annual teacher training. I also met a few urban teachers who do not have much experience in rural areas, and find the teaching is quite challenging for them, as some students who could not read or write Karen fluently and have very little knowledge of Karen history. Sometimes they are feeling homesick. Some teachers would like to continue to study further education but many schools and colleges in Burma are closed and unsafe to live with their families. Therefore, by teaching they can learn at the same time. A few teachers have a very difficult journey and dangerous to travel across places to places, in the middle of a Civil War.

Many teachers mentioned to me that the school building is small or not enough space or falling apart, so they must use the church building or hall to teach with no classroom divider and very noisy etc. Teachers receive very small stipends annually. They don't have regular salary. They made it clear that they have been fleeing over 70 years, from the time of their great grandparents and no longer want to move. The villagers were like their families and children live together peacefully in their homeland. They prefer to grow their own vegetables, rice, and raise animals and be able to protect their lands - rather than having to flee again into the jungle.

During the ceasefire, my family and I travelled to the area nearly every year during our school holidays, but since pandemic and coup in Burma, we could not travel as a family anymore. In 2019-2020 academic year, with the support from The Slingshot Development Fund, the community high school's latrines/wash and water for schools, and Free the Oppressed help with latrines for the dormitories. In 2020-2021 academic year, this Slingshot, Free the Oppressed, CMIS Interact Group, H4FA, Karen abroad and other individuals donated for emergency food, hygiene, water filter, and medicines for COVID. We were particularly pleased to get the donation from the boys'school (CMIS). The schoolchildren at TTT High School Community really appreciate it.

On behalf of the community, I very much appreciate for all your help and support Karen people. Last but not least we deeply thanks Help for Forgotten Allies (H4FA) and Karen in Amarillo, Saint Paul, Omaha, Utica and Milwaukee for the Mergui/Tavoy Education Department to build better school buildings and other's needs.

## Saw Joshoo

A chance meeting with Saw Joshoo (right) at the Kwai River Christian Hospital in Sangkglaburi. He was living in the convalescent wing of the hospital with his daughter who had learning difficulties. He was very thin and looked very poor. I asked him what I could do to help him and he said he would like me to "inform his officers". I went back home and thought about this and on my son in law's advice went to the British Legion who sent me to the Royal Commonwealth Ex-Services League and Col Sam Pope. Sam began the work of a list of 2nd WW veterans in Burma and in the refugee camps on the Thai Burma border and ended up with around 4,000. They were then all given annual welfare grants. However two years later the Burma Welfare Association who had taken over the work, and which was no longer under the guidance of Col Sam, cut the grants to those in the refugee camps and H4FA was formed by myself and Col Sam. This photo is Saw Joshoo when young.

Daw Aye Nyo. She cannot see very well. High blood pressure and look after by her son's family

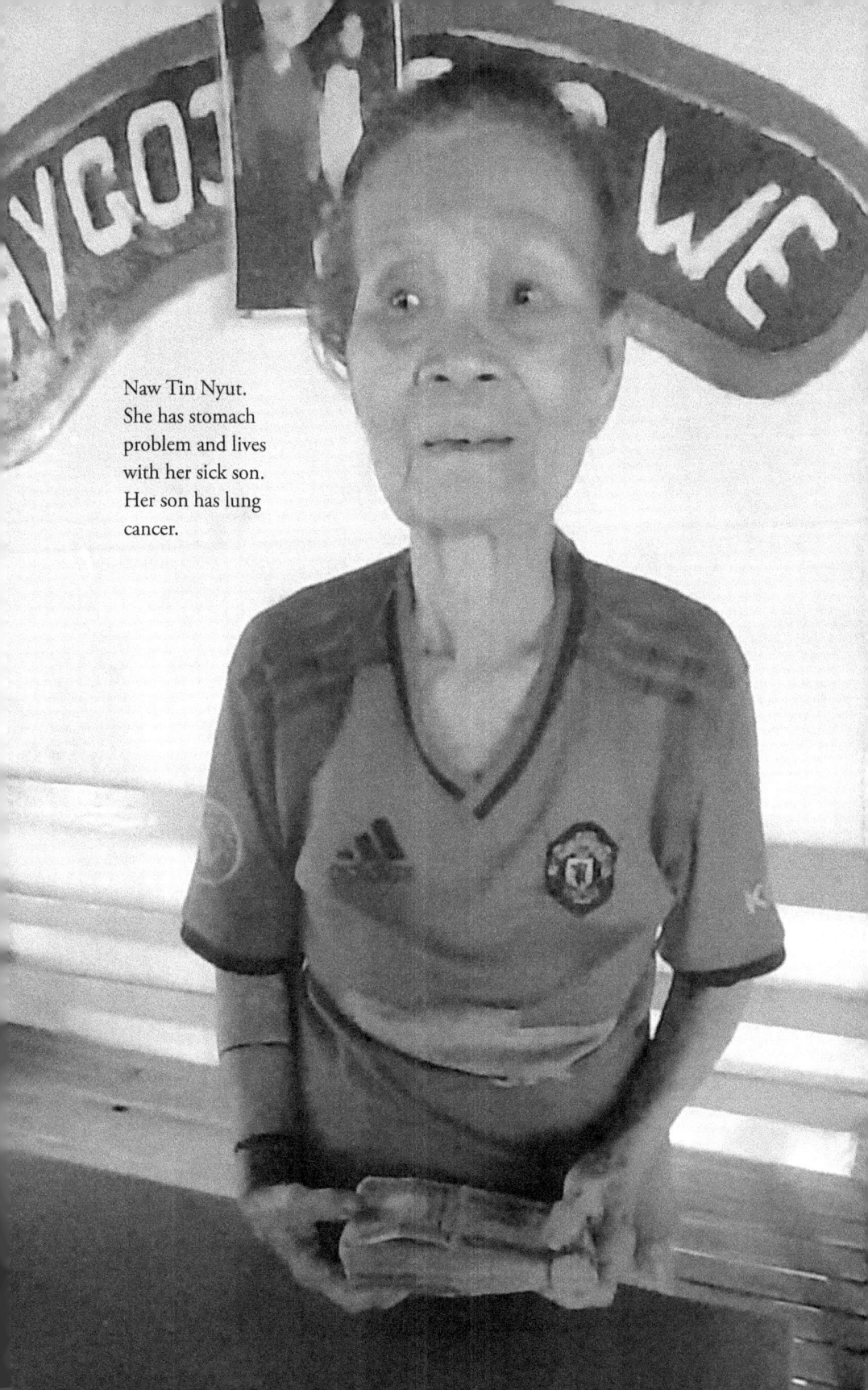

Naw Tin Nyut. She has stomach problem and lives with her sick son. Her son has lung cancer.

Po Htin, 92 yrs old in the photo, with his wife Pe Naw Gaw. He was blind and she is partially sighted. Joined the Burma Rifles in 1936.

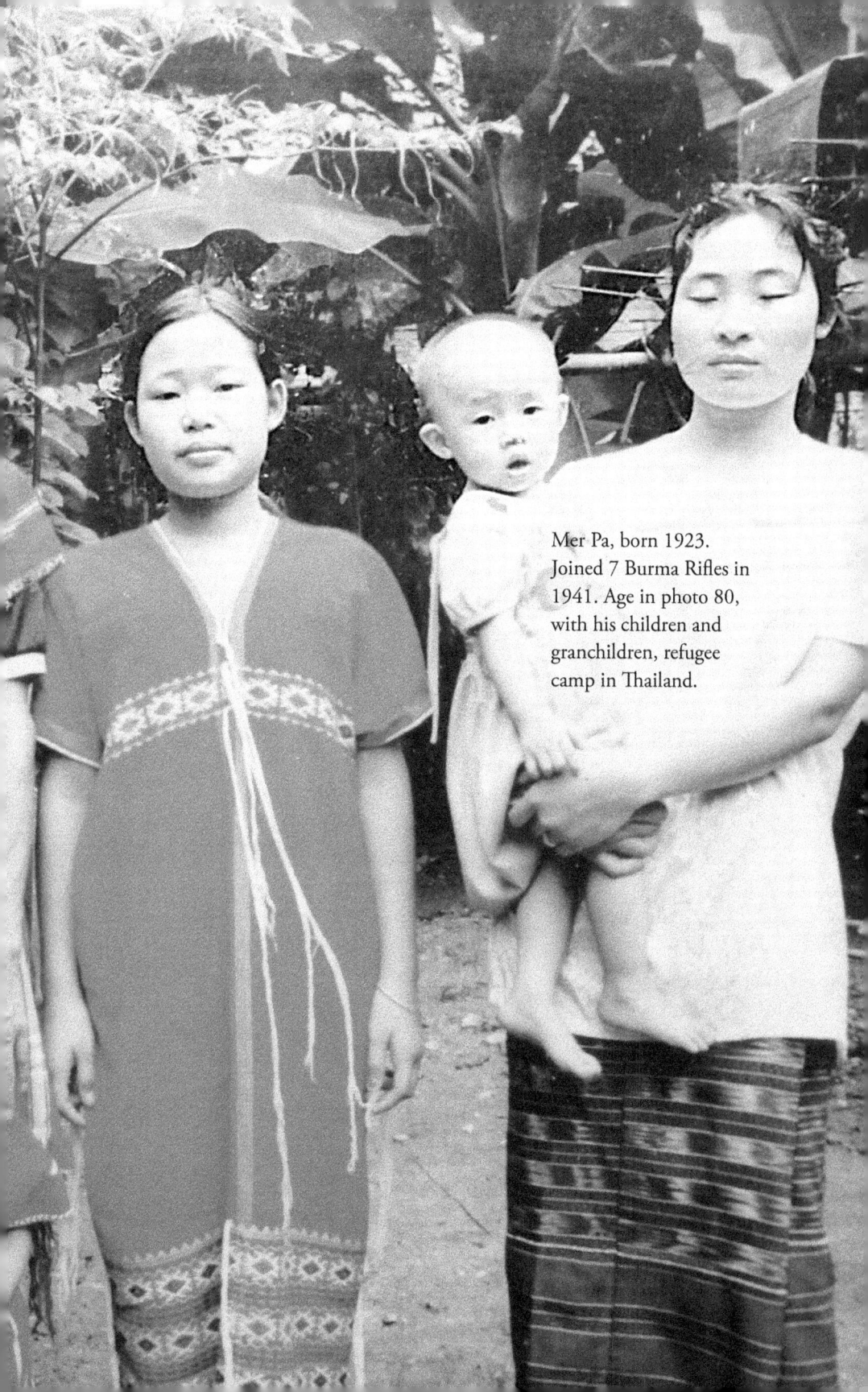

Mer Pa, born 1923. Joined 7 Burma Rifles in 1941. Age in photo 80, with his children and granchildren, refugee camp in Thailand.

Saw Ma Na's family. Jemadar Saw Ma Na joined the Burma Military Police, 1 Rangoon Battalion. He later joined Major Seagrim. He died in 1990. This is one of his four children and grandchildren in a refugee camp in Thailand.

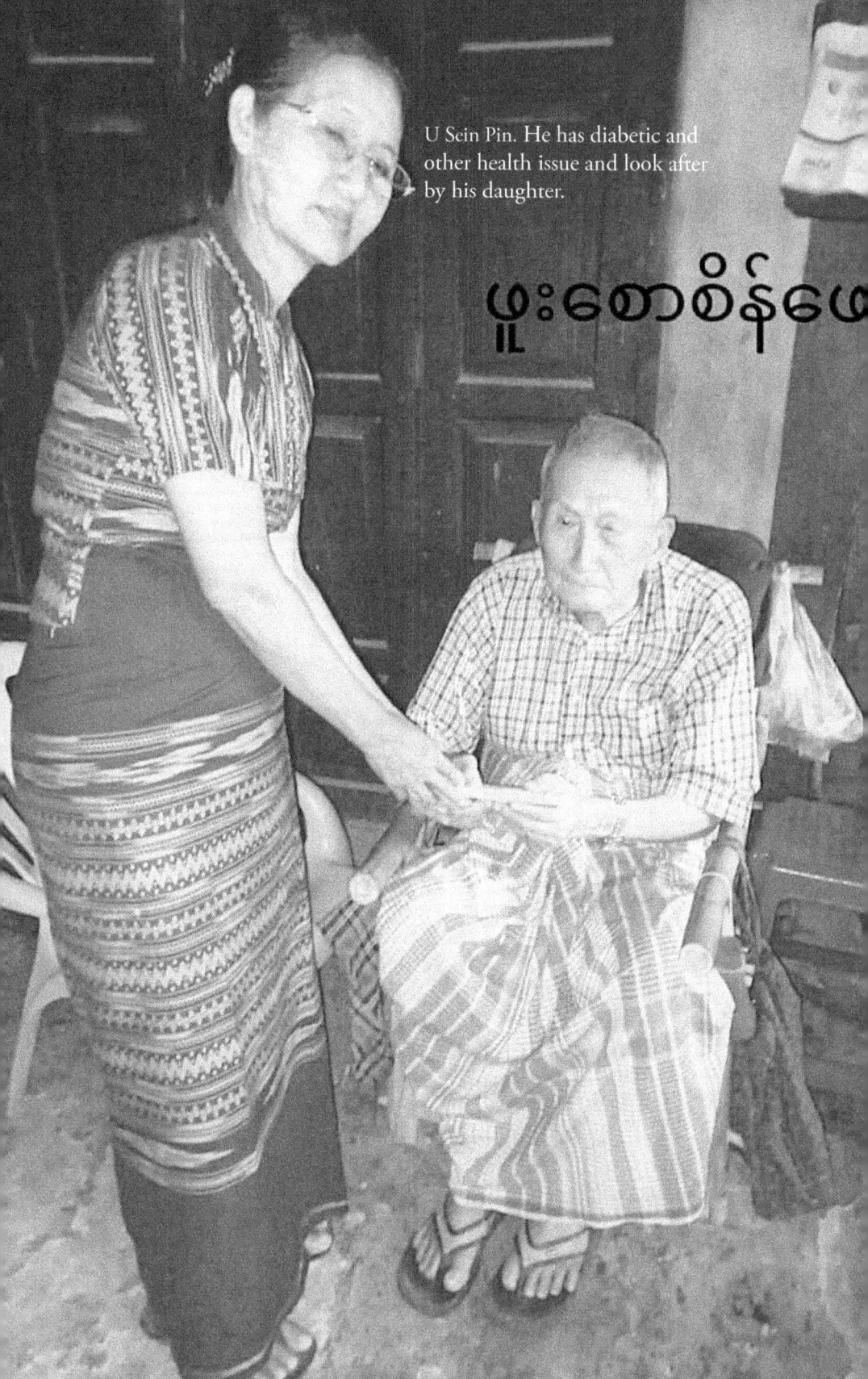

U Sein Pin. He has diabetic and other health issue and look after by his daughter.

ဦးစောစိန်ဖေ

Naw Ah Mu. She is weak and look after by her son.

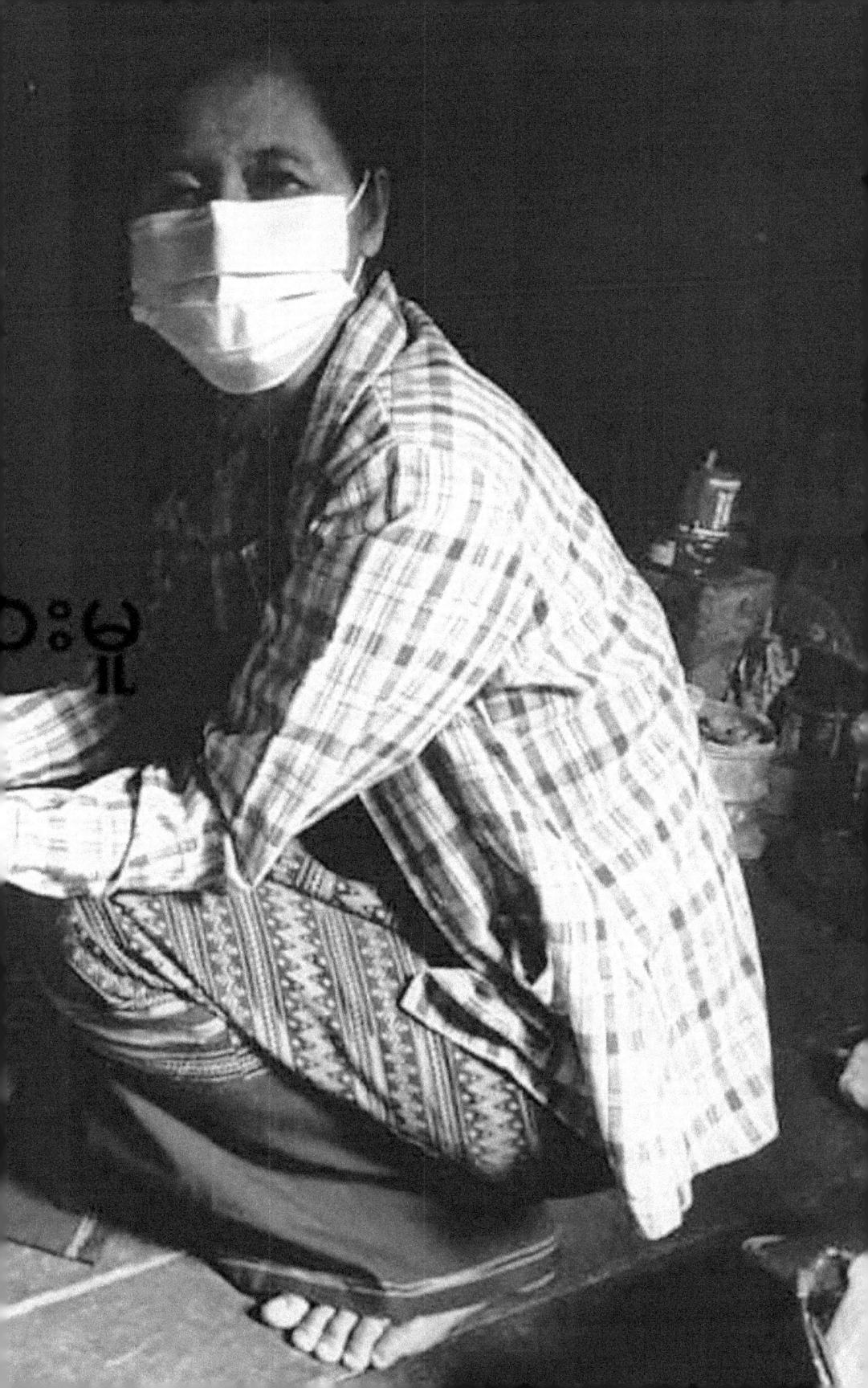

# Sources and Bibliography

## Private Collections
Captain Tony Bennett's papers courtesy of his daughter Priscilla Church

Major Fred Milner's papers courtesy of David Mattey

Sergeant Roger Leney's photographs, courtesy of his son, Simon Leney

Lt.Col. (retired) Sam Pope RM

Martin Smith

The Trofimov Literary Estate

c/o Brethertons Solicitors, Franklins House, Manorsfield Road, Bicester, Oxon OX26 6EX United Kingdom

## Archives
### The National Archives (TNA), London
CAB 66 – War Cabinet and Cabinet: Memoranda

CAB 129 – Cabinet: Memoranda

FO 371 – Foreign Office: Political Departments: General Correspondence from 1906-1966

HS 1 – Special Operations Executive: Far East.

HS 7 – Special Operations Executive: Histories and War Diaries.

HS 9 – Special Operations Executive: Personnel Files (PF Series)

KV 2 – The Security Service: Personal (PF Series) Files

WO 203 – War Office: South East Asia Command: Military Headquarters Papers, Second World War.

WO 325 – War Office: General Headquarters, Allied Land Forces (South East Asia) War Crimes Group: Investigation Files

WO 373 – War Office and Ministry of Defence: Military Secretary's Department

*Opposite left* Saw Po Way's wife, Naw Mut Mut, then 70yrs old. Saw Po Way died age 78. He joined the Burma Army Signals in 1939. He later joined Major Seagrim and then Operation Character in 1945.

## The British Library (BL)
### India Office Records
Records of the Military Department (IOR L/MIL)

Burma Office Records (IOR M)

Official Publications (IOR V)

## Books and Articles

Aldrich, Richard, *Intelligence & the War Against Japan: Britain, America and the Politics of Secret Service* (Cambridge: Cambridge University Press, 2000).

Aldrich, Richard, 'Legacies of Secret Service: Renegade SOE & the Karen Struggle in Burma 1948 – 1950', *Intelligence and National Security*, 14, 4, (1999), pp.130-48.

Allen, Louis, *Burma: The Longest War 1942 – 1945* (London: Phoenix Giant, 1998).

Appleton, George, 'Burma Two Years After Liberation', *International Affairs*, 23, 4 (Oct 1947), pp.510-21.

Bailey, Roderick, *Forgotten Voices of the Secret War: An Inside History of Special Operations During the Second World War* (London: Ebury Press, 2008).

Balfour-Oatts, Lieutenant Colonel, *The Jungle in Arms* (London: NEL Books, 1976).

Bornat, Joanna. 'Oral History and Remembering.' *Research Methods for Memory Studies*, edited by Emily Keightley and Michael Pickering, Edinburgh University Press, Edinburgh, 2013, pp. 29 – 42. JSTOR, www.jstor.org/stable/10.3366/j.ctt1g0b78k.5.

Braund, Harold, *Distinctly I Remember: a Personal story of Burma* (Victoria: Wren Publishing, 1972).

Davies, Philip, *Lost Warriors* (Croxley Green: Atlantic Publishing, 2017).

Duckett, Richard , *The Special Operations Executive in Burma: Jungle Warfare and Intelligence Gathering in World War Two* (London: IB Tauris, 2017).

Dun, Smith, *Memoirs of a Four-Foot Colonel* (New York: Cornell University, 1980).

Fellowes-Gordon, Ian, *Amiable Assassins* (London: Panther, 1958).

Ghosh, Parimal, *Brave Men of the Hills: Resistance and Rebellion in Burma, 1825 - 1932* (London: Hurst, 2000).

Glass, Leslie, *The Changing of the Kings* (London: Peter Owen 1985).

Gravers, Mikael, 'The Karen Making of a Nation' in *Asian Forms of the Nation*, edited by Stein Tonneson and Hans Antlov (London: Routledge, 2003).

Keong, Voon Phin, 'The Rubber Industry of Burma, 1876-1964', *Journal of Southeast Asian Studies,* 4,2 (September 1973), pp.216 – 28.

Kirby, S.W, *The War Against Japan,* Vols. I-IV (Uckfield: Military & Naval Press, 2004).

Lunt, James, *A Hell of a Licking: The Retreat From Burma 1941 – 42* (London: Collins, 1986).

McEnery, John H., *Epilogue in Burma 1945 – 48* (Tunbridge Wells: Spellmount, 1990).

Morrison, Ian, *Grandfather Longlegs* (London: Faber, 1947).

Naw, Angelene, *Aung San and the Struggle for Burmese Independence* (Copenhagen: NIAS, 2001).

Okihiro, Gary Y. 'Oral History and the Writing of Ethnic History: A Reconnaissance into Method and Theory.' *The Oral History Review*, vol. 9, 1981, pp. 27 – 46. JSTOR, www.jstor.org/stable/3675323.

Peacock, Geraldine, *The Life of a Jungle Walla: Reminiscences in the life of Lieutenant-Colonel E.M. Peacock* (Ilfracombe: Arthur Stockwell Ltd, 1958).

Pointon, A.C., *Bombay Burmah Trading Corporation, 1863-1963* (Southampton: Millbrook Press, 1964).

Portelli, Alessandro. 'The Peculiarities of Oral History.' *History Workshop*, no. 12, 1981, pp. 96 – 107. *JSTOR*, www.jstor.org/stable/4288379.

Redding, Tony , *War in the Wilderness: The Chindits in Burma 1943-1944* (Stroud: Spellmount, 2011

Sadan, Mandy (ed.), *War and Peace in the Borderlands of Myanmar* (Copenhagen: Nias, 2016).

Serikaku, Laurie R. 'Oral History in Ethnic Communities: Widening the Focus.' *The Oral History Review*, vol. 17, no. 1, 1989, pp. 71 – 87. JSTOR, www.jstor.org/stable/3675240.

Slim, Field Marshal Sir William, *Defeat into Victory* (London: Pan, 1989).

Summerfield, Penny, 'Oral History as an Autobiographical Practice', Miranda [Online], 12 | 2016, http://journals.openedition.org/ miranda/8714; DOI: 10.4000/miranda.8714

Thompson, Julian, *Forgotten Voices of the Burma Campaign* (London: Ebury Press, 2009).

Thompson, Paul, *The Voice of the Past: Oral History* (OUP, Oxford: 1978).

Webster, Anthony, *Gentleman Capitalists: British Imperialism in Southeast Asia 1770-1880* (London: IB Tauris, 1998).

Woods, Philip, *Reporting the Retreat: War Correspondents in Burma* (London: Hurst, 2016).

Woods, Philip, *Managing the Media in the India-Burma War: Challenging a 'Forgotten War'* (London: Bloomsbury, 2023).

## Websites

BBC Timewatch, 'Forgotten Allies', 1997 [online] https://www.youtube.com/watch?v=xTJ3q5yg38Q

'Blaber Family Genealogy' [online] http://www.blaberfamily.org.uk/trees/blaber04/b343.htm

Bogget, David, 'JAPAN' S BURMA ROAD; Reflections on Japanese Military Activities in Northern Thailand' [online], http://www.kyoto-seika.ac.jp/researchlab/wp/wp-content/uploads/kiyo/pdf-data/no18/David.pdf

'British Army Officers, 1939-1945' [online], http://www.unithistories.com/officers/Army_officers_A01.html

Commonwealth War Graves Commission [online], www.cwgc.org

Downing, Jared, 'Myanmar History 101: How Britain defeated Burma', Frontier Myanmar [online] https://frontiermyanmar.net/mm/node/3951

Days Not to be Forgotten published by Drum Publications, *see* http://www.lulu.com/shop/drum-publication-group/days-not-to-be-forgotten/paperback/product-5524024.html

Duckett, Richard, 'The Special Operations Executive in Burma' [online] https://soeinburma.wordpress.com/

Fisher, Jonah, 'The man who carried out one of the world's earliest hijackings', BBC, 27 June 2014 [online], https://www.bbc.co.uk/news/magazine-28014394

Gerry Holdsworth Trust [online], http://holdsworthtrust.org/

Hansard, House of Commons Debate, 21 June 1948, vol 452 cc931-2 [online], https://api.parliament.uk/historic-hansard/commons/1948/jun/21/anglo-burmese-treaty

Help for Forgotten Allies, Registered Charity, Help for Forgotten Allies [online] http://www.h4fa.org.uk/about-us

Holmes, Oliver, 'Myanmar airstrike kills 60 people at concert, says Kachin sepaaratist group', *The Guardian*, 24 October 2022 [online] https://www.theguardian.com/world/2022/oct/24/myanmar-military-air-strike-kills-dozens-at-concert-says-kachin-separatist-group

'Japan in Northwest Thailand During World War II' [online], https://www.lanna-ww2.com/frontpage.html

Linn Htin, 'Myanmar military bombs Karen State town from air as Karen resistance alliance strikes junta targets', *Myanmar Now*, 21 October 2022 [online] https://myanmar-now.org/en/news/myanmar-military-bombs-karen-state-town-from-air-as-karen-resistance-alliance-strikes-junta

The London Gazette [online], https://www.thegazette.co.uk/

Lundy, Darryl, 'The Peerage' [online] http://www.thepeerage.com/p58596.htm#i585956

Myanmar Humanitarian Update No. 21, 2 September 2022, UN Office for the Coordination of Humanitarian Affairs (OCHA) [online] https://reliefweb.int/report/myanmar/myanmar-humanitarian-update-no-21-2-september-2022

'Myanmar Rebel Leader Dies After Long Illness', Reuters [online], https://www.reuters.com/article/us-myanmar-rebels-leader/myanmar-rebel-leader-dies-after-long-illness-idUSBKK2996520061224

National Archives, Kew Gardens, London, online catalogue, http://discovery.nationalarchives.gov.uk/details/r/C153

P&O Heritage 'Ship Fact Sheet: Sir Harvey Adamson' [online] http://www.poheritage.com/Upload/Mimsy/Media/factsheet/94487SIR-HARVEY-ADAMSON-1914pdf.pdf

Richardson, Dave, (Yank, the Army Weekly British Edition Vol 3. No.3), July 2 1944 [online] http://www.marauder.org/yank27.htm

Rothwell, Steve, 'The Burma Campaign' [online], http://www.rothwell.force9.co.uk/burmaweb/index.html

Singh, S.B. 'Nepal and the World War II', Proceedings of the Indian History Congress, vol.53, 1992, pp.580 – 585; [online] www.jstor.org/stable/44142873.

Sithu Kyaw Thein Lwin, 'The Navy's Most Important Ship' [online], http://frankstaylorfamilyandroyalnavyhistory.net/HMSScarabBurmaTheNavysMostImportantShip.htm

Taylor, Ronnie, 'FEPOW Family' [online] http://www.britain-at-war.org.uk/WW2/Death_Railway/html/tha_muang.htm

'Treaty between the Government of the United Kingdom and the Provisional Government of Burma' (London: HMSO, 17 October 1947) [online], https://www.cvce.eu/en/obj/anglo_burmese_treaty_on_the_independence_of_burma_london_17_october_1947-en-cd1357f8-0e15-41a7-ae41-f39aa1a6db9b.html

# Biographies

## Dr Richard Duckett

Richard is a graduate of the Universities of Essex (BA, 2000) and Reading (MA, 2001), and was awarded a PhD in 2015 by the Open University. He has published two books on the Special Operations Executive in Burma, and continues to lecture widely on the subject. He also maintains a website (www.soeinburma.com) where more of his latest research can be accessed for free. Richard has taught History and Politics since 2004 and is currently employed at Leighton Park School where he is Head of Politics and Assistant Head of Sixth Form.

## Bellay Htoo South

Born in Burma (Myanmar), and when I was 9 years old my parents left my birth place and moved to Mergui/Tavoy area (Tanintharyi Region) where I grew up and finished my high school in a Karen Nation Union controlled area (KNU 4 Brigade). I taught in a KNU school for 4 years, and attended Karen Teacher Training College for 2 years. In 1996, I came to study English in Bangkok and in 1997 I got married to Ashley South; the same year, my parents and sister were refugees because of a major Myanmar Army offensive. They fled to Thailand and lost everything we owned in Burma. I then moved to the UK with my husband to start my new life. On 13 Feb 2003, we lost my father from stomach cancer, then 10 days later my father-in-law died from pancreatic cancer, and on 16 Nov we lost my mother-in-law from Pneumonia. However, in April 2004, and Dec 2006, we have two sons, Joseph and Benjamin. We have traveled from the UK to Thailand and Burma/Myanmar several times. Currently we live in Chiang Mai, northern Thailand where my sons have been attending the international school for nearly 5 years.

## Dr Robert Lyman FRHistS

A writer and historian. He is a Research Fellow at the Changing Character of War Centre, Pembroke College, University of Oxford.

After finishing a twenty year career in the British Army in 2001 he has published widely on the Second World War in Europe, North Africa and Asia.

He is Field Marshal Bill Slim's military biographer. His presentation of the case for Slim won a National Army Museum debate in 2011 for Britain's Greatest General and his case for Kohima/Imphal won a National Army Museum debate in 2013 for Britain's Greatest Battle.

He was the BBC's historical adviser for the VJ commemorations in 2015 and 2020 and is a regular contributor to documentary films on aspects of the war.

He is currently finishing a new narrative account of the war in the Far East ('A War of Empires') due for publication by Osprey in November 2021. Also in the pipeline is an account of the two Chindit campaigns (Operations Longcloth and Thursday), an account of American experiences of living under Nazism ('Jackboot'), the story of the British Army between 1918 and 1940 and a combined biography of Britain's greatest generals of the Second World War, Bill Slim and Bernard Montgomery.

# Index

**A**

Akyab Island 74
Alexander, Defence Minister A.V. 136
Amarapura 61
Ambulance 19, 46, 49, 60
Andrews, Mr Peter 52, 68, 93
Anglo-Burmese War 42–44, 49, 54, 194
Arakan 42, 74–75
Assam 94
Aunglan 61, 148–149
Aye Kyaw, Saw 40, 49, 60, 80, 119, 145

**B**

Ba Aye, Saw 193
Ba Kyaw, Saw 20, 23, 188
Bago 97, 119
Bamar 18–19, 28, 36, 44
Barrackpore 94
Baw Nay, Saw 53, 72, 99, 126, 162–163
Beik 53, 124, 126, 154, 157, 161, 163
Berlin Conference 44
Blaber, Company Commander Major 51
Botahtaung 119
Bunny, Saw 67, 92, 125
Burdett, Lt.Col. Ernest 47–48
Burma rifles 12, 19, 28, 36, 38, 44–47, 51, 54–55, 58, 63–64, 67–70, 72, 77, 79, 81, 83, 113, 118, 121, 129, 135, 148
Burmese Rebellion 47

**C**

Champion, Saw 56, 77
Chin 19, 28–29, 36, 44–45, 58, 64, 67, 74, 78, 81, 86, 89, 121, 129, 147, 149, 151, 202
Chindits 12, 19, 36, 74, 98
Critchley, Lt. Colonel R. 107

**D**

Daniel Tun Baw, Saw 53, 99, 159
Darjeeling Hill Station 79
Delta 15, 49, 78, 95, 128, 141, 153
Dibrugarh 79
Dun, Supreme Commander, General Smith 137
Dway Maung, Saw 182–184

**E**

East India Company 39, 42

**F**

Fair Play, Saw 50, 63, 88, 121, 147
Fletcher, Major Roger 48
Force 136 12, 36, 38, 61, 75, 77, 79, 82, 87–88, 92, 95, 97, 100–101, 106, 126, 134, 136, 138, 141–142
Ford, Frank Major 47, 48, 138, 142, 144
Fort Hertz 74, 94
French Indochina 52, 54

**H**

Harcher, Saw 185–186
Haswell, Division Commander 60
Hla Tin, Saw 178–180
Hoshiarpur 79, 92
Htakanan 121

227

Htaw Tha Heh, Saw also known as Saw Kway Kwi  64, 89
Hteemoepawar  163
Htoo Mar, Saw  53, 126, 161

**I**
Imphal  95
Indian Mutiny  42
Insein  138, 140, 155, 160–161
Irrawaddy River  71, 147, 198

**J**
Johnny Htoo, Saw  13, 20, 47, 58, 78, 118, 144–145

**K**
K'Hsaw, Saw  50, 65, 91
Kachin  60, 74–75, 80, 91, 95, 97, 118, 125, 135, 140–141, 151–153, 170–171, 202
Kalaywa  66
Kalewa  61, 71–72
Kaleymo  198
Kanchanaburi  121
Karen  10, 12, 18–22, 24–29, 36–39, 44–46, 50, 52–53, 55, 61–63, 67, 72, 75–77, 79–80, 82–83, 85, 88–90, 92, 95–96, 98–104, 106–110, 112–113, 115, 117–138, 141–155, 158–163, 166–169, 171–174, 176–178, 180, 182–186, 188, 190, 192–197, 201–205
Karutu  67
Kaw Lo Klo  89
Kawlo River  160
Kawpor  162
Kawthoolei  163
Kay Ray, Saw  50, 66, 91, 125
Kaymarhtar  163
Kempeitai  112
Kengtung  96
Klawmawsoe  53
Klerpu  162

Kya-in  100–101
Kyantaw Cemetery  92
Kyaukkyi  88, 91
Kyaw Po  110, 112
Kyettaik  114

**L**
Lashio  170
Lebyaunbya  96
Ledo  94
Lerdoh  52, 98
Lerwetkhi  52, 98
Levies  36, 58, 60, 74, 78, 82, 90–91, 107, 109, 118, 125, 137, 185
Lipyekhi  91
Longcloth, Operation  74

**M**
Mahler, Saw  169–172
Manipur  61
Martin, Lt. Col. James  51
Maung Sein  176–178, 181
Maw Ler, Saw  69, 71, 94, 97, 159, 169
Mawchi  77, 185–186
Mawlamyine  66–67, 124, 127, 160
Maymyo  46–47, 49, 52, 58, 68, 71, 77, 80, 92–93, 97, 126, 147, 150–152, 155
Maytarkalelki  63
McDonald, Tancy  194–201
Meiktila  61, 71–72, 95, 147, 149, 152, 198–200
Mel Du, also known as Pu Hla Kyi Pa, Village Headman  52, 72, 98, 159
Mergui  53, 146, 163, 194–195
Mewaing  107
Michael Shwe, Saw  58, 79–80, 118
Minbu  61
Mindwin  143
Mingaladon  49, 51, 58, 148–149
Moei River  60

Momeik 93
Monywa 66
Moore, Captain F. 51
Moore, Sergeant Jack 87–90
Muree 71
Myaungmya 134
Myawaddy 60
Myeik 66
Myitkyina 94–95
Myitkyo 70

**N**

Naw Bellay Htoo South 10, 18, 26, 202
Ngarhtetkyi 67
Nimmo, Major Jimmy 112
Nyaung 67
Nyaunglebin 152

**O**

Ohn Pe, Saw 138, 142–143

**P**

Pa Nar Mee 155
Palaw 53
Papun 66–67, 82, 92, 107, 113–115, 129, 153, 155, 160, 166–167, 178
Pathein 78
Paycha 53, 163
Pearl Harbor 28, 54
Penwegon 87
Percy, Saw 181–182
Phar Gaw 92
Pheh Tho 90
Po Htin, Saw 109, 141
Pinlaung 96
Prome 71, 193
Putao 60, 95, 97
Pyapon 49
Pyawbwe 199
Pyay 72, 148–149
Pyin Oo Lwin 47, 58, 92
Pyinmana Sawmill 119
Pyu 124–125
Pyuntasa 67

**R**

RAF 20, 46, 54, 88
Ranchi 94
Rangoon 29, 65, 75, 112
Rangoon (Yangon) 17, 39, 55, 58, 60, 63, 69–70, 72, 78, 80, 82, 91, 94–95, 107, 113, 115, 119–120, 124–125, 130, 136–138, 142, 148, 154, 157, 160, 193, 195, 199
Rangoon 123
Rupert, Saw 82

**S**

Sagaing 95
Sale Barracks 49
San Aye, Saw 51, 67, 93, 126, 158
San, General Aung 125
Sandakan 120
Sangkhlaburi 146
Sarukhi 63
Seagrim 190
Seagrim, Major Hugh 28–29, 61–62, 66–67, 72, 78–79, 82–83, 92, 95, 98, 113, 125, 132, 166–168, 170, 178–180, 185–186, 192–193
Sein Aye 173–176
Shanker, Major Bhavani 49
Shillong 61
Sholo 186
Shwebo rising 129
Shwegyin 71
Shweli River 95, 97
Shwenayungbin hills 113
Shwenyaingbin 114
Siam 52, 54
Sittang River 88
Slim, General William 17, 54, 75

229

Smile Paul, Saw  38, 55, 61, 82, 109, 121, 146
Special Operations Executive (SOE)  10, 12, 17, 36, 38, 75–76, 99, 112, 118, 121, 125, 178, 220
Spider Group  13, 178–180
Stringer, Captain A.  51–52
Sumprabum  97

**T**

Ta Phoe Htar  154
Tamu  61, 66, 71–72, 95, 196
Tanintharyi  53, 155, 163
Tanissary  154
Tarkholaw Monastery  52
Tatamadaw  15
Taukkyan  70
Taunggyi  52, 199
Taungoo  53, 67, 77, 88, 91, 124, 126, 149, 153, 161, 166, 193
Tavoy  50, 53–54, 56–57, 69–70, 72, 80, 88, 126, 137, 146, 153, 163, 205
Tenasserim  42, 54, 66, 77, 88, 94, 140, 163
Tha Din  192
Thandaung  114
Thart'gay, Saw  186–188
Thaton  57, 124, 140, 143, 157, 160
Thawthikho  185, 190
Thayet  61
Thibaw, King  44
Thra Charles  10, 18, 28
Thu Po Mu, Saw  166–169
Tinsukia  60, 79
Toe Kin, Jemadar  112

Toungoo  17, 71, 82, 93–94, 113–114, 121, 141
Training  28, 46–47, 49, 51–52, 59, 63, 75, 77–79, 81, 91, 93–94, 99, 117–118, 122, 126–127, 145, 147, 154, 176–177, 181, 186, 193, 198, 204
Tulloch, Lieutenant Colonel Cromarty  136
Twante  201

**U**

U Tun Baw  112–113

**V**

Victoria Point  64
Victoria Point (Kowthoung)  28, 54, 69

**W**

Wai, Major Phoe  156
Wavell, General Archibald  54
Win, Major General Ne  147

**Y**

Yaytwinkone  90

PB ISBN 978-1-7394402-0-6
HB ISBN 978-1-7394402-1-3
Ebook ISBN 978-1-7394402-2-0

# A Most Irregular War
## SOE Burma, Major Trofimov's Diary 1944–45

### Richard Duckett
Richard is a graduate of the Universities of Essex (BA, 2000) and Reading (MA, 2001), and was awarded a PhD in 2015 by the Open University. He has published two books on the Special Operations Executive in Burma, and continues to lecture widely on the subject.

### GH Bennett
Harry is Associate Professor at Plymouth University where he has taught history, including that of the Second World War since 1992. Author of more than 20 volumes on Military, Diplomatic and Political history he has appeared in TV documentaries on the Second World War.

In early 1945 small teams of Allied special forces soldiers were parachuted into the Burmese jungle far behind enemy lines. Their task was to work with local tribespeople who had suffered at the hands of the Japanese occupiers and the majority Burman population to raise irregular forces for guerilla warfare. Their goal was to assist advancing Allied forces by disrupting the rear area of the Japanese Army as it tried to hold the Allied advance. Recruiting, training, supplying and fighting with indigenous peoples Allied special forces created powerful local forces that learnt all the skills of demolition, ambush and infantry attack. As the war in Burma turned into a rout for Japanese forces in 1945 those forces, instead of trying to disrupt the rear areas of the enemy, found themselves squarely in the way of the retreating Japanese Army trying to get out of Burma. The fight would turn desperate as Allied special forces and tribespeople stood against a Japanese Army in headlong flight. This is the story, through the unvarnished diary and photographs, of one of those Allied special forces soldiers.

PB ISBN 978-1-73944-026-8
HB ISBN 978-1-73944-027-5

# Raiding Support Regiment
## The Diary of a Special Forces Soldier 1943–1945

### GH Bennett

Harry is Associate Professor at Plymouth University where he has taught history, including that of the Second World War since 1992. Author of more than 20 volumes on Military, Diplomatic and Political history he has appeared in documentaries on the Second World War as well as historical series such as *Who Do You Think You Are* and *Combat Ships*. He is also a regular contributor to BBC National, Local Radio and to Gem Collector TV.

The Second World War in Yugoslavia is an area neglected by historians and other commentators. This is perhaps surprising as Yugoslavia was the only country in Europe to be conquered by the Germans and then, later, to free itself solely as a result of guerrilla activity. Other countries had to be liberated by Allied armies. The British played an important role in supporting the activities of Tito's guerrilla army. This is the story of Walter Jones's service and the operations of the Raiding Support Regiment.

A precursor to the modern SAS the Raiding Support Regiment fought alongside the commandos and Tito's partisan in Yugoslavia. Based on the Island of Vis in the Adriatic they provided heavy weapons support to British and partisan forces trying to drive the Germans out of Yugoslavia. Later they served in Albania and Italy. This is a brutally honest account of one man's service with the Regiment and a neglected period of European history. It documents the transformation of a young man into a combat veteran as he witnesses the effects of bombing, the deliberate killing of POWs and partisan savagery against those who transgress the partisan code.

www.ingramcontent.com/pod-product-compliance
Lightning Source LLC
Chambersburg PA
CBHW070532090426
42735CB00013B/2961